The Macroeconomics of
Open Economies

The Macroeconomics of Open Economies

An Introduction to Aggregate Behaviour and Policy

Richard Morley

EDWARD ELGAR

Published by
Edward Elgar Publishing Limited
Gower House
Croft Road
Aldershot
Hants GU11 3HR
England

and distributed in the United States by
Gower Publishing Company
Old Post Road
Brookfield
Vermont 05036
USA

ISBN 1 85278 070 3
    1 85278 071 1 (pbk)

British Library Cataloguing in Publication Data
Morley, Richard, *1930–*
    The macroeconomics of open economies : an
    introduction to aggregate behaviour and
    policy.
    1. Open economics. Macroeconomic aspects
    I. Title
    330.12′2

Library of Congress Cataloging-in-Publication Data
Morley, Richard, 1930–
    The macroeconomics of open economies.
    Bibliography: p.
    Includes index.
    1. Macroeconomics. 2. Capitalism. I. Title.
    HB172.5.M66   1988   339   88–1197
Printed in Great Britain at the University Press, Cambridge

Contents

Preface   *ix*
Notation   *xi*

I THE LONG RUN   1
1 *Prices*   *3*

1.1 The supply of output and the demand for labour
1.2 The labour market 1.3 Aggregate income 1.4 Aggregate demand 1.5 The government's budget 1.6 The
market for loanable funds 1.7 Money and the price
level 1.8 Imports, exports and gold flows 1.9 The
model with no international market for loanable
funds 1.10 An international market for loanable
funds 1.11 Increases in capital equipment 1.12 Summary Problems for chapter 1 Further reading

II THE MEDIUM RUN   31
2 *Money*   *33*

2.1 Fiduciary money 2.2 The New Quantity Theory of
the demand for money 2.3 The original Phillips
curve 2.4 The aggregate supply function 2.5 Monetary
expansion and contraction 2.6 Increased labour
productivity 2.7 The Monetary Rule 2.8 Expected
inflation 2.9 The expectations-augmented Phillips
curve 2.10 Money senorage 2.11 Purchasing Power
Parity 2.12 Summary Problems for chapter 2 Further
reading

3 *Government Borrowing*   *66*

3.1 Crowding out 3.2 The bond market 3.3 Bond
senorage 3.4 The sustainable budget deficit 3.5 Interest parity and exchange risk 3.6 Government borrowing from foreign banks 3.7 Summary Problems for
chapter 3 Further reading

III THE SHORT RUN   83
4   *Quantities and the Interest Rate*   85

4.1 The balance of payments constraint   4.2 The goods sector   4.3 The monetary sector   4.4 Monetary changes and the balance of payments   4.5 Expansionary policies with fixed exchange rates   4.6 Income multipliers 4.7 Summary   Problems for chapter 4   Further reading

5   *Quantities and the Exchange Rate*   *109*

5.1 Devaluation   5.2 The Marshall–Lerner conditions 5.3 Problems of Devaluation   5.4 Floating exchange rates   5.5 Fiscal expansion with floating rates 5.6 Monetary expansion with floating rates   5.7 Monetary policy and uncertainty   5.8 Managed floats and the need for reserves   5.9 Summary Problems for chapter 5 Further reading

6   *Quantities and the Price Level*   *127*

6.1 The aggregate demand function   6.2 A rise in the price level   6.3 Rules versus discretion   6.4 Inflation 6.5 Consumption, income and inflation   6.6 Summary Problems for chapter 6   Further reading

IV ADJUSTMENT   143
7   *Tradeables and Non-Tradeables*   145

7.1 Two methods of disaggregating output   7.2 Absorption and switching   7.3 The structuralist theory of inflation   7.4 The effect of oil price rises on oil importers   7.5 The Dutch disease   Problems for chapter 7   Further reading

8   *Adjustments and Misperceptions*   *169*

8.1 The speculative demand for money   8.2 Rational expectations equilibrium with misperceptions   8.3 Exchange rate overshooting when output lags   8.4 Exchange rate overshooting when the price level lags   8.5 Hysteresis and tradeables   8.6 Hysteresis and unemployment 8.7 Summary   Problems for chapter 8   Further reading

Chapter 9 *Towards Harmony*   *191*

9.1 Harmonious monetary policies 9.2 Harmonious
fiscal policies 9.3 Absorption, switching and the
FEER 9.4 Institutions 9.5 Summary Problems for
chapter 9 Further reading

Bibliography   *202*
Author Index   *207*
Subject Index   *209*

Preface

Each country is capable of generating its own economic problems but most are also effective in creating problems for others. Particularly in the United Kingdom and the United States, a change of government is followed by a short period of attempting to implement policies which focus on domestic problems but which are thwarted by the reactions of the rest of the world. There is then a long learning period while policy-makers absorb the complexities of managing an open economy.

This book attempts to prevent analogous problems arising for the student of macroeconomics. Inflation, unemployment and the slowing growth of aggregate income in the main industrialised countries cannot be explained by focusing only on behaviour and policy within each domestic economy. The foreign sector is too important to be left to the last chapter. Here it is introduced at the start and incorporated throughout. The cost is a small early addition in complexity but the benefit is the avoidance of the tedious reworking of analysis required when a simple model of a closed economy is extended to bring it nearer to the world as it is.

The book achieves brevity by avoiding retelling the controversies of the past two decades. The main schools of economists have contributed to our understanding of the way economies adjust over different periods of time. Their achievements are complementary. One economist need not be wrong just because another is right. Chapter 1 shows how price changes bring about consistent plans which are realisable, though sometimes only in the long run of a decade; the economists who formulated this analysis are known as the Old Neoclassicists, who also laid the foundations for microeconomics. Chapter 2 analyses the effects of dramatic monetary changes over the medium run of four or five years: the contributions of the Monetarists. Chapter 3 examines the danger of large borrowing by government when repeated for several years; these dangers are too widely accepted for a recognisable school to be labelled. Chapters 4, 5 and 6 examine macroeconomic behaviour and policy in the short run of a year or two, the period of relevance to standard Keynesian analysis. Taken by themselves, each of these six chapters describes one or other of the economic primitivisms which sometimes grasp people whose time for economics is limited. Chapter 7 draws the distinction between that part of an economy's output which is internationally tradeable and that which is not. Chapter 8 examines some of the problems which result because modern financial sectors adjust to events within minutes but producers of goods require years to bring about quantity changes. The final chapter discusses some of the problems of bringing stability to a world of developed international financial markets, credible and incredible governments, volatile exchange rates, current account imbalances and long-lasting unemployment.

This is an introductory text aimed at first- or second-year students. Only elementary algebra is used. The reader is assumed to be unfamiliar with econometrics at this stage of his course. The text contains few empirical examples but the theory elucidates the reports found in the financial press, bank reviews and OECD *Economic Outlook*.

The book is the result of explanations and questions from colleagues and students at the University of Durham, advice on brevity from Edward Elgar, and on promptness from Kathryn Cowton, who also typed the manuscript.

Notation

Ad	Aggregate demand; expenditure on domestically produced output
B	Stock of government bonds
C	Consumption expenditure (including its import content)
c	Propensity to consume (in Chapter 6 only, c is the rate of growth of C)
D	Domestic assets of Central Bank
Def	Government's budget deficit excluding interest payments
Dip	The outflow of dividend, interest and profit payments to service past surpluses on the capital account
E	The price of foreign exchange; the exchange rate expressed as units of domestic currency per unit of foreign currency
e	Rate of change of E (positive for depreciation of domestic currency)
F	The net inflow of loanable funds from abroad; the surplus on the capital account
G	Government orders for goods (including the import content)
H	High-powered money; the monetary base
h	The base multiplier M/H
I	Investment expenditure (including its import content)
k	The liquidity ratio Md/PQ
LOOP	The Law of One Price: $P = EP^*$
M	The money supply, M1, currency in circulation plus demand deposits
Md	The demand for M1
N	Person-years of labour services
Nd	The demand for labour
Ns	The supply of labour
P	The price of domestic output in domestic currency
P^*	The price of foreign output in foreign currency
Q	Domestically produced output; aggregate supply; income
q	Rate of growth of Q
R	Foreign reserves held by Central Bank
Rri	Real rate of interest

r	The domestic rate of interest
Rer	The real exchange rate; competitiveness; EP^*/P
S	Savings
s	Propensity to save
T	Taxes less subsidies
u	Unemployment rate
W	The nominal wage rate
w	Rate of change of W
X	Exports (including any import content)
x	Expected rate of depreciation
Y	Disposable income $Q - T$
y	Rate of growth of Y
Z	Imports
z	Propensity to import
η	Elasticity
π	Inflation rate

Superscripts *foreign; ^{e}expected; ^{n}natural.

PART I
The Long Run

1. Prices

Thou didst the scattered atoms bind,
Which, by thy laws of true proportion joined,
Made up of various parts,
One perfect harmony.

Nicholas Brady,
'Ode on St Cecilia's Day', 1692

Sometimes economies behave as if St Cecilia were the patron saint of buyers and sellers as well as of musicians. Work, inventiveness and capital accumulation increase the supply of output. Selling the output creates income, and spending the income creates the demand for the output. Economic activity is supply-led; it is constrained only by the quantity and quality of labour and capital. What is the process which causes this result? What conditions are necessary to ensure that the process does indeed bring about some harmony, in the limited sense that the plans of buyers and sellers coincide and are realised? This chapter investigates how people's plans respond to changes in prices, and how prices respond to changes in people's plans. The changes in prices change economic actions until each person's plans become consistent with those of other people. The plans are then realisable and the changes in behaviour cease: the economy is in equilibrium. The price changes provide signals about disequilibria and incentives to remove the disequilibria.

1.1 THE SUPPLY OF OUTPUT AND THE DEMAND FOR LABOUR

Firms organise the services of labour and capital equipment to produce output. Some may buy raw materials and use their labour and capital to add value to the raw materials. Others buy semi-finished goods and add value to them. Firms such as lawyers simply sell services. The *aggregate supply* of output is the sum of all the values added by all the firms in an economy. In national accounting terms we would be measuring domestic product. However, the national accounts provide rough measures of what actually was produced; they measure the outcome after the event, *ex post*. Here we are investigating what would be produced in equilibrium. We are studying likely outcomes before they happen, *ex ante*.

Value-added is measured in money terms and changes when either prices or quantities change. Writing P for the price index and Q for real output, nominal value-added is PQ. For this chapter, we are not interested in changes in the price of one component of output relative to another. Such changes may cause firms to transfer their resources of labour and capital from producing one component of output to another, and they may cause consumers to substitute one sort of consumption good for another. Provided both P and Q, the general levels of prices and quantities, remain unchanged the aggregate effects on economic activity are assumed to be sufficiently small to be ignored. Although Q is value-added, it can be considered as the number of bundles of goods produced; P is the price of each bundle. Ignoring depreciation, the *ex post* measure for Q is real gross domestic product. P is that price index known as the gdp deflator.

Assume for the moment that capital services and the techniques of production are constant. Output depends on employment. Writing N for person-years of labour services

$$Q = f(N) \tag{1.1}$$

This aggregate production function has two characteristics familiar from microeconomics. Output increases as N increases (the marginal product of labour is positive), but each additional increase in N leads to a smaller increase in Q (the marginal product of labour decreases). Considering the effort and ingenuity which are involved in making things and the many human problems involved in the process of production, equation (1.1) may seem to be carrying abbreviation almost to the point of aridity. Nevertheless it provides a helpful starting-point when considering the economic decisions which households and firms make about employment.

The wage rate W is the cost to firms of employing an additional worker, and the extra worker provides revenue equal to P times his or her product. Provided W is less than this value of the marginal product of labour, firms wish to employ more workers, but the more workers they employ the smaller is the marginal product. Their demand for labour is that number of workers which results in

P × marginal product of labour = W

or: the marginal product of labour = W/P.

This ratio of the wage rate to the product price is known as *the real wage*. Writing Nd for the demand for labour and Nd( ) for the demand function, we can express this as:

$$Nd = Nd\,(W/P) \underset{-}{} \tag{1.2}$$

Because the marginal product of labour diminishes as more workers are employed, a rise in W/P causes a fall in the number of workers demanded. The minus sign under the price ratio shows the direction of the influence of W/P on Nd.

Figure 1.1 illustrates the production function of equation (1.1) in the top diagram where the vertical axis measures output per annum and the horizontal axis labour services per annum. The bottom diagram shows the marginal product of labour. This information is already available in the top diagram because the marginal product curve is given by the slope of the production function for each value of N. The vertical axis of the bottom diagram has as its dimension output per person, which is the same unit of measurement as output per marginal person. It is also the same dimension as the real wage since

$$\frac{W}{P} = \frac{\text{dollars per person per annum}}{\text{dollars per bundle of output}} = \text{output per person}$$

1.2 THE LABOUR MARKET

The supply function for labour is labelled Ns in Figure 1.1. As the real wage rises more labour services are offered:

$$Ns = Ns\,(W/P) \underset{+}{} \tag{1.3}$$

The plus sign shows the direction of change of Ns when W/P increases. The upward slope of the function is an empirical discovery. Theory gives no clear direction to the response because households enjoy both leisure and goods: they might react to a rise in the real wage by purchasing only slightly more goods but selling less labour. Changes in social conventions, household technology, conditions at work and demography made this discovery a delicate task for econometricians.

When W/P is such that Ns = Nd, the plans of the suppliers and demanders of labour are consistent: the labour market is in equilibrium.

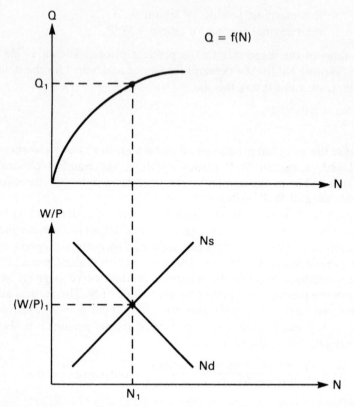

Figure 1.1   The production function and the labour market.
Nd shows the demand for labour as a function of the real wage. It is derived
from $Q = f(N)$, being the slope of this curve for each value of N. The labour
supply function is the result of the tastes of households. W adjusts to ensure that
Ns = Nd. At the equilibrium real wage $(W/P)_1$ the N_1 workers produce Q_1 of
output.

If the real wage is above its equilibrium value, firms ration employment
at a level which is less than households wish to supply. There is an excess
supply of labour, people who are job-hunting and are prepared to
accept a lower money-wage W. Firms respond by lowering W and hence
the ratio W/P. Conversely, if W/P is below equilibrium there is an
excess demand for labour as households ration employment. Firms bid
up W because more employment is profitable provided the marginal
product of labour exceeds the real wage. W changes unless the following
equilibrium condition holds:

Ns = Nd   (1.4)

Equilibrium in the labour market is described by the demand function (1.2), the supply function (1.3) and the equilibrium condition (1.4), thereby determining the equilibrium value of the ratio W/P. The dynamics of the move to this equilibrium are set in motion by the reactions of firms and households which respond to disequilibrium values. Workers hunting for jobs provide signals of excess supply to firms, or firms hunting for workers provide excess demand signals to households. The nominal wage W adjusts to bring the ratio W/P to its market-clearing level.

1.3   AGGREGATE INCOME

The previous section explained why employment is at a particular level. This employment is then plugged into the production function to explain *how* output is produced as a technical process combining labour and capital. We have yet to explain *why* the output is produced. The short answer is that firms expect to be able to sell their output at a price which will not result in bankruptcies, but the previous section has shown that the money wage will adjust in the long run so that any output price can be made profitable. The problem, therefore, is to ensure that the *volume* of output that is produced will be demanded. We have to explain why aggregate supply and demand should be equal in equilibrium.

The nominal or money value of output is PQ. The wage bill, again in money terms, is WN. Profit is the surplus which is left after labour has been paid, so profit is PQ − WN. This definition of profit is extremely broad. It covers monopoly profit, entrepreneurial profit and the return to the owners of capital; in competitive equilibrium, the first two are bid away, leaving only the return on capital. If profit is measured in real terms, the units of measurement would be the bundles of goods which the receivers of profit are able to buy with the funds they receive.

$$PQ = \text{nominal profit} + WN$$
$$\text{or} \quad Q = \text{real profit} + (W/P)\,N \qquad (1.5)$$

This equation states that real output results in real profit income or real wage income. Either profit is distributed to the households which own the firms, or the profit is retained by the firms, in which case the value of the equity owned by households will increase. Provided the market in equities has time to react to profit retentions by firms, the stock of wealth owned by households will increase. An increase in the stock of wealth is a flow of income. The result is that output and income are the same. All value added by firms is returned to households either as wages or profit income, the latter taking the form of interest on loans, dividends on equity, or capital gains on the value of the equity.

In an economy without government, households can spend their income on current consumption or they can save it. However, all economies have governments, which raise revenues by taxes and often pay back part of this revenue to households in the form of subsidies. If T is the real value of the net transfers to government, the taxes less the subsidies, then the real disposable income available for households to decide whether to spend or save is $Q - T$. Income, therefore, is spent on consumpton or saved or transferred to government. Using three bars on the equals sign for 'equals by definition':

$$Q \equiv C + S + T \tag{1.6}$$

1.4 AGGREGATE DEMAND

The domestic economy has three sources of demand. Households place orders with firms for consumption goods; firms place orders with other firms for investment goods, and the government orders goods from firms. The same notation C can be used for both the decision by households on how to dispose of their real income and the orders placed with firms for consumption goods. The symbol I denotes the volume of orders placed by firms for investment goods and G denotes the orders placed by government. The sum of these is sometimes labelled *domestic demand* and sometimes *absorption*.

$$\text{Absorption} \equiv C + I + G \tag{1.7}$$

In an open economy firms are also receiving orders from abroad for exports X. The total of orders received by firms is $C + I + G + X$. However, we defined aggregate supply as the sum of the values added by firms in the domestic economy. Aggregate demand is defined analogously to ensure that when the total of orders equals the total of output, aggregate supply and demand are equal and the goods market is in equilibrium. The orders for C, I, G and X are not orders for value added because each of these components of aggregate demand has an import content which has to be deducted to discover the demand for the value added by firms within the domestic economy. Writing Z for imports and Ad for aggregate demand:

$$\text{Ad} \equiv C + I + G + X - Z \tag{1.8}$$

In the previous section, aggregate supply or output was shown to be the same as income, and households dispose of this income in three ways: consumption, savings or transfers to government

$$Q \equiv C + S + T \tag{1.6}$$

Our problem is to discover how aggregate supply and demand are brought into equilibrium, so that the plans of the producers and demanders of output are consistent and realisable. Households' decisions to consume are immediately translated into orders for consumption goods. Hence the equilibrium condition $Q = \text{Ad}$ will be satisfied provided we can show that the economy adjusts to ensure that

$$S + T = I + G + X - Z$$

1.5 THE GOVERNMENT'S BUDGET

Government acts partly as an agent for households, purchasing goods from firms for collective provision. It also acts as a producer, running 'firms' which produce such outputs as defence, law and order, education and health services. The total demand generated by government includes both demand for the output that government itself produces, and the orders placed by government with firms on behalf of households. The total demand generated by government for goods and services is labelled G.

In most modern economies, governments have three sources of revenue: taxation, borrowing and the creation of new money. In this chapter we make the two simplifying assumptions that the monetary base is gold, which cannot be created by governments, and that the electorate does not approve of government borrowing. Therefore, the only source of government revenue is taxation. The electorate expects the government to redistribute income, collecting taxes from some households, and providing subsidies to others. The government's net revenue is the net transfers from households to government T. With borrowing and money-creation denied it, the government must balance its budget:

$$T = G \tag{1.9}$$

1.6 THE MARKET FOR LOANABLE FUNDS

Firms with profitable investment opportunities will seek to borrow
funds to finance the investment. The lower the rate of interest charged
for loans, the greater will be the number of potentially profitable
investment opportunities. The relationship between investment plans
and the rate of interest constitutes the demand for loanable funds.
Figure 1.2 illustrates this demand function, where r is the rate of
interest and I is the amount of funds demanded for investment. Firms
are borrowing funds in order to spend them, hence I is also part of the
demand for output.

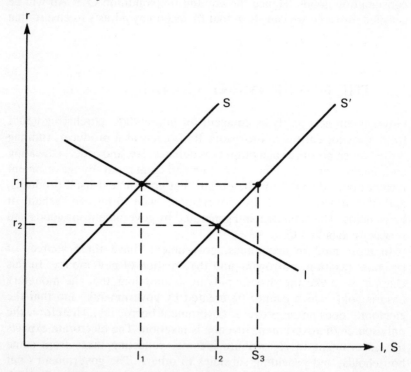

Figure 1.2   The market for loanable funds.
The demand is from firms to finance their investment expenditure I. The supply
is from households offering their savings S. The initial interest rate is r_1 which
results in both savings and investment being the amount I_1.

An increase in thrift moves the savings function to S'. The initial interest rate
now causes an excess supply of funds equal to $S_3 - I_1$ which drives down the
rate of interest to r_2. Investment increases, a movement down the unchanged I
function. Consumption falls by $I_2 - I_1$, which is the increase in investment.
Total expenditure remains constant.

The supply of loanable funds is that part of the *disposable income* Q − T which households do not spend on consumption. The decision to save is really a decision to postpone consumption until a later period. By lending money, households are able to receive interest.

The amount of saving, hence the supply of loanable funds, will be influenced by the rate of interest. If the rate rises, a decision to postpone consumption this year enables an individual household to consume more next year: the opportunity cost of this year's consumption has increased. A rate of 4 per cent allows £100 of this year's saving to purchase £104 of consumption next year. The price of next year's consumption relative to this year's is $1/(1 + r)$. A rise in r lowers this relative price and makes next year's consumption more attractive: if r increases saving increases.

The market for loanable funds consists of firms demanding funds for investment but being deterred by increases in the interest they have to pay on their borrowing, and households lending their savings more readily when the interest they receive increases. The market is summarised by two functions and an equilibrium condition

$$I = I\,(r) \qquad\qquad\qquad\qquad (1.10)$$
$$\underset{-}{}$$

$$S = S\,(r) \qquad\qquad\qquad\qquad (1.11)$$
$$\underset{+}{}$$

$$S = I \qquad\qquad\qquad\qquad (1.12)$$

If there is a change in tastes by households so that their desire to save increases, the S function of Figure 1.2 shifts to S'. For each level of the rate of interest there is now an increased flow of loanable funds offered to the market. The previous equilibrium rate of interest r_1 now causes an excess supply of loanable funds which results in a decrease in the rate of interest and moves the loanable funds market to its new equilibrium so that decisions to save are again matched by decisions to invest. By postponing present consumption, households buy claims on future consumption. An increase in the desire to save leads to a fall in the interest rate and persuades firms to increase investment, thereby increasing future productive capacity so that, when households decide to spend their extra savings, the extra consumption goods will be available. The decline in the demand for output caused by the fall in orders for consumption goods is exactly matched by the increased orders for investment goods.

A crucial feature of the argument is that additional savings should be used to buy claims on assets which are reproducible by firms. Saving by

buying land, old paintings and other non-reproducible assets depends
on individual tastes and involves transfer payments between households. Taking the household sector in the aggregate, such transfers
cancel out and can be ignored. Massive movements of funds into such
assets are caused by destabilising speculation and are temporary
disequilibrium phenomena. Saving by hoarding money is irrational
because the saver forgoes interest. A postponement of consumption by
the household sector results in more investment by firms in preparation
for the future increase in demand for consumption goods. An increase
in saving causes an increase in real assets.

1.7   MONEY AND THE PRICE LEVEL

This section presents a simplified version of the money market. The
analysis of the demand for money is confined to the main reason why
people wish to hold money: it facilitates exchange. The 'supply' of
money is whatever things or arrangements meet this requirement. In an
open economy, money must facilitate international exchange. Until
1914 gold was the most widely acceptable medium for international
payments. During the occasional moments of tranquillity between 1914
and 1969, and particularly from 1952, the United States dollar was more
acceptable. It combined the advantage of gold, into which it could be
converted at a fixed rate of $35 an ounce, with the convenience of
currency. A dollar standard is analogous to a gold standard. With the
currencies of the main trading nations tied to the dollar and the dollar
tied to gold, the rate of exchange between one currency and another is
fixed. (When currencies are not tied to each other, exchange rates are
determined in the international currency market. The consideration of
floating exchange rates is postponed to later chapters.)

Gold is the *monetary base*. Households and firms find currency more
convenient than gold. The Central Bank issues currency in exchange for
gold, treating the currency as liabilities in its accounts and the gold as
assets. For large transactions, currency also is inconvenient. The non-
bank public deposit some of their currency with commercial banks and
exchange cheques for goods instead of currency for goods. Such cheques
have to be encashable into currency on demand if they are to be
acceptable. Provided the cheques are believed, the demand deposits act
as money.

Once cheques become widely accepted, the commercial banks are
able to lend part of the currency deposited with them, keeping a reserve
which is sufficient to cover the requirements of those customers who

might wish to draw currency out of the banks. As the banks lend, the borrowers write out cheques which in turn are deposited back with the banking system. The total amount of demand deposits is a multiple of the amount of currency held by the commercial banks. The banks receive interest on their loans, and try to push the amount of their lending as far as is commercially prudent, but they must also maintain confidence in their ability to pay cash on demand. The medium of exchange is the currency in circulation (not held as reserves by the banks) together with the total of demand deposits. This definition of money is known by the abbreviation M1.

Currency in circulation is a roughly constant proportion of total currency, the proportion being determined by the relative convenience of using currency and cheques. The total of demand deposits is a multiple of the currency held as reserves by the banks, the multiple being prevented from falling by the banks' desire to lend profitably, but prevented from rising by banking prudence. These constancies ensure that M1 is a roughly constant multiple of the gold stock, the monetary base. If the gold stock increases by £1 million, M1 would increase by, say, £2 million. For this reason the monetary base is sometimes known as *high-powered money*, here abbreviated as H. The link between the money supply M and the monetary base is

$$M = h\,H \qquad (1.13)$$

where h is known as the *base multiplier*. In stable times, the behaviour of the commercial banks ensures that h is roughly constant. In many countries, the Central Bank imposes reserve requirements on the banks which place a maximum value on h. When the banking system is de-regulated and the banks engage in financial innovations, h will rise. Here h is assumed constant.

The stock of money which firms and households wish to hold depends upon the money value of their expenditures and the timing of receipts and expenditures. Although people can make minor alterations to the timing, the analysis can be greatly simplified by focusing on the main variable which affects the demand for money, nominal income. The average stock of money demanded during the period is a fraction of the flow of nominal income during the period.

$$Md = kPQ \qquad (1.14)$$

k is the *liquidity ratio*. Its unit of measurement is the £s in which Md is measured divided by the £s per annum in which PQ is measured. The dimension of k is therefore 'time'. It is a figure such as 1/4, implying that people wish to hold enough money to finance their transactions for three months ahead. Variations in k are usually small and for the present chapter k will be treated as constant.

In equilibrium the stock of money is willing held:

$$M = Md \qquad (1.15)$$

Hence from (1.13) and (1.14), hH = kPQ. If the monetary base increases, there is initially an excess supply of money and condition (1.15) would not hold. When people find themselves holding more money than they want they spend the excess on goods, thereby creating an excess demand for goods. Firms react by raising prices, which increases the demand for money until it equals the increased supply and equilibrium is restored. A fall in the money supply would reverse the process and cause a fall in the price level.

In an economy where output is determined in the goods and labour markets via the signals and incentives provided by relative prices, the quantity of money determines the price level. The next sections show that money also has an indirect influence on the blend of expenditures on output, but not on total output. The hypothesis that money determines P but not Q is known as the *Old Quantity Theory of Money*.

1.8 IMPORTS, EXPORTS AND GOLD FLOWS

This section examines an economy where the only payments made to other countries are for imports and the only payments made by other countries are for exports. Many goods which enter international trade are substitutes for goods produced and sold domestically. The volumes of exports and imports can be considered as numbers of rather similar bundles of goods. If the domestic economy is the United States, a potential buyer could choose a domestically produced bundle at the price P, or he could purchase foreign exchange and use it to purchase imports. If E is the price of foreign exchange (say, \$4.80 per £1) and P* is the foreign price of a bundle, the bundle of imports will cost EP*. With transport costs, tariffs, the transaction costs of purchasing foreign exchange, information problems, local loyalty and any differences between domestic and foreign goods, everyone does not switch to foreign products as soon as EP* falls below P. However, imports increase as the ratio EP*/P decreases. This ratio is known as the *real exchange rate*, abbreviated below as Rer. It is an indication of *competitiveness*: the higher its value the more competitive are the economy's goods in international markets.

$$Rer \equiv EP^*/P \qquad (1.16)$$

where P is the domestic price level, P* is the foreign price level and E is the price of foreign currency in terms of domestic currency. When all currencies are tied at a fixed rate to gold and hence to each other, E is constant; any change in the Rer is brought about by changes in P or P*.

The volume of imports demanded Z decreases when the Rer increases

$$Z = Z(Rer) \qquad\qquad (1.17)$$
$$\underset{-}{}$$

The volume of exports demanded X increases with the Rer:

$$X = X(Rer) \qquad\qquad (1.18)$$
$$\underset{+}{}$$

The value of exports is PX and the value of imports, measured in units of the same domestic currency, is EP*Z. If export value exceeds import value during the year, more gold flows into the country than flows out, gold being the medium of international exchange. Using the Greek letter delta to mean 'an increase in', ΔH is the change in the high-powered money stock brought about by this gold flow. The *trade surplus* is identical to the gold flow:

$$PX - EP^*Z \equiv \Delta H \qquad\qquad (1.19)$$

The increased gold allows the banks to increase their lending, which in turn leads to a rise in deposits so that M1 increases proportionately with H. The supply of money exceeds the demand, and people react to this disequilibrium by attempting to purchase goods. The goods price is bid up until the demand for money $Md = kPQ$ has risen to the same extent as the supply.

What is the effect of the rise in P on the identity (1.19)? The Rer falls and domestic goods become less competitive relative to foreign goods. If the economy is small, the loss of gold to foreign economies will have a negligible effect on P*. If the economy is large, both the rise in P and the fall in P* will be significant. The quantity variable X falls and Z rises, but the effect on (1.19) is ambiguous. The value of exports PX may move either way if P rises but X falls. The value of imports EP*Z is unambiguous only if the change in P* is negligible. These ambiguities can be removed with information about the elasticities of response of X and Z to changes in Rer.

Suppose the gold flow during the year raised P by 10 per cent and lowered P* by 1 per cent. For convenience, set the Rer at the start of the year at unity so that its value by the year's end is 0.99/1.10 or 0.9 of its value at the start. Provided the elasticity of X in response to changes in the Rer is greater than unity, X will fall proportionately more than the rise in P and the value of exports PX will fall. For the value of imports, the fall in Rer would raise Z by more than 10 per cent if the elasticity of imports was greater than unity. With E constant and P^* down by only 1 per cent, import value increases. The evidence for most countries in most years supports the thrust of this example. Provided exporters and importers have time to adjust, the Rer-elasticities of exports and imports are both greater than unity. The effect of the inflow of gold is to eliminate the trade surplus. The gold flow is a transitory, disequilibrium phenomenon which triggers changes in the relative price P^*/P, thereby changing the quantities of exports and imports demanded. In equilibrium

$$PX - EP^*Z = 0$$
$$X = (EP^*/P)\, Z$$
$$\text{or} \quad X = (\text{Rer})\, Z \tag{1.20}$$

This equation shows balance of payments equilibrium in an economy where the only payments across frontiers are for imports and exports. In the eighteenth century, gold was most acceptable in the form of coins and gold coins were called 'specie'. The adjustment process became known as the *price specie-flow mechanism*. It was first propounded in 1752 by David Hume. As trustworthy institutions developed, the gold would often stay in vaults and its ownership would be changed by a book-keeping entry. During disequilibrium claims to gold rather than the gold itself would move across frontiers and change the high-powered money stocks. A trade surplus generates a net inflow of either actual gold or certificates of ownership. The price level rises. The quantities of exports and imports are taken to be sufficiently sensitive to price changes for the trade surplus to be eliminated and move the economy to the equilibrium described by (1.20).

If the price of goods produced in the domestic economy P rises sufficiently above the price of imports EP^* to outweigh transport costs, tariffs and other factors which reduce the attraction of imports, the value of imports will exceed the value of exports and a trade deficit will develop. Gold will flow out and the price level will fall. There is a tendency for the price of similar goods to be the same in each country when these prices are converted to the same currency by using the fixed exchange rate E. This tendency is known as the *Law of One Price* (LOOP). Expressed in terms of the domestic and foreign price levels of the aggregates of goods in the domestic and foreign economies, the LOOP states that

$$P = EP^* \tag{1.21}$$

The LOOP is an approximation which is most likely to apply when there are stable conditions for international trade, unobtrusive governments, cheap transport and efficient information flows. It is a convenient approximation for analytical purposes because it implies that the real exchange rate is unity:

$$Rer \equiv EP^*/P = 1 \qquad (1.22)$$

hence, from (1.20), $X = Z$ $\qquad (1.23)$

In Figure 1.3, the left diagram shows the marked responses of import and export volumes to changes in the Rer. The centre diagram shows the smaller responses of the values of imports and exports. The difference between these two values are settled by gold movements, shown in the right diagram. If exports exceed imports, gold flows into the economy, raises P and lowers Rer. The Law of One Price ensures that the equilibrium value of the Rer is unity. In later chapters the definition of high-powered money will be widened to include those other assets besides gold which modern economies use as international

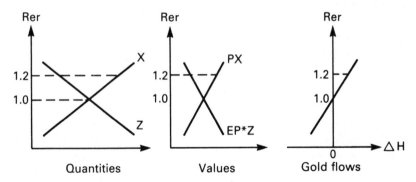

Figure 1.3   The price specie-flow mechanism.
Left. When the real exchange rate is 1.2, the import price EP* is 20 per cent above the export price P. Exports are competitive and their volume is high. The gentle slopes to the X and Z functions show the significant responses of volumes to changes in competitiveness.
Centre. A fall in P would raise the Rer, but PX increases because the rise in export volume outweighs the fall in P; hence PX increases with the Rer. Analogously, the value of imports falls as the Rer increases.
Right. A high Rer generates an inflow of gold ΔH which raises P and lowers the Rer. With the Law of One Price operating, equilibrium occurs when the Rer = 1. The flows of exports and imports stay constant, equal in value and equal in volume. Net gold flows are then zero.

(If there are international flows of loanable funds, replace X by $X + F - Dip$ for a debtor country, or Z by $Z - F + Dip$ for a creditor country.)

media of exchange, and the Law of One Price will be demoted to a long-run approximation. However, the basic principles of Figure 1.3 apply to modern economies which are tied by fixed exchange rates. These principles are known as the *Monetary Approach to the Balance of Payments*. The price specie-flow mechanism is the application of the approach to a world on a gold standard.

1.9   THE MODEL WITH NO INTERNATIONAL MARKET FOR LOANABLE FUNDS

The purpose of the model is to demonstrate how the behaviour of domestic and foreign firms and households can ensure that what is produced will be demanded. We assume that the market for loanable funds is a domestic market, perhaps because it depends upon trust and detailed information the lack of which inhibit international lending. In this section, only the equations which describe equilibrium are numbered, with the numbers at the beginning of the line to avoid confusion with those in the rest of the chapter.

1. The production function $Q = f(N)$
2. The demand for labour is derived from 1 $Nd = Nd\,(W/P)$
3. The supply of labour $Ns = Ns\,(W/P)$
4. Labour market equilibrium $Ns = Nd$

These four equations constitute the *supply side* of the output market. They drive the model of the economy as a whole. The labour market clears because the participants in it adjust W to P. The three equations 2, 3 and 4 are solved for Ns, Nd and W/P. The N in equation 1 is that N which results in $Ns = Nd$. Hence Q is determined. This variable is output, or income, or aggregate supply. The remaining equations show that aggregate demand adjusts to equal aggregate supply, ensuring that the output market also clears.

5. The disposal of income $Q \equiv C + S + T$
6. The components of aggregate demand $Ad \equiv C + I + G + X - Z$

These two equations are definitions, convenient ways of subdividing income and aggregate demand. C appears in both because the decision to consume income is also the decision to demand goods.

7. The government's budget $T = G$

The government decides G by a process which is not explained in the model: G is exogenous. The balanced budget then determines T.

8. Firms' demand for loanable funds $I = I(r)$

9. Households' supply of funds $\qquad$ $S = S(r)$

10. Equilibrium $\qquad$ $I = S$

Changes in r bring equilibrium to the loanable funds market. The three equations determine I, S and r.

11. The demand for money $\qquad$ $Md = kPQ$

12. The supply of money $\qquad$ $M = hH$

13. Equilibrium $\qquad$ $M = Md$

Here k and h are behavioural constants. Q is determined in the goods and labour markets. H is determined in the foreign sector. P is the variable which adjusts to bring equilibrium in the monetary sector.

The foreign sector interacts with the monetary sector because a change ΔH in the gold stock occurs when the value of exports exceeds the value of imports.

$$PX - EP^*Z \equiv \Delta H$$

This is the balance of payments *identity*. Since it is not an equilibrium condition it is not numbered. Only when ΔH is zero can the economy be in equilibrium, otherwise the price specie-flow mechanism changes P via changes in H.

14. The foreign demand for exports $\qquad$ $X = X(EP^*/P)$

15. The domestic demand for imports $\qquad$ $Z = Z(EP^*/P)$

16. Balance of payments equilibrium $\qquad$ $X = Z$

When both domestic and foreign currencies are tied to gold (or to a dollar which is tied to gold), E is fixed. If the domestic economy is small relative to the foreign economy, the impact of gold flows on P* can be ignored, leaving P* constant. Changes in P affect competitiveness and cause changes in X and Z. The Law of One Price ensures that gold flows continue until

$$P = EP^*$$

However, the LOOP is omitted from the list of equations because it is already implicit in equation 16. To obtain this equilibrium *two* conditions have to be applied to the balance of payments identity: the LOOP to signify that price changes have ceased, and $\Delta H = 0$ to signify that the specie flow has ceased.

The sixteen equations form the model of the economy and allow us to deduce that aggregate demand equals aggregate supply in equilibrium. From equations 5 and 6, we have to show that

$$S + T = I + G + X - Z$$

but S = I from 10, T = G from 7 and X = Z from 16. The supply of output is created by the inventiveness and industry of firms and households, whose plans are harmonised by the labour market. Behaviour in the loanable funds market and the combined monetary and foreign sector ensures that the output is demanded. In equilibrium

$$Ad = Q$$

There are three exogenous variables: E, P* and G are treated as constants. The sixteen equations determine the endogenous variables. Three of these are prices: r, W and P. Ten are flows: Ns and Nd, S and I, X and Z, C, T, Q and Ad. The remaining three are stocks: H, Ms and Md.

The equations merely describe the equilibrium. The behavioural dynamics of the equilibriating process involves three 'laws'. Two of these were discussed in the previous section: the price specie-flow mechanism and the LOOP. The third 'law' is implicit throughout this and the next chapter. It is the *Law of Supply and Demand*. Excess demand in a market causes deals to occur at rising prices. When there is excess supply, the price of what is traded falls. These price adjustments change the quantities supplied and demanded (movement along the supply and demand functions) until the markets clear.

1.10   AN INTERNATIONAL MARKET FOR LOANABLE FUNDS

Deals between the residents of one country and another do not occur only for the exchange of goods for money. There are also deals involving financial paper such as bonds and equities. Firms demanding funds for investment may obtain them from either domestic or foreign households. Savers may supply funds to either domestic or foreign firms. When the loanable funds market is international, the interest rate is determined in the world market. If the domestic economy is too small to influence this rate and is free of imperfections, it takes the world rate of interest r* which is exogenous to our model of one particular economy.

When r* is high, saving in the domestic economy is encouraged and investment discouraged; savers will send funds abroad. When r* is low, domestic saving is discouraged but domestic firms will see investment opportunities and will borrow more than domestic savers are offering. There will be an inflow of funds from abroad to buy the financial paper offered by firms who use the funds to finance their investment expenditure. Foreign savers will buy the domestic firms' shares in the expectation of future dividends and the firms' bonds in the expectation of future interest payments. In some cases foreigners may buy entire firms in the expectation of future profits. Shares, bonds and ownership documents flow out of the country. This outflow of financial paper is matched by an inflow of funds which are recorded as positive items in the *capital account* of the balance of payments.

If a country were entering the international capital market for the first time, all of this inflow on the capital account would be available to meet firms' demand for loanable funds. When the capital account has been in surplus in past years, domestic firms have incurred obligations to pay dividends and interest. If a domestic firm had been purchased by residents of a foreign country, that firm's profits will be repatriated to the owners' country. The net addition to the domestic supply of loanable funds, the savings of domestic households, is the inflow to purchase financial paper *less* the dividends, interest and profits resulting from past purchases of financial paper. Writing F for the inflow on this year's capital account, and Dip for the dividends, interest and profit which flow out of the country as a result of past surpluses on the capital account, the net addition to the domestic supply of loanable funds is F-Dip. Equilibrium in the domestic loanable funds market occurs when the supply from both domestic and foreign lenders is equal to the demand by domestic firms

$$S + F - Dip = I \tag{1.24}$$

In Figure 1.4, the world interest rate of r^*_1 leads domestic firms to demand more funds than domestic households wish to supply. During the disequilibrium, the domestic interest rate rises but this attracts funds from abroad. The temporary rise in the domestic interest rate lowers the price of bonds. Foreign buyers bid up bond prices and hence bid down the rate of interest until the domestic rate equals the world rate r^*_1. The variable which causes the equilibriating process is F, which responds to the excess demand in the domestic loanable funds market. The reason F responds is the rise in the domestic interest rate above the world rate r^*_1. but this rise is only temporary. By adding to the domestic supply of loanable funds, F drives the domestic rate down to r^*_1. Any deviation of the domestic rate from the world rate will trigger a change in F which will restore the equilibrium.

If the world rate of interest had been r^*_3 in Figure 1.4, domestic savers are supplying more funds than domestic firms wish to borrow. There is an outflow of funds to purchase foreign financial paper or firms. (Since F is defined as an inflow, a net outflow makes F negative.) The figure assumes that this is a new situation for the economy: the surpluses on

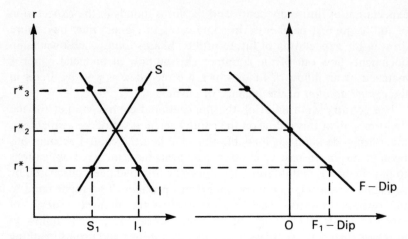

Figure 1.4   Domestic savings, domestic investment and the international flow of loanable funds.
Left. The world interest rate determines domestic savings and investment, which are equal only if the world rate happens to be r^*_2. At a world rate of r^*_1 domestic demand exceeds domestic supply.
Right. The gap is filled by an inflow from abroad, but not all the payment for financial paper is available for borrowing by domestic firms. The inheritance of past obligations causes an outflow of dividends, interest and profit Dip which must be subtracted from F_1. The gap $I_1 - S_1$ is filled by $F_1 - $ Dip.

the capital account in past years leave Dip positive. Repeated capital account deficits, outflows of funds, will change Dip in future years. (Since Dip is defined as the outflow of dividends, interest payments and profits, a net inflow of these from abroad would mean a negative value for Dip.)

With an international market for loanable funds, a country gains gold by selling both exports and financial paper. It loses gold by buying imports and by meeting its obligations on its sales of financial paper in past years. Present foreign lenders are buying claims on the country's future exports, and past lenders now receive claims on the country's present exports. Although F and Dip refer to financial transactions, the people involved are implicitly judging the volume of such transactions by comparing them with a bundle of exports, the unit of measurement of X. The value of the gold inflow is $P(X + F - $ Dip$)$ and the value of the outflow, again measured in the domestic currency, is EP^*Z. If the gold flowing in exceeds that flowing out, there is a surplus on the balance of payments and an increase in the gold stock. The *balance of payments identity* is

$$P(X + F - Dip) - EP^*Z \equiv \Delta H \tag{1.25}$$

When F is positive, the *capital account* is in surplus. The inflow of gold pays for the outflow of financial paper which carries obligations for debt servicing or profit payments in future years.

When the *trade account* is in surplus, the value of exports exceeds that of imports. However, this trade surplus may be insufficient to finance the commitments of dividends, interest and profit payments to foreigners which resulted from past surpluses on the capital account.

The *current account* refers to all payments except F. It is in surplus if export value exceeds the sum of import value and Dip. The current and capital accounts combine to give the balance of payments identity (1.25). Hence an overall surplus on the balance of payments may be due to the capital account, the current account or both. The effect of the surplus is to trigger the price specie-flow mechanism, change the volumes of exports and imports until both the surplus is eliminated and the LOOP then holds constant the existing flows of exports and imports. Balance of payments *equilibrium* occurs when

$$X + F = Z + Dip \tag{1.26}$$

When loanable funds have an international market, will all domestic output be demanded? From equation (1.24), an excess domestic demand for loanable funds is met by an inflow from abroad:

$$I - S = F - Dip \tag{1.27}$$

From equation (1.26), a trade deficit is financed by the excess of capital inflow over Dip:

$$Z - X = F - Dip \tag{1.28}$$

Hence $I - S = Z - X$

or $I + X - Z = S$

Add the government's balanced budget $G = T$

$$I + G + X - Z = S + T$$

Add consumption to both sides

$$C + I + G + X - Z = C + S + T$$

and we have deduced that

$$Ad = Q$$

The domestic goods market is in equilibrium. Aggregate demand equals aggregate supply, although the inflow of funds from abroad allows imports to exceed exports.

(The model of section 1.9 is modified by introducing the new variable F. With r* exogenous, the domestic interest rate r drops out. The term Dip is also exogenous since it is an inheritance from previous periods. Equations 10 and 16 are replaced by:

10′ I − S = F − Dip
16′ Z − X = F − Dip

to give again sixteen equations and endogenous variables.)

1.11   INCREASES IN CAPITAL EQUIPMENT

The assumption in previous sections was that investment adds to aggregate demand but has no effect on aggregate supply. Firms demanded capital goods but had not yet plugged them into the production process. This section investigates the effects of increases in the stock of capital. For simplicity we shall assume a constant utilisation rate for each item in the stock, hence an increased stock results in an increase in capital services. The many problems of measuring capital can be avoided by focusing attention on the changes in the relations between employment and output and between employment and the marginal product of labour. The production function now includes capital services K as well as labour services N:

$$Q = f(N, K) \tag{1.29}$$

When K increases, output at each level of employment is greater than before. This is illustrated in Figure 1.5 by the counter-clockwise shift in the production function. With employment remaining at N_1 output increases from Q_1 to Q_2. Each worker is more productive than before (the new production function is higher than the old). Also, an additional worker adds more to production than before (the new production function is steeper), and this means that the marginal productivity of labour has shifted (the new demand function for labour, Nd_2 in the lower diagram, is higher than the old function Nd_1). Firms are prepared to pay a higher real wage to their present employees if this results in more employment and output. The rise in the real wage from $(W/P)_1$ to $(W/P)_2$ causes a movement along the labour supply function Ns. Households offer more labour services; their offer is accepted by firms and output increases further to Q_3.

Why is the increased output matched by an increase in expenditure? The matching results from the actions of firms and the demanders of money. For the firm facing a downward-sloping demand curve for its

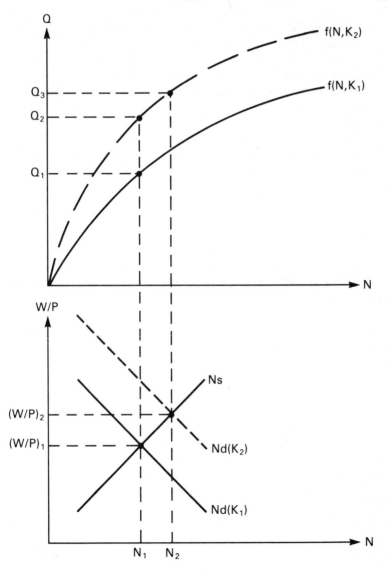

Figure 1.5   An increase in the amount of capital equipment.
Top. The production function shifts counter-clockwise. More is produced for each value of N, and the slope is steeper for each value of N.
Bottom. When capital increases from K_1 to K_2, the labour demand function shifts. The production from N_1 workers increases from Q_1 to Q_2. The higher equilibrium wage entices more workers into employment and the extra workers raise output further to Q_3.

particular product, a successful investment involves both increased output and unit cost reductions enabling the price to be reduced. Firms which do not immediately reduce prices will later be forced to do so by the behaviour of the holders of money. With P constant, the increase in Q leads to an increase in the demand for money Md = kPQ. With the money supply fixed initially, people withhold from purchasing goods while they attempt to build up their stock of money. The excess demand for money leads to an excess supply of goods and firms react by reducing prices. The fall in P reduces Md back to equality with Ms. If the money supply stayed constant, the fall in P would exactly counter the rise in Q.

As differences between domestic and foreign prices become noticeable, the demand for exports increases and the demand for imports decreases, allowing domestic production to replace imports as well as being sold abroad. The balance of payments moves into surplus and gold flows into the domestic economy, raising the money supply and moderating the fall in prices. However, imports have a positive income-elasticity of demand (ignored in previous sections where income was treated as steady at the level determined by the labour market and the production function, with no change in the amount of capital). Extending the import function of equation (1.17) to include the effect of rising income:

$$Z = Z\,(\text{Rer},\, Q) \qquad\qquad (1.30)$$
$$-\quad\ +$$

The fall in the domestic price level increases the real exchange rate, and lowers imports, but the rise in income raises imports. Imports might increase or decrease but even if imports rise, the increase in exports will be greater because the increased output must be sold.

The sequence of events is as follows. Last period's investment becomes this period's increase in the capital stock which causes output and income to increase. The price level falls and exports increase. Imports fall if the price effect dominates the income effect, rise if the strengths of the effects are reversed, but the rise in imports is less than the rise in exports. The price specie-flow mechanism then reverses the price fall, slows the rise in exports and hastens the rise in imports until the balance of payments surplus disappears. Once again,

$$X + F = Z + \text{Dip}$$

Each of the components of this equilibrium condition may change between the previous period and the present period. The rate of interest determines how a given income is divided between consumption and savings. With income varying, the savings function given in equation (1.11) is extended to

$$S = S(r, Q) \qquad (1.31)$$
$$ + \ +$$

The rise in income leads to increased savings which may now exceed the domestic demand for loanable funds. Funds flow abroad and there is a deficit on the capital account, a negative value for F. A country which financed investment by foreign borrowing in one decade might lend abroad in the next, eventually becoming a net creditor. The outflow of dividends, interest and profit would turn into an inflow: Dip would be negative.

1.12 SUMMARY

This chapter has shown how the behaviour of firms and households can move an economy to equilibrium. The equilibrium is conveniently described by a set of equations giving the supply and demand functions and the equilibrium condition for each market. The markets interact: the demands for imports and exports and the international market for loanable funds affect the balance of payments, which then affects the domestic money market, which in turn influences the domestic price of goods, a price change which feeds back to the demands for imports and exports.

The supply and demand functions shift with changes in tastes, technology, capital or population. Such shifts may be followed by periods of disequilibria when the excess demands or supplies trigger price changes which move the economy to its new equilibrium. The economists who developed the approach are now known as the *Old Neoclassicists*. They emphasised the importance of marginal changes. The Neoclassical label was applied to distinguish them from the Classical economists writing before marginal analysis was developed in the 1870s. The Old Neoclassicists considered that disequilibria were frequent but short, with the move to a new equilibrium being rapid because key people quickly respond to excess supplies or demands by becoming price-makers instead of price-takers and others quickly react to the signals and incentives provided by the price changes.

Adjustment could be immediate if economic actors anticipate change. When people form their expectations by using theory to predict the future, and if their predictions are correct, the economy changes without excess demands or supplies appearing; it is always in equilibrium. The economists who are developing such theories of continuous equilibrium and comparing their predictions with reality are known as the *New Neoclassicists*.

Expectations are not always formed in this forward-looking way. If we are trying to predict the price level, for example, we may not focus on measuring the money supply (or whatever causal variables are most able to predict the price level). Instead we might examine the past behaviour of the price level and use this to predict its future, as if we were extrapolating a graph. Such backward-looking expectations can lead to sluggish adjustment. They are one reason why a dramatic economic shock may be followed by a long period of disequilibrium. The present chapter, with its concentration on equilibria, then becomes an exposition of the behaviour of an economy in the long run. It gives the position to which the economy would move many years ahead.

Taken by itself, this chapter could be interpreted as a recommendation to leave economic decisions in the hands of firms and households, where an economy's inventiveness, industry and application originate. Invention causes disequilibrium but the price system moves the economy to a new equilibrium, coordinating individual actions to restore harmony at a higher level of income than before. The government confines itself to providing those goods and services which are not in the interests of each individual to provide but are in the interests of society as a whole. These public goods and services are financed by taxation but taxes can shift the labour supply or demand functions and reduce employment. They may shift the supply or demand for loanable funds and reduce capital accumulation. Although these supply-side effects are difficult to measure, there is less controversy about the effect of taxes on the demand side of the goods market: taxes indeed reduce demand. The implication of Neoclassicism whether Old or New is that minimal government is best. The next two chapters reinforce this view by examining what happens when a government runs a budget deficit, filling the gap between expenditure and tax revenue by creating money or borrowing. Erratic or immoderate deficit policies inhibit market adjustments. The apparent inability of firms and households to adjust rapidly to change can sometimes be explained by the confusions which governments create.

In practice, economies where income per capita grew rapidly during periods of fixed exchange rates were not those whose governments participated minimally in economic activity. On the supply side, rapid economic growth is encouraged by government-provided information, incentives and persuasion. Governments organise investment in infrastructure and people. They can hasten adjustments towards real wages which clear labour markets, price levels which encourage competitiveness and a climate which encourages business optimism and investment. Chapter 4 examines the ability of governments to encourage adjustment when aggregate demand lags behind supply. Optimal government need not be minimal government. However, three of the very different economies which enjoyed 'miraculous' growth during the period of fixed exchange rates had one feature in common. The bureaucrats of West Germany, Japan and South Korea had a knowledge of markets. Prices were not ignored.

Three price ratios are particularly important in explaining aggregate behaviour: the real wage, the real exchange rate and the rate of interest. Policies are often thwarted if they are designed in ignorance of such behaviour. This chapter has shown some of the reasons why these ratios change and how firms and households respond to the information conveyed by the changes.

PROBLEMS FOR CHAPTER 1

1. An increase in population causes an increase in the labour services offered at each real wage. What are the effects on the volumes of output and exports? Show that the price level falls initially and then returns to its previous level.
2. An economy is in equilibrium and is part of the international market for loanable funds. There is a fall in the world rate of interest. Trace the effects on C, I, X and Z in the short run before the increase in capital equipment has an effect. (Hints: Q is constant and Ad = Q, hence increases in some components of Ad must be matched by falls in others.)
3. Why would a country's money stock change if the price of its output was higher than the output price of its trading partners?
4. For many years of the nineteenth century, Britain had an approximate equilibrium on its balance of payments. Show that a constant surplus on the trade account would lead to deficits on the capital account which increased from year to year.
5. Show that a nation which accumulates capital equipment and improves the productivity of its workforce will increase its gold stock if it trades in a world on a gold standard. Show also that a nation can increase its gold stock in the short run by becoming an international debtor. Criticise the Mercantilist view that the objective of trade policy is to accumulate gold.

6. A country has a money supply which is twice the monetary base. The banking system then innovates and the money supply becomes three times the monetary base. Show that in a gold standard world with all output demanded, the effect of the innovation is not a permanent increase in the price level but instead a temporary increase in imports.

FURTHER READING

An account of Classical monetary theory is given in Chapter 6 of O'Brien (1975). Jones (1933), Beach (1935) and Fetter (1965) give accounts of banking policy and gold movements during the period of British hegemony. Jeffrey G. Williamson (1964) describes the American experience during the same period.

The simplifying assumption that bundles of goods are similar is criticised in Isard (1977) and Kravis and Lipsey (1978). However, the Law of One Price survives the test in Officer (1986), provided it is considered as a long-run approximation. These three references require some familiarity with econometrics. References about the sluggishness of wage adjustments are given at the end of Chapter 2.

Cohen (1978) and Grubel (1984) are good introductory texts on the world monetary system.

Yusef and Peters (1985) show that rapid economic growth can occur under government which is far from minimal.

PART II:
The Medium Run

2. Money

This chapter examines the effects of dramatic changes in the money supply on output, employment and the price level. The opening section shows how modern monetary systems have ceased to rely on gold. Chapter 1 assumed that commercial bankers were prudent, with their prudence reinforced by rules set by the Central Bank. Epidemics of bank failures were not considered, although these were often the cause of sudden contractions in the money supply which in turn caused low output and high unemployment during the long period of ensuing adjustment. Monetary expansions create longer-run problems when repeated year after year. Most of the chapter examines the effects on the labour market of such monetary changes.

When minor economic events occur and are within the experience of firms and households, enough people know both the direction and the approximate extent of the required adjustments for the resulting changes to be fairly smooth and rapid. Workers and entrepreneurs provide the innovations and the banking system provides the caution, as in the world of Chapter 1. Occasionally, the Central Bank or the commercial banks generate dramatic happenings, with firms and households reacting with caution. This chapter is about such happenings and the adjustments which follow them.

2.1 FIDUCIARY MONEY

When a Central Bank promises to pay gold for its currency it needs to hold only enough to meet expected demand. The currency which it prints may be used to purchase bonds as well as gold, with the currency appearing in the accounts as a liability and both gold and bonds appearing as assets. The Central Bank can also use this printing facility to maintain confidence in the commercial banking system. If one imprudent commercial bank is unable to pay cash on demand to its depositors, people who have deposits with other banks may decide to convert the deposits into currency. There is a 'run on the banks', even though other banks have an asset structure which is sound enough for all reasonable circumstances. The Central Bank can lend currency to the sound banks, confining the bank failure to the one imprudent bank. The Central Bank is acting as *lender of last resort*. Once confidence is restored, the banking system returns the currency to the Bank, whose liabilities are thus reduced, matched by a reduction in its assets because the commercial banks no longer owe the Bank. Sudden fluctuations in the demand for currency can also be met by the Bank in the same way. Banking prudence is encouraged by the Central Bank charging high interest rates for this service.

When part of the currency is backed by government bonds instead of gold, the Treasury (the printer of the bonds) owes debt to the bank (the printer of the currency). An amalgamated account of these two departments would show no increase in assets but the Bank's liabilities have increased because the public is holding the currency. Similarly, if the Bank's assets are increased because the commercial banks owe it debt in return for currency, an amalgamated account of the Bank and the commercial banking system would show no increase in assets in spite of the increase in currency. In both cases, the currency is not backed by gold but by faith; it is known as a *fiduciary issue*. The Bank may still be able to exchange currency for gold on demand, provided only a part of the currency is presented. Confidence is maintained until the idea of a fiduciary issue becomes accepted. The Bank may then refuse to pay gold to domestic residents. The monetary base ceases to be gold.

In a world on fixed exchange rates, the Bank must still hold assets suitable for an international medium of exchange. Such assets can include the fiduciary issues of the main trading partners as well as gold. The assets backing the high-powered money stock are either domestic or foreign. In practice, most of the domestic assets are government bonds: the fiscal branch of government owes debt to the Central Bank branch. Writing H for high-powered money, R for the reserves of foreign exchange and gold, and D for the domestic assets held by the Bank, the following accounting identity must hold

$$H \equiv R + D \tag{2.1}$$

H is the liabilities of the Central Bank. It consists of currency, whether held by the public (currency 'in circulation') or the commercial banks. H also includes demand deposits placed by the commercial banks with the Central Bank. Such a deposit could be converted to currency if a bank wished; it acts as potential currency. Replacing it by currency would change neither the Central Bank's total liabilities nor the commercial banks' total assets. The system allows the fiscal branch or Treasury to pay for goods by cheque. The firm receiving the cheque deposits it with a commercial bank which then deposits it with the Central Bank. The Bank's liabilities have increased. The Treasury provides the Bank with bonds of the same value to raise the Bank's assets, both H and D have increased in identity (2.1). The effect of the cheque is the same as when the Treasury prints bonds, the Bank prints currency and exchanges it for the bonds. An increase in the commercial banks' deposits with the Central Bank has the same effect as printing money.

A surplus on the balance of payments results in a rise in foreign reserves R. If the international demand for the currency exceeds the supply, the Bank can intervene by creating the domestic currency and using it to purchase gold or foreign currencies. The buyers of the domestic currency are demanding it to pay for exports or domestic financial paper, hence the new currency finds its way into the domestic economy although it was introduced via the international economy. The *exchange market operations* therefore raise both H and R.

There is a third way in which the high-powered money stock may change. Past government borrowing involved selling bonds to households. The Bank could buy these bonds (adding to D) and use new money for the purchase (adding to H). Such an operation helps to smooth transactions when there is a seasonal rise in the demand for currency. At other times the Bank may mop up excessive currency by selling part of its holding of bonds, withdrawing part of H from circulation at the same time that part of its assets D are sold. These changes are known as *open market operations*.

The identity (2.1) can be written in terms of changes in the stocks.

$$\Delta H \equiv \Delta R + \Delta D \tag{2.2}$$

A change in liabilities can be brought about by three types of operation. Foreign exchange operations involve the Bank and foreign currency holders: $\Delta H = \Delta R$. 'Printing money' involves the Bank and the Treasury: $\Delta H = \Delta D$, where the ΔD are new bonds. Open-market operations involve the Bank and the bond-holding public: again $\Delta H = \Delta D$, but the ΔD are old bonds.

A modern monetary system is very different from one where the monetary base is entirely backed by gold. Domestic assets are fiduciary. Foreign reserves include gold but are mainly the fiduciary issues of other countries. Until 1969 most of the main currencies were convertible into US dollars at a fixed rate, and the dollar was convertible into gold. These convertibilities survived only because such little use was made of them. Sterling convertibility could not survive if most sterling-holders wanted dollars, and most dollar-holders must not want gold. Monetary systems are based upon confidence.

As in Chapter 1, the money supply is defined as currency held by firms and households plus the deposits placed by them with the commercial banks, the M1 definition here abbreviated to M. That part of the high-powered money stock which is held as an asset by the commercial banks is excluded from the definition, whether held as currency or as deposits with the Central Bank. However, it is this part which enables the banks to lend prudently, and the loans return as deposits to the banking system. Hence the behaviour of the banks ensures that M is a roughly constant multiple of H.

$$M = hH \tag{2.3}$$

In many countries the Bank reinforces the constancy of h by imposing rules on the banking system, insisting that the banks place deposits with the Central Bank in proportion to firms' and households' deposits with the commercial banks. (Britain is an exception. An unusually small proportion of H is commercial banks' deposits with the Bank of England, which relies on other methods of ensuring prudent banking. In Britain, h is less constant than in most countries.)

2.2 THE NEW QUANTITY THEORY OF THE DEMAND FOR MONEY

The Old Quantity Theory treated the demand for money as a transactions demand which is proportional to nominal income PQ. The economists of the time combined it with a view of an economy where relative prices adjusted rapidly and people's behaviour responded quickly to such adjustments. These relative prices determined Q and the quantity of money determined P, the absolute price level.

In his restatement of the Quantity Theory, Milton Friedman extended our understanding of why people want to hold money. The critics of the Old Quantity Theory had pointed out that money is only one of many assets. It is part of a portfolio of assets held by each firm and household. The amount which is held depends on the advantages of holding money relative to bonds, shares and goods produced in the past, as well as those goods produced in the present whose output creates present income. The desired stock of money is influenced by many factors, including the sentiment of the moment in financial markets. The critics of the Old Quantity Theory thought the demand for money was unpredictable. The effects on the economy of a change in the money supply were also considered unpredictable because we did not know the actions which people would take to ensure that the actual money stock was willingly held.

Friedman accepted that money is held for reasons other than the financing of foreseen transactions. Readily available purchasing power is a convenient insurance against unforeseen emergencies or can enable the holder to take advantage of unforeseen opportunities. Holding money for these reasons is known as the *precautionary demand*. Friedman also accepted that money is only a part of a portfolio of assets and the demand for it could be influenced by changes in other assets. He and his colleagues engaged on a series of historical investigations to discover the extent of these influences. Their conclusions were that the influences were indeed present, but their effects were usually small and, above all, they were predictable. The demand for money is not just a simple proportion of nominal income, but it depends upon nominal income, together with a short list of other observable variables. Provided the demand function is correctly specified, a manageable task, the function is stable.

During periods when the price level is constant, the opportunity cost of holding money is the interest forgone on the bonds which could have been held instead. When interest rates are high, people rearrange the timing of their expenditures and, sometimes more difficult, their receipts. With a closer synchronisation of the two, each firm and household need hold less money on average over the year but still finance the same transactions. The demand for money falls when the interest rate rises.

When prices are expected to rise people expect that the purchasing power of their money-holdings will fall. If the expected inflation rate exceeds the rate of interest, they would be better off buying real assets or goods instead of bonds. The opportunity cost of holding money would be the goods which could be bought rather than the interest on bonds, because goods purchases are the next best use of money rather than bond purchases. The liquidity ratio falls with expected inflation as people rush to spend their money before it has lost its value.

The New Quantity Theory includes other variables whose influences have been found to exist but are small. Its main features can be captured by writing

$$Md = k\,PQ \tag{2.4}$$

$$\text{and} \quad k = k\,(r, \pi^e) \tag{2.5}$$

Equation (2.4) states that an increase in either the price level or real income will lead to a proportionate increase in the demand for money:

the elasticities of demand with respect to P and Q are both unity. These are empirical findings, approximate but close enough for analysing behaviour in the medium run of, say, two to ten years.

In equation (2.5) π is the rate of inflation and π^e the rate which people expect. Unlike the Old Quantity Theory, k is here recognised as being variable. The desired ratio of money to nominal income falls if the rate of interest rises, or if the expected inflation rate increases. Although important, the interest-elasticity of demand for money is well below unity. An increase of 10 per cent in the rate of interest (by half a percentage point from 5 per cent, say) might reduce the demand for money by only 1 per cent. P and π^e are two distinct variables. More money is demanded as the actual price level increases; less is demanded if there is a rise in the rate at which P is expected to increase.

Equilibrium occurs when the money supply M is willingly held:

$$M = Md \qquad\qquad (2.6)$$

An increase in high-powered money allows the money supply to increase. Immediately following the increase, people are holding more money than they wish and spend the surplus on goods, real assets and financial assets such as bonds. Initially, each firm interprets the rise in the demand for its output as a microeconomic phenomenon. It may produce more or raise the price, but usually employs a blend of the two. Both P and Q increase. To the extent that the surplus money is spent on bonds, the price of bonds rises and drives down the rate of interest, encouraging investment expenditure. The fall in the interest rate raises the demand for money by its effect on k, but this effect is small and is dwarfed after a year or two by the effect of the increases in P and Q. It is these two variables whose increase is the main cause of lifting the demand for money to equality with the increased supply. In the medium run the close causal link is *from* the money supply *to* nominal income PQ. Allocating the effects between P and Q is a more complex matter which depends upon the reaction of the labour market.

What of the possibility that the statistical support for the link between money and nominal income is really describing a causal sequence which runs from nominal income to the money supply? Business optimism might encourage investment plans. Firms might borrow from the banks and the Central Bank might accommodate the banks' lending by raising the high-powered money stock. The Bank might use open-market operations in response to the needs of trade, buying old bonds with new money when it notices an increase in the demand for money. Friedman accepted this possibility and found evidence that this does sometimes happen. However, the timing of events usually shows the monetary cause preceding the effect on nominal income. When the timing is reversed, the Central Bank has over emphasised day-to-day and seasonal open-market operations to smooth the money market and has lost control of the year to year growth of money.

2.3 THE ORIGINAL PHILLIPS CURVE

The Law of Supply and Demand states that excess supply in a market will cause a fall in the price of what is traded in that market, and that the greater the excess supply the faster is the fall in price. Strictly, the law refers to the price of what is traded relative to the prices of other goods and services, because relative prices rather than an absolute price determine the decisions of firms and households. This section investigates the effects of an excess supply of labour on nominal wages.

The law says nothing about how the excess supply developed in the first place. We can think of some event beyond the control of firms and households – an exogenous shock such as a decline in export markets causing a drain in foreign reserves, or an open-market operation by the Central Bank which sells bonds to households and withdraws from circulation the money received. Either event would reduce the monetary base and the money supply. Households are holding less money than they wish and they refrain from purchasing goods while they attempt to build up their stocks of money. Firms react by reducing prices, and the fall in the price level reduces the demand for money to match the reduced supply. With no change in the nominal wage W, the real wage W/P has risen and caused excess supply in the labour market. This is illustrated in Figure 2.1 where the labour market clears at the real wage $(W/P)_2$ but Ns is greater than Nd at the higher real wage $(W/P)_3$. The diagram to the right of the labour market shows excess supply expressed as a proportion of labour supply $(Ns - Nd)/Ns$. The ratio is zero at the equilibrium real wage and negative when there is excess demand for labour.

The Australian economist A. W. Phillips realised that labour services are one of the few things that are traded for which there is an indicator of excess supply. Long runs of data exist on the numbers unemployed and the total labour force (employed plus unemployed). The per cent of the labour force unemployed is in the lower diagram of Figure 2.1. It increases when $(Ns - Nd)/Ns$ increases. However, the continuing microeconomic changes which occur mean that some unemployment will be present even if the aggregate labour market is cleared. The unemployed people are engaged in routine job-changing, or have the

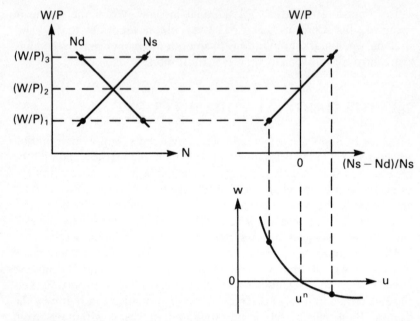

Figure 2.1   The Law of Supply and Demand as it operates in the labour market.
Top left. The labour market clears at a real wage $(W/P)_2$. At $(W/P)_3$ N_s exceeds N_d. At $(W/P)_1$ there is excess demand.
Top right. The horizontal axis measures excess supply as a ratio to total supply. This is negative when the real wage is below $(W/P)_2$.
Lower diagram. The Phillips relation uses u as an indicator of excess supply with the natural rate u^n corresponding to a cleared labour market. The rate of change in the money wage is high and positive when there is excess demand, slow and negative when there is excess supply.

(Note that the Ns and Nd functions are fixed in this example.)

wrong skill and have not yet retrained, or are in the wrong location and have not yet moved. The rate associated with labour market equilibrium has since become known as *the natural rate of unemployment*. Unemployment below this rate means that job-changing is unusually rapid; firms are unusually ready to retrain recruits or to open new plants in areas of high unemployment. Low unemployment is an indication of excess demand for labour. Clearly the unemployment rate cannot be negative.

The Phillips curve is a test of the Law of Supply and Demand. It compares the indicator of excess supply with changes in the nominal wage, which is that part of the real wage under the control of the participants in the labour market. In Figure 2.1, w is the per cent per annum change in the nominal wage W. The curve shows rapid wage increases when unemployment is low, but sluggish falls in wages when unemployment is high. Expressing w as a decreasing function of u

$$w = f(u) \tag{2.7}$$
$$\underset{-}{}$$

Figure 2.1 pictures no change in money wages when excess labour supply is zero. This would be correct if the Ns and Nd functions remained fixed, but during most peacetime years the Nd function shifts upwards as the marginal product of labour increases with capital accumulation, education and technical change. The Ns function shifts to the right as population increases or as an increasing proportion of the population join the labour force. During most years, the effect of the upward shift of Nd outweighs that of the rightward shift in Ns and the equilibrium real wage rises. If the price level were constant, nominal wages could rise each year and still preserve equilibrium. In Figure 2.2, the natural rate of unemployment is shown as 2.4 per cent, implying that nominal wage increases of 2 per cent per annum would preserve labour market equilibrium. At greater levels of unemployment, wage increases would be less than the growth in labour productivity and the market would move to equilibrium. Provided prices are constant, wages can still increase but the gap between the real wage and the marginal product of labour narrows because the former grows more slowly than the latter.

The Phillips curve therefore shows the Law of Supply and Demand in operation. When there is excess demand for labour, wages rise rapidly. Wages may not fall when there is excess supply but they rise less quickly than labour productivity: their rate of change falls. Nominal wages actually fall only when there is considerable excess supply, as shown by an unemployment rate of 5.4 per cent in Figure 2.2. The crucial feature of the curve is the asymmetry between rapid adjustment to excess demand and very sluggish adjustment to excess supply. A second feature is the way in which changes in the price level seem to have no direct influence on wage adjustment. A monetary shock may be the cause of a price level change but the influence on nominal wages is only indirect via a disequilibrium real wage, a change in unemployment, and only then a change in the rate of increase in nominal wages. The causal sequence seems to be:

$$M \rightarrow P \rightarrow W/P \rightarrow u \rightarrow w$$

Each stage in the sequence takes time, particularly if there is a monetary contraction. The correction of the disequilibrium starts only when the

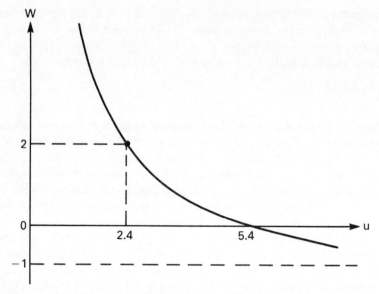

Figure 2.2   The original Phillips curve derived from British data from 1861 to 1913.

The curve also fits data for the peacetime years up to the mid-1960s. If the natural rate of unemployment was 2.4 per cent, nominal wage increases of 2 per cent per annum would preserve equilibrium. With no trend in the price level, this rate for w allows real wages to rise in line with labour productivity. Wages fall when u rises above 5.4 per cent but are unlikely to fall by more than one per cent per annum even when unemployment is very high. The equation for the curve is

$$w = -0.9 + 9.6u^{-1.4}$$

The negative power to which u is raised implies that the smaller is u the larger is w. High values of u reduce the influence of the term on the right but wage decreases are not more than 0.9 of a percentage point per annum.

last stage in the above sequence is reached, when the change in the rate w causes a change in the ratio W/P. This is the corrective feedback which slowly causes a movement along the Phillips curve towards that w which corresponds to the natural rate of unemployment.

In retrospect, the century of stability of the Phillips curve for Britain, and the decade of stability shown by the curves for other countries during the 1950s and early 1960s, can be attributed to the fixed exchange rates which prevailed during most of the peacetime years which provided the data for the curves. Until 1913, the main currencies were tied to gold. For some of the interwar years, and for the postwar period up to the late 1960s, currencies were tied to the US dollar, which itself was tied to gold. Changes in the price level might be up or down. Short-term economic forecasting was rudimentary. By the time the actual price changes had been noticed, the unemployment had already changed. Wage negotiations would have been influenced by firms' knowledge of the price they could obtain for their output, but the workers would have been influenced by their knowledge of unemployment rates. In a statistical exercise, a high value for the u variable would also be capturing the effects of a low value for the P variable, which could therefore be omitted. The exceptions to the stability of the Phillips curve were those years when import prices rose noticeably. Phillips had warned in his article that nominal wage increases were higher than predicted by the curve in such years. We postpone to a later section the analysis of wage changes when inflation is expected.

2.4   THE AGGREGATE SUPPLY FUNCTION

The aggregate supply function is the relation between the price level and the output offered by firms. It shows how a change in nominal income is split between price and quantity changes in the short run of, say, a year. Its derivation draws upon our understanding of behaviour in the labour market, particularly the different responses to excess labour supply compared with excess labour demand. These responses can be captured in the analysis by treating the nominal wage W as the result of a contract negotiated at the end of the previous year. The negotiators took into account the unemployment rate then prevailing and the price level which they then expected for the present year. If they overestimated P, the W contract will lead to W/P above equilibrium. The contract refers to wages, not employment, and firms react by reducing the number of workers and output. Most workers are still in jobs and insist that the wage contract is kept until the next routine round of negotiations. Figure 2.3 shows the labour market and the aggregate supply function when the price level is less than was expected.

When the price level is surprisingly high, the response of the labour market and output is more complicated. The explanation can be developed in three stages. First, we consider what would happen if workers and employers stuck to the wage contract. The real wage would be below equilibrium and households would ration employment. This reduction in employment would reduce output and a higher price level would be associated with lower output. This possibility is illustrated in Figure 2.4 where the contracted money wage W_1 combines with the

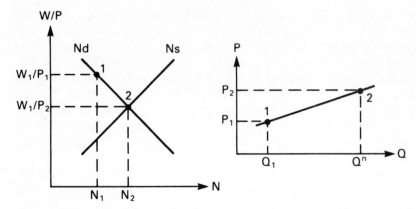

Figure 2.3   The aggregate supply function when there is excess supply of labour.
In the short run, the wage contract fixes the nominal wage at W_1. If the output price is P_2 the real wage is at equilibrium. N_2 workers are employed and produce Q^n of output. At the lower output price P_1, the real wage is above equilibrium and firms ration employment to N_1 workers who produce only Q_1 of output. The right-hand diagram shows the response of aggregate supply to the price level when the nominal wage is fixed.
Point 1 in the left diagram shows excess labour supply and in the right diagram the resulting low output.
Point 2 shows the employment associated with equilibrium and the natural level of output Q^n which results.

high output price P_3. Households ration employment to N_3 to yield output Q_3 which is less than Q^n. With excess demand for labour, this aggregate supply function shows Q decreasing as P rises. We now consider why this does not happen.

The second stage of the explanation is that the interests of both parties to the negotiations would be furthered by recontracting when there is an excess demand for labour. Firms want more workers and are prepared to pay more for them until the marginal product of labour ceases to be above the real wage. Workers in jobs will not resist rises in money wages. With recontracting, any excess demand for labour is eliminated during the period. If P is higher than was expected during the original negotiations, W rises to bring the real wage to equilibrium. If all parties were aware of the true real wage, employment would be constant and output at Q^n. The aggregate supply function would be vertical. Implicitly, this was the supply response of Chapter 1 when all prices are flexible.

The third part of the explanation of supply behaviour involves the different capacities of firms and households to absorb information. Firms

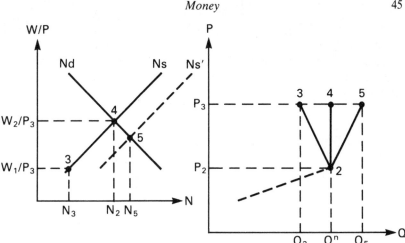

Figure 2.4   The possible responses of aggregate supply to a surprisingly high output price.

The negotiators expected P_2 and set a wage of W_1. The actuality is P_3 and the real wage is below equilibrium at W_1/P_3. If this real wage holds, households ration employment to N_3 and firms produce only Q_3 of output. Point 3 in the left diagram shows the excess demand for labour and in the right diagram the low output.

If the nominal wage is renegotiated to W_2 the real wage clears the market. Point 4 shows the full-information equilibrium on the left diagram. On the right, the high price level combines with Q_1^n and the aggregate supply function is vertical. The upward flexibility of W allows neoclassical adjustment to maintain equilibrium as in Chapter 1.

If households misinterpret the rise in W as a rise in W/P, the Ns functions shift to Ns' while the misperception lasts. Point 5 in each diagram shows the N_5 workers employed and the Q_5 of output they produce. The increase in P is associated with a short-run increase in Q.

know the price of their own product and the wages they pay. They are approximately aware of the other prices and wages which make up the indexes P and W. Households are fully aware of their own wage increases, but underestimate any price increases in the short run. Until they have had time to gather information about P, they think that the real wage has risen. As the nominal wage increases, they offer more labour services at each actual real wage than they would if they had full information. On a diagram with actual W/P on the vertical axis, the labour supply function shifts to the right. In Figure 2.4, the renegotia-tion of the nominal wage from W_1 to W_2 has been fully taken into account by households, but the extent to which P_3 exceeds the expected P_2 has been only partially appreciated. The labour supply function shifts to Ns' enabling firms to employ N_5 workers at a real wage which is below that which would result if households had full information. Output rises to Q_5 which is above Q^n. This confusion of a nominal or money wage increase with a real wage increase is known as *money illusion*.

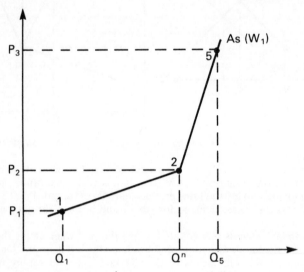

Figure 2.5   The aggregate supply function when the initial nominal wage was negotiated to be W_1.
Between points 1 and 2 the excess labour supply diminishes as W_1 remains constant but P increases. As P rises above P_2 the nominal wage is recontracted. More labour is supplied than if there were no money illusion. The function is labelled As (W_1) to show the initially agreed nominal wage. The actual nominal wage will exceed this if P exceeds P_2.

   The complete short-run aggregate supply function is shown in Figure 2.5. P_2 is the price level which was expected when the wage negotiations were in progress. Firms and households are aiming at an equilibrium real wage for the present period. If P_2 is indeed the present price level, output is Q^n and the labour market again clears. At lower price levels, the function has a gentle slope. There is an excess supply of labour but small increases in P would be associated with large increases in Q until output reaches Q^n. For surprisingly high price levels, the function has a steep slope. The renegotiations of the nominal wage eliminate any excess demand for labour but the suppliers of labour overestimate the real wage.

2.5 MONETARY EXPANSION AND CONTRACTION

During the eighteenth century, Sweden had a currency which was mainly a fiduciary issue. The quantity would be determined by the state. The political parties debated on the relative merits of increasing or decreasing this quantity. A decrease lowered the cost of living particularly the cost of imports. By creating a scarcity of Swedish crowns on the foreign exchanges, each crown could buy more foreign money and hence more imports. However, when the government printed money the increase could be used to finance beneficial public works. The argument was between those who thought more money raised output and employment, and those who thought less money lowered the cost of living. The Swedish philosopher P. N. Christiernin argued against both these views. He was the first writer to point out the unfortunate asymmetry between monetary expansion and contraction: more money raised prices but less money raised unemployment. This section uses modern theories and evidence to elaborate and support Christiernin's lectures, which were delivered in 1761.

Monetary equilibrium occurs when the money supply M equals the demand for money kPQ. In Figure 2.6, the curve labelled M is a rectangular hyperbola giving the different combinations of P and Q which equal $(1/k)\,M$. The aggregate supply function As (W_1) shows the output which would be supplied by firms at each price level if the nominal wage negotiated for the period is W_1. The negotiators expected the price level P_1. They were correct and the real wage is at its equilibrium with output at its natural level Q^n. The nominal income curve M cuts the aggregate supply function at its kink.

For the next period, firms and households again expect P_1 and agree a wage W_1 leaving the aggregate supply function unchanged. The authorities expand the money supply to M'. During the disequilibrium, the excess supply of money causes an excess demand for goods and raises P; the lower real wage causes an excess demand for labour leading to recontracting of the nominal wage W which rises above the W_1 of the contract at the start of the period. Households have money illusion and supply more labour than they would do with full information. The economy moves up the steeply sloping section of As (W_1) to point 2, where output is larger than Q^n and the price level is now P_2. However, point 2 is only a temporary equilibrium because the misperceptions of households will soon be corrected as they appreciate the extent of price rises.

In the third period, the money supply stays at M' and there is no

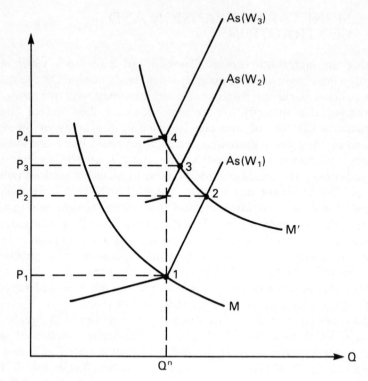

Figure 2.6   A major expansion of the money supply shifts nominal income from M to M'.
Point 1 is the initial equilibrium with the nominal wage of W_1 combining with P_1 to clear the labour market and the equilibrium number of workers producing Q^n of output.
Point 2. Nominal income increases to the M' curve. W is recontracted during the period. Misperceptions increase employment and output.
Point 3. The wage negotiated for the third period is W_2 in the expectation of P_2. (The As (W_2) function is vertically above As (W_1) and the kink is at P_2.) The actual price level is P_3 and again there is some recontracting during the period.
Point 4 is the new equilibrium without misperceptions. P_4 is expected and W_3/P_4 is the equilibrium real wage. The effect of the monetary expansion was a temporary rise in output and a permanent rise in the price level. Each point is a position of equilibrium in both the goods and labour markets, but points 2 and 3 are equilibria with misperceptions.

change in nominal income. The wage for this period was decided by disillusioned households, who realised the extent of the price rise by the end of the previous period, and profitable firms able to offer a higher wage. If P_2 is the price level expected, the nominal wage of W_2 is expected to clear the labour market, but when this third period arrives firms find they can raise prices above P_2. Recontracting of W again occurs, although on a smaller scale than in period 2. The economy moves to point 3 for period 3. In Figure 2.6 the misperceptions have disappeared by period 4. The effect of the monetary expansion has worked its way through entirely into a rise in the price level with output reverting back to its natural level Q^n. The example refers to a once-only increase in the money supply. Repeated increases of erratic size would lead to wrong expectations about the price level and misperceptions of the real wage.

A monetary contraction reduces the price level but has its main initial effects on output and employment because job-holders refuse to recontract a lower money wage during the period. The adjustments are confined to the regular wage negotiations at the end of each period. The labour market responds sluggishly to excess supply (the gently sloping section of the Phillips curve) and the inter-period adjustment is small. A major reduction in the money supply is followed by many years with unemployment above its natural rate, output below its natural level, prices falling slowly, and money wages falling only slightly faster to push the real wage back down to its level before the monetary contractions. Figure 2.7 illustrates a major contraction which shifts nominal income from the curve marked M to that marked M''. Initially, the aggregate supply function is fixed. The money wage stays constant and the decline in nominal income is mainly a fall in Q with only a slight fall in P. This short-run fall in output will be explained more realistically in Chapter 4 which focuses on the short-term demand for goods. Here we can note that such a fall would be consistent with an elastic demand for labour: the rise in the real wage causes a major fall in employment and output, a supply-side effect caused by the sticky nominal wage. The fall in the money supply causes an excess demand for money and an excess supply of goods. The excess demand for money is eliminated by the fall in PQ. Relative prices do not adjust immediately and the disequilibrium is pushed into the labour market where the excess supply of labour will influence the next round of wage negotiations.

In subsequent periods money wages fall. The fall in wage costs enables firms to reduce prices slightly and hence sell more goods. The price reductions are not as great as the wage reductions and the fall in the real wage increases the demand for labour. The reluctant reductions in money wages slowly move the economy back to equilibrium. In Figure 2.7 the falls in the nominal wage are shown as the downward shifts in the As function.

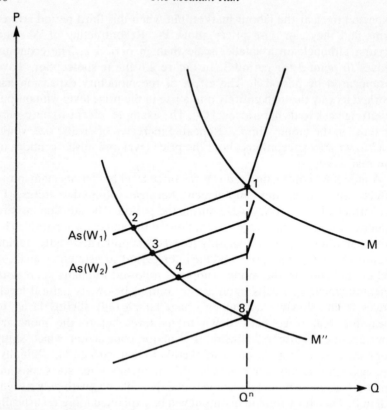

Figure 2.7 A major monetary contraction is followed by many years of adjustment before employment returns to equilibrium and output reverts to its natural level.
Point 1. The initial equilibrium.
Point 2. Nominal income falls to M″. The nominal wage stays at W_1 during period 2. Employment and output fall.
Point 3. The wage negotiators respond to high unemployment by lowering the nominal wage to W_2. With no intra-period recontracting and slow inter-period falls in W, the return to full employment is a lengthy process.
Point 8 is the final equilibrium with the labour market again cleared. Each point shows equilibrium in the goods market but only points 1 and 8 show no excess supply in the labour market.

2.6   INCREASED LABOUR PRODUCTIVITY

Throughout the previous section, the exposition was simplified by assuming that labour productivity did not change between periods. In most years the marginal product of labour increases due to innovations and investments in equipment, training and health. The equilibrium real wage increases as the demand for labour shifts in response to increased productivity. A cleared labour market could result from a constant money wage combined with a fall in the price level, or a constant price level and a rise in the money wage which was in the same proportion as the rise in productivity. Figure 2.8 illustrates these two possibilities. The kinks in the As functions denote the points where the wage negotiations before the period began produced a money wage which combines with the output price to give a market-clearing real wage.

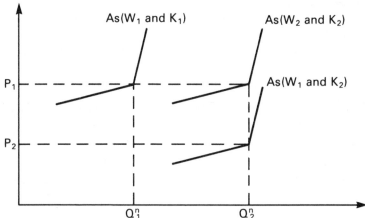

Figure 2.8   Shifts in aggregate supply caused by increased labour productivity. Capital increases from K_1 to K_2, allowing an increase in the equilibrium real wage either by raising W from W_1 to W_2 or by lowering P from P_1 to P_2 where $W_1/P_2 = W_2/P_1$ which is greater than W_1/P_1. The natural level of output increases from Q_1^n to Q_2^n in either case.

P is the index of all output prices. If P remains constant, any change in individual product prices or money wages are also changes in relative prices or real wages. Such changes provide signals and incentives for those adjustments to quantities which increase microeconomic efficiency. Constant P has the advantage of simplifying the information system.

2.7   THE MONETARY RULE

The close link between the money supply and nominal income enables the monetary authorities to maintain constant P. They estimate the sustainable growth rate of real output and expand the money supply at the same rate. This policy is known as *the monetary rule*. In addition to the informational advantages, the rule also encourages stable growth. If actual output fell below its natural level, the demand for money would be less than supply. People would be holding more money than desired and would spend the extra, encouraging firms to expand output. If output grew beyond its sustainable rate, pushing actual output above its natural level, the demand for money would exceed the supply. Each person would attempt to build up his stock of money although the total stock is controlled by the authorities. Each person reduces his spending and firms reduce output back to its sustainable level. The rule helps to eliminate both under- and overproduction of output.

Figure 2.9 illustrates the rule working as intended. Aggregate supply has shifted from As to As' with W rising in line with labour productivity so that the higher natural level of output occurs at the same price level as before. The money supply increases from M to M' to ensure that actual output again equals natural output.

The rule is advocated with caution. Estimating the sustainable growth rate of output is difficult, and there are often errors in predicting the behaviour of the monetary sector. The authorities can control the monetary base H and they can use banking legislation in an attempt to maintain h constant in $M = hH$. However, bank failures reduce h. The commercial banks may innovate in a way which skirts the legislation and increases h. Careful monitoring is needed to ensure that the growth in H leads to the required growth in M.

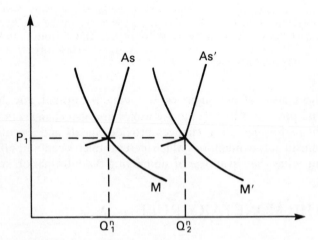

Figure 2.9   The monetary rule.
If natural output grows at 4 per cent per annum, the price level will stay constant if $M' = (1.04) M$.

Monetary equilibrium occurs when

$$M = k\,PQ$$

To convert this equation to rates of change, write m for the growth rate of M, π for the growth rate of P and q for the growth rate of Q.

$$m = \text{(the change in k)} + \pi + q \qquad (2.8)$$

If k is constant, π is zero and q is at its sustainable rate q^n, then (2.8) becomes

$$m = q^n \qquad (2.9)$$

The liquidity ratio increases over the years as the wealth of households increases. When two people have the same nominal income their transactions demand for money tends to be the same, but if one has a greater stock of wealth than the other his precautionary demand for money is greater. The convenience of money to meet unforeseen contingencies leads him to increase his holdings as his total portfolio of assets increases. An increase in the community's stock of wealth raises the demand for money.

Equation (2.5) is extended to include this influence of wealth.

$$k = k\,(r, \pi^e, \text{wealth}) \qquad (2.10)$$

The object of the monetary rule is to eliminate inflation. If expectations are forward-looking, knowledge that the rule is operating ensures that $\pi^e = 0$. If they are backward-looking, some years' experience of zero inflation will have the same result. With stable monetary growth, r will be mainly influenced by the loanable funds market and changes in it will be minor. The low interest-elasticity leads to an even smaller effect on the demand for money. This leaves wealth as the main long-run influence on k. Its effect is difficult to measure precisely because most countries have poor data on wealth, but its effect is to raise the demand for money by perhaps a percentage point per annum. For this reason Friedman advocated that monetary growth should be slightly above the sustainable rate of output growth.

2.8 EXPECTED INFLATION

The study of wage increases reveals that people in the labour market behave as if they are often surprised by the rate of inflation. They seem to form their expectation about next year's inflation from their experience of past inflation. At the beginning of period t, the inflation rate expected during the period $\pi^e{}_t$ seems to be formed from observations of actual inflation in preceding periods π_{t-1}, π_{t-2} and so on. The expectation is formed by looking back at past values of the same variable, with the more recent past having the most influence on the view of the future.

People also learn from their mistakes, adapting their expectations in the light of past errors. *The Adaptive Expectations Hypothesis* (AEH) states that

$$\pi^e{}_t = \pi_{t-1} + b\,(\pi^e{}_{t-1} - \pi_{t-1}) \tag{2.11}$$

If b were zero, people would put all the weight on last year's inflation, which would also be the expected rate for this year. If b were unity, this year's expected rate would be the same as last year's expected rate, with the actual rate last year having no influence. In practice, b is between zero and unity. For example, with $b = 0.6$ and $\pi^e{}_{t-1} = 10$ per cent, this year's expected rate depends on last year's rate in the following way:

If π_{t-1} was 5, then $\pi^e{}_t$ is 8
If π_{t-1} was 10, then $\pi^e{}_t$ is 10
If π_{t-1} was 15, then $\pi^e{}_t$ is 12

The AEH predicts that expectations will slowly catch up with actual inflation provided it stays constant for some years after its initial change. If inflation accelerates, expected inflation will lag further and further behind. Decreasing inflation results in expectations which are greater than the actuality. The hypothesis provides an explanation of why money wage increases sometimes result in real wage changes which, *ex post*, are either too low or too high for labour market equilibrium.

Unfortunately, there is a shortage of survey data about people's expectations of inflation. This makes the AEH difficult to test by itself although it can be tested as one of a group of hypotheses about labour markets or, as it was originally presented by Cagan (1956), about people's behaviour when there are hyperinflations. Its appeal lies in its assumptions that people make economical use of information, and that people learn from their mistakes.

When inflation increases for many years in succession, the AEH implies that people do not learn from their mistakes sufficiently rapidly. After several years of larger and larger under-predictions of inflation, attention shifts from the inflation rate to increases in the rate. Writing $\Delta\pi$ for the percentage points increase in inflation, expectations are formed by taking

$$\Delta\pi^e{}_t = \Delta\pi_{t-1} + b\,(\Delta\pi^e{}_{t-1} - \Delta\pi_{t-1}) \tag{2.12}$$

There has been a *change of gear* between equations (2.11) and (2.12). This gear-changing modification to the AEH is due to Flemming (1976). If actual inflation accelerated for several years and then fell for several years, expectations might lag particularly far behind while the process of forming them changed gear, first up from π^e to $\Delta\pi^e$ then down from $\Delta\pi^e$ to π^e.

2.9 THE EXPECTATIONS-AUGMENTED PHILLIPS CURVE

Consider an economy where actual and expected inflation are both zero. The labour market is cleared and unemployment is at its natural rate. Money wage increases are also real wage increases, rising at the same rate as the increase in labour productivity, thereby preserving equilibrium (assuming for simplicity no increase in labour supply). This position is illustrated in Figure 2.10 as point 1 on the lower curve.

The authorities now provide a monetary stimulus which raises the price level by 5 per cent. The real wage falls and there is an excess demand for labour, driving unemployment down to u_2 which is below the natural rate. Although this change in unemployment is not predicted by the curve, the results of the change are: wages rise at the high rate of w_2 to eliminate the excess demand. If the exchange rate is fixed, the rise in prices will cause a loss of competitiveness and the balance of payments will be in deficit. Foreign reserves are lost as the exchange rate is preserved. Prices return to competitive levels, perhaps with a period when unemployment is above its natural rate. The effects of the monetary stimulus are reversed before inflation enters people's expectations. The economy moves along the curve labelled $\pi^e = 0$. This is the original Phillips curve estimated from the data generated during regimes of fixed exchange rates.

Suppose the economy is at point 2 in Figure 2.10, instead of reversing the monetary expansion the authorities continue it at the same rate. Prices continue to rise and the wage negotiators start to expect inflation. The Phillips curve shifts upwards. Eventually the constant inflation rate will be anticipated. The economy is now on the curve labelled $\pi^e = 5$ per cent. With accurate expectations, workers and firms arrange wage deals which clear the labour market and unemployment reverts to its natural level. This is point 4 on the diagram. The journey from point 1 to point 2 and then point 4 involves a temporary fall in unemployment but leaves a continuing inflation rate.

The authorities could maintain unemployment at its low level of u_2 but

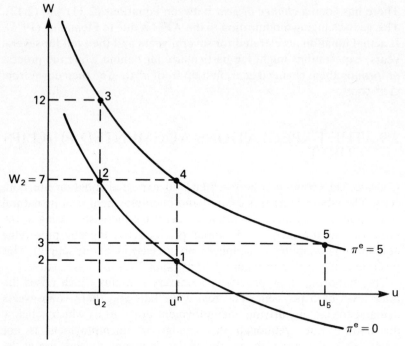

Figure 2.10   The expectations-augmented Phillips curve.
Point 1 shows $w = 2$ when unemployment is at its natural rate and inflation is not expected; nominal wages grow at the expected rate of increase of productivity.
Point 2 shows $w = 7$ to remove the excess demand for labour signified by u_2 below u^n and π^e still zero.
Point 3. If 5 per cent inflation is expected, u_2 causes w of 12.
Point 4. If $u = u^n$, $w = 7$ is expected to clear the labour market.
Point 5. High unemployment causes $w = 3$ when $\pi^e = 5$.

only by generating ever-increasing inflation. They have to keep ahead of the expected inflation rate to ensure that the negotiators keep setting a money wage increase which will generate excess demand. It is unanticipated inflation which moves u. It is expected inflation combined with u which determines wage increases. The actual inflation which occurs during the period of the wage contract holds down the increase in real wages and maintains the excess demand for labour. After a few years of noticeably increasing inflation, expectations will change gear. Low unemployment can then be achieved only by increasing the rate of increase of inflation. There is no long-run trade-off between unemployment and inflation. The cost of holding unemployment below its natural rate is accelerating inflation leading to hyperinflation.

The authorities can resign themselves to maintaining actual inflation at the same rate as expected inflation. In this case the labour market is unsurprised by the inflation and unemployment is at its natural rate. Provided it is expected, any inflation rate can be consistent with natural unemployment. Money wage increases will exceed the inflation rate by the amount justified by the growth of productivity (adjusted for any changes in labour supply). The long-run Phillips curve is vertical, if we define 'the long run' in the rather special sense as the period required for expectations to catch up with reality.

In practice, expectations are difficult to discover and often seem to depart from actuality. The natural rate of unemployment is not constant. The authorities are criticised for actual inflation, and periods of rising inflation are followed by periods of falls. Then firms and households arrange wage contracts in the expectation of high inflation, raising the real wage above its equilibrium level and unemployment above its natural rate.

Point 5 in Figure 2.10 shows the high unemployment of u_5 which resulted from a past real wage increase. With inflation expected to be 5 per cent, this unemployment is high enough to generate a money wage increase of only 3 per cent, a cut in expected real wages. If actual inflation is zero, however, what was expected to be a real wage cut turns out to be an actual increase which is greater than the rise in productivity and unemployment rises during the period. Only in the next period will expected inflation fall and shift the Phillips curve to a position between those marked $\pi^e = 5$ and $\pi^e = 0$, lower w and reduce excess supply.

Equilibrium in the labour market would be preserved if labour supply were constant and $w = \pi +$ productivity growth. Departures from equilibrium would be short if high unemployment moderated wage increases.

$$w = \pi + \text{productivity growth} - a(u - u^n)$$

where the parameter a shows the impact of disequilibrium unemployment on w. The wage negotiators have to estimate inflation and productivity growth. Monetary shocks make π^e depart from π. The erratic monetary expansions in many countries from the mid-1960s to the late 1970s created many of such monetary surprises. Shocks to aggregate supply reduce productivity growth below expectation, as occurred when much oil-using equipment was made obsolete by the oil price rises of 1973 and 1979. The equilibrating processes are the revision of expectations about inflation and productivity, and the impact of excess supply as u departs from u^n.

For a government observing the labour market the position is further complicated by changes in the natural rate of unemployment. In most European countries this has been rising throughout the 1970s and 1980s. In particular, the long-term unemployed have little impact on wage negotiations. Sometimes this is because they have given up offering their labour services. More usually, their offers are rejected by firms which do not perceive them as part of the supply of labour, the lack of a work record being taken as an indicator of poor quality. There are many policies which can reduce the natural rate: information, counselling, training, the provision of work experience to provide a work record to prospective employers. The lesson of the expectations-augmented Phillips curve is that monetary expansions have only short-run effects on unemployment. Permanent effects require policies which are directed at the natural rate.

2.10   MONEY SENORAGE

Originally 'senorage' was the profit made by a ruler from minting coins. His prestige backed the coin as the image of his face fronted it. If the coin's gold content was reliable, the coin was more convenient than uncoined gold and was therefore worth more. Senorage was the coin's value less the gold's value and less the cost of minting. Modern governments have almost perfected the art of senorage by eliminating the gold content. Money senorage can be used to finance a government's budget deficit. It is one of the temptations to break the monetary rule. The problem is to achieve senorage without totally losing prestige.

This section considers the size of the budget deficit which can be financed by continually expanding the monetary base at a rate faster than implied by the monetary rule. The monetary growth rate is taken to be constant for many years. The inflation rate is also constant and the wage negotiators have adapted to this constant rate: real wages are at equilibrium and are perceived to be so. With inflation and monetary growth both constant, there is also a constant growth rate of real output. We are considering long-term trends over a period of a decade or more.

The budget deficit is government expenditure on goods and services plus transfer payments paid by government less the taxes paid to government. In order to simplify the analysis which follows, we shall assume that output growth is determined by firms and households. This implies that we are excluding two types of government expenditure: investment projects which would influence the economy's output by their long-run effects on aggregate supply, and those short-run government expenditures or tax reductions which expand aggregate demand when the government notes that output is temporarily constrained by a shortage of orders to firms. (Short-term deficits incurred to boost aggregate demand are considered in Chapter 4.) We are examining a rather smaller deficit than that which appears in a government's accounts but the simplification allows us to focus on the main effects of senorage on the size of the deficit. We are attempting to discover the proportion of nominal income which can be captured by the government via printing money rather than taxation.

During each period the deficit Def is financed by an increase ΔH in the monetary base:

$$Def = \Delta H \tag{2.13}$$

Expressing the deficit as a ratio to nominal income, and writing H for the average stock of money during the period:

$$\frac{Def}{PQ} = \frac{\Delta H}{PQ} = \frac{\Delta H}{H} \bullet \frac{H}{PQ} \tag{2.14}$$

Reserve requirements ensure some constancy of h in the money supply relation $M = hH$, which means that the monetary base is a constant fraction of the money supply: $H = M/h$. The demand for this money stock is kPQ, and monetary equilibrium implies that $PQ = M/k$. In equilibrium, therefore

$$\frac{H}{PQ} = \frac{M/h}{M/k} = \frac{k}{h} \tag{2.15}$$

and equation 2.14 becomes

$$\frac{Def}{PQ} = \frac{\Delta H}{H} \bullet \frac{k}{h} \tag{2.16}$$

$\Delta H/H$ is the rate of growth of the monetary base, which allows an equal rate of growth of the money supply, which in turn causes growth in nominal income. Provided k and h are constant, nominal income grows at the same rate as the monetary base. However, the liquidity ratio varies in response to changes in three variables. Repeating (2.10),

$$k = k \ (r, \ \pi^e, \ wealth)$$

Constant monetary growth causes a constant inflation rate which becomes the expected rate if it continues for many years. Variations in the interest rate are small if monetary growth is constant. The main long-run influence on k is the slow increase brought about by increasing wealth.

Equation (2.16) referred to a particular period. We are interested in the sustained ratio of the deficit to nominal income over many periods, d in equation (2.17) below. Monetary base growth causes nominal income growth at a rate which is the sum of inflation π and real income growth q. The relation between d, π and q is

$$d = (\pi + q)\, k/h \qquad\qquad (2.17)$$

Suppose that the sustained growth of output is 4 per cent per annum, the liquidity ratio 0.3, and the monetary base multiplier 2. For zero inflation the sustainable deficit which can be financed by money creation is

$$d = (0 + 0.04)\, 0.3/2 = 0.006$$

A steady price level entails the modest money senorage of only 0.6 per cent of gross domestic product.

For inflation of 10 per cent,

$$d = (0.10 + 0.04)\, 0.3/2 = 0.021$$

and the government can capture 2.1 per cent of gdp.

For inflation of 100 per cent,

$$d = (1.00 + 0.04)\, 0.3/2 = 0.156$$

Provided we accept the price level doubling each year, the government can finance a deficit equal to 15.6 per cent of gdp.

The demand for money rises slightly as real wealth increases but the effect on d is small. A decade of increasing wealth might raise k from 0.30 to 0.33, raising d by one-tenth. There may be spectacular reductions in d if deregulation of the banking system and financial innovations raise h. The following table gives illustrative percentages for d when real output grows at 4 per cent per annum, k increases from 0.3 to 0.33 over a decade, and financial innovations raise h from 2 to 3.

π per cent	k = 0.30 h = 2	k = 0.33 h = 2	k = 0.30 h = 3	k = 0.33 h = 3
0	0.60	0.66	0.40	0.44
10	2.10	2.30	1.40	1.54
100	15.60	17.16	10.40	11.44

These illustrations suggest that the inflation rate is the main influence on the deficit which can be sustained by money senorage. In effect, money creation acts as an *inflation tax*, providing the government with a command over resources by shrinking the purchasing power of the money held by firms and households.

2.11 PURCHASING POWER PARITY

Under a regime of fixed exchange rates there is a sense in which the world has only one money. One country's gain in gold or foreign reserves is another country's loss. Movements of money occur when there is balance of payments disequilibrium. The price of imports is EP^*, where E is the fixed price of foreign currency and P^* the foreign price level. The price of exports is P. International movements of money change P and P^*. Imports and exports then change, until there is no net movement of gold and foreign reserves across frontiers. The flows of imports and exports remain constant when $EP^* = P$, the condition discussed in Chapter 1 and known as the Law of One Price.

When countries adopt independent monetary policies, the purchasing power of the different monies falls at different rates. The LOOP would cease to hold even as a rough approximation unless the exchange rate changed. The currency of a country with high inflation would otherwise lose export markets as its competitiveness fell. The real exchange rate $Rer = EP^*/P$ would fall further and further below unity as P rose faster than P^*, unless the nominal exchange rate E rose. With exporters receiving less foreign currency and importers demanding more to purchase the lower-priced imports, the excess demand for foreign currency raises its price E. Competitiveness would remain constant if the price of foreign exchange were

$$E = P/P^* \qquad (2.18)$$

This is known as the *Absolute Purchasing Power Parity* theory of exchange rates. Clearly one would not expect it to hold at all times because then the Rer would always be unity. The flows of imports and exports would change only in response to influences other than relative price changes. In practice, the Rer for most pairs of currencies most of the time lies within the range of 0.7 to 1.3. Even this vague statement has to be qualified by the difficulties of accurately measuring P and P^*, the indexes of the absolute price levels in the domestic and foreign economies.

The dynamic version of (2.18) involves comparing domestic and foreign inflation rates. These can be more accurately measured than price levels because a proportionately consistent error in P_t and P_{t-1} will cancel out in $(P_t - P_{t-1})/P_{t-1}$. Write e for the rate of increase in the price of foreign exchange, which is the rate of *depreciation* of the domestic currency:

$$e = \pi - \pi^* \qquad (2.19)$$

where π and π^* are the domestic and foreign inflation rates. This is the *Relative Purchasing Power Parity* theory of exchange rates (RPPP). During the 1970s and 1980s, there was a limited sense in which RPPP often provided good predictions of exchange rate movements: the greater the gap between e and $\pi - \pi^*$ in the recent past the more likely that the gap would narrow in the near future. Even this limited version of RPPP is not totally reliable, particularly for those currencies whose price is affected by major changes in the movement of financial capital. Nevertheless it has a better track record than other theories or combinations of theories.

During the 1960s many economists who emphasised the importance of moderation in monetary policy also advocated floating exchange rates. They expected that the foreign exchange market would adjust exchange rates in conformity with RPPP. Such adjustments would allow monetary policy to be detached from the foreign sector. Zero inflation in one country and high inflation in another would cause nominal exchange rate changes which would leave the real exchange rate unaltered and allow international trade to grow in response to the real influences provided by firms and households in the trading countries. This section has shown how such adjustments could occur. The last two decades have shown the very limited extent to which they actually occurred.

2.12 SUMMARY

This chapter showed how governments can create the monetary base. This activity releases gold for industrial or artistic use and avoids excessive reliance on gold-mining countries, mainly South Africa and the Soviet Union. It enables the Central Bank to maintain orderly conditions in financial markets by varying the base with the day-to-day needs of trade. The Bank can also create money to avoid epidemics of bank failures when there are runs on the commercial banks.

The temptation is to create too much. Sometimes this is to finance the government's deficit. At others, the authorities may underestimate the natural rate of unemployment and use new money to bring about their view of equilibrium in the labour market, but with only a short-run increase in employment and output.

The emphasis has been on the monetarist causal sequence from money to nominal income. When analysing changes in one period, the New Quantity Theory shows how M can determine PQ. The aggregate supply function shows how nominal income is split between P and Q. The labour market behaves asymmetrically in response to excess labour supplies and demands. Those in jobs refuse to recontract during the period if there is excess supply. Both firms and workers agree to recontract when there is excess demand. Rapid increases in nominal wages can lead to money illusion in the short run and more labour is offered than when households have full information. The asymmetry is supported by the empirical evidence summarised in the Phillips curve, with its steep slope for excess labour demand but small slope for excess supply. The Phillips curve also provides evidence on the inter-period shifts in the aggregate supply function: rapid when the price level rises but sluggish when it falls. Continually rising prices lead to expectations of inflation which are incorporated in the expectations-augmented Phillips curve.

Erratic monetary policy causes surprises for firms and households in their wage negotiations, and surprising monetary expansions cause households to misperceive the real wage. Wage negotiators seem to be influenced by indicators of past events: adaptive expectations for inflation and existing unemployment for the extent of disequilibrium. Stable inflation would assist market adjustment. Zero inflation of the general level of prices would encourage more rapid microeconomic adjustments, because each absolute price change would then be a relative price change providing a signal for quantitative responses. The monetary rule would ensure zero inflation. Elected governments have medium-run terms of office and sometimes dither between the short-run advantages of monetary expansion and the medium-term advantages of zero inflation.

In countries such as the United Kingdom, the Central Bank ensures the prudence of the commercial banks by insisting they maintain ownership of reliable assets as a proportion of those accounting assets which they obtain by making loans, rather than insisting on a fixed proportion of base money to the money supply. In such countries the monetary base multiplier varies, the authorities often adjust the monetary base in response to the needs of trade, and the monetarist causal sequence is reversed. The historical evidence for such countries seems to support the view that the more usual sequence runs *from* nominal income *to* the money supply. Even in such countries there have been periods when the authorities have initiated dramatic monetary expansions or periods of rapidly falling monetary growth. For such events, the analysis of this chapter remains relevant. Long periods of disequilibrium are often caused by the monetary authorities who create shocks which are beyond the experience of firms and households.

PROBLEMS FOR CHAPTER 2

1. Show how the monetary base increases as a result of (a) an open-market operation, (b) an operation in the foreign exchange market, (c) the government selling new bonds to the Central Bank, and (d) the government paying a firm for goods by writing a cheque.
2. You observe a negative correlation between unemployment and nominal wage increases. Devise an argument to show that high wage increases cause low unemployment.
3. Why were there both increased unemployment and rising rates of change of nominal wages during the 1970s in many countries?
4. What are the main causes of changes in the liquidity ratio?
5. Why might financial deregulation reduce the amount of senorage which a government can obtain?
6. If equation (2.11) is true, then the following is also true:

$$\pi^e_{t-1} = \pi_{t-2} + b\,(\pi^e_{t-2} - \pi_{t-2}) \tag{2.11a}$$

   Plug (2.11a) into (2.11), note that $0 < b < 1$, and show that expected inflation depends upon past inflation.
7. The authorities wish to use senorage to capture 20 per cent of an economy's output. If $q = 0.04$, $k = 0.03$ and $h = 3$, what rate of inflation would develop?
8. An economy's export sector is uncompetitive. Show that the currency must depreciate more rapidly than predicted by Relative Purchasing Power Parity if competitiveness is to be restored.

FURTHER READING

A short and sympathetic account of the main tenets of Monetarism is given by Congden (1978). A more detailed study is in Chapter 1 of Laidler (1982). Miller (1985) investigates the problems of money-financed deficits. Crump (1981) is a fascinating and detailed study of money by an anthropologist.

Phillips (1958) is the seminal article. Friedman and Laidler (1975) discuss the effect of expectations. The interpretation of the Phillips curve given in this chapter is that of Desai (1975). An econometric criticism of Monetarism in Britain is given by Desai (1981). Butler (1986) provides a readable survey of Friedman's main works.

McKinnon (1984) presents evidence on the break in the link between money and nominal income which occurred in the US with the advent of floating exchange rates. Frankel (1985) discusses some of the reasons for the dollar's departure from Purchasing Power Parity.

Eagly (1971) translates and provides an historical background to the remarkable lectures of P. N. Christiernin.

3. Government Borrowing

Since the early nineteenth century economists have been concerned about the problems created when a government borrows to finance its current expenditures. The Classical economists considered that such expenditures should be financed by current taxes at the time when the payers could clearly see the cause of the expenses, as during wartime. Borrowing merely postponed the burden to future taxpayers whose resentment would mount as the cause faded further into the past.

During the 1960s and 1970s many governments financed large deficits by both borrowing and money-creation but with new money dominating and generating inflation. The inflation reduced the real value of the bonds sold. Nominal income rose more rapidly than the nominal value of the debt stock, and taxing the inflated current income provided a progressively easier method of servicing the debts incurred in the past. Money-creation generated misinformation in the labour market and inequity for past purchasers of bonds, but the burden of debt-servicing was correspondingly light. Inflation was the main macroeconomic problem of these decades.

During the 1980s, the United States ran large budget deficits financed almost entirely by new borrowing. As the stock of debt accumulated from year to year, the problem facing prospective purchasers of bonds was to guess whether the deficit would fall before the debt became unserviceable, or whether future deficits would have to be financed by money-creation which would lower the real value of interest payments. US bonds would be worthwhile investments in the first case but not in the second. The demand for funds by the US government combined with uncertainty over the purchasing power of the dollar to raise interest rates throughout the world.

This chapter analyses the main effects of government borrowing. Are the funds which firms need for financing investment more expensive to obtain? How does the total stock of bonds influence each year's flow of lending and borrowing? What is the effect of expected inflation on the yield which a lender demands on his loan? If we combine the findings of the present chapter with those of Chapter 2, how large a deficit can be financed by both new money and new bonds?

A later section discusses the special form of borrowing adopted by many Third World countries during the 1970s. This took the form of dollar loans from foreign banks at rates of interest which varied each quarter as the market rate varied, unlike a bond whose interest is fixed at the time of the bond sale. During the 1970s, sovereign borrowers seemed reliable to the banks who provided the loans, and the terms seemed attractive to the borrowers when interest rates were low. A decade later, the borrowing countries found increasing difficulty in obtaining the dollars to service the loans as interest rates increased.

3.1 CROWDING OUT

When the economy is producing its natural level of output, an increase in the goods and services used by government prevents their being used by the private sector. The state sector crowds the private sector out of the markets for resources. This *resources crowding out* occurs because supplies of real resources are limited. Its extent depends on the size of the public sector rather than the method of financing its activities. *Financial crowding out* occurs when the government enters the market for loanable funds in order to finance its deficit by borrowing. The increase in the demand for funds drives up the rate of interest and investment by firms is reduced. The public expenditure financed by the borrowing has crowded out private investment expenditure. If the government's expenditure is also on investment it is behaving like a firm; the optimal extent of such expenditures can be discovered, in principle, by the techniques of investment appraisal. In this chapter we discuss the effects of a government deficit financed by bond sales but incurred for spending on 'consumption' by government. Financial crowding out then leaves a legacy to later years of slower growth in the supply of output because investment is reduced.

Figure 3.1 illustrates the simple theory of crowding out. The investment intentions of firms form the demand function for loanable funds I. Households' savings provide the supply of funds S. With no government borrowing the interest rate would be r_1 and the loanable funds market is in equilibrium. The government now decides to obtain funds from the market. It prints ΔB of new bonds and sells them for \$1 each, but it has to offer a higher interest rate of r_2 in order to find buyers. The demand function has shifted to $I + \Delta B$. Households respond to the higher interest rate by offering more savings, a movement up the S function (implying a reduction in consumption due to the higher r). Firms respond by reducing investment. They have been crowded out of the loanable funds market. With a steep S function, the fall in investment would be almost equal to the ΔB of government borrowing.

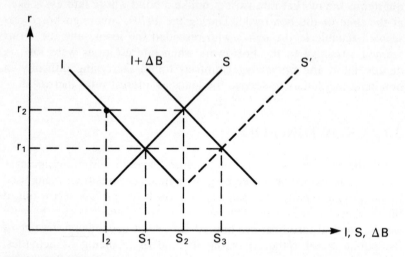

Figure 3.1   Financial crowding out.
With no government borrowing, the demand function for loanable funds is I and the supply function is S. The equilibrium interest rate is r_1. When the government sells bonds to the value ΔB during the period, it shifts the demand function to the right. It must offer r_2 interest to persuade households to supply funds. Investment falls from $I_1 = S_1$ to I_2.

During much of the last four decades the puzzle was to discover whether such crowding out occurred at all. An industrialised country might devote 10 per cent of GDP to investment and government borrowing might vary from 2 to 5 per cent of GDP with little apparent effects, although the expectation from Figure 3.1 is of a dramatic change in the rate of interest in response to the variation in borrowing. A possible implication was that households treated government bonds in a different way from other assets. In the early nineteenth century, the economist David Ricardo had pointed out that the community is behaving irrationally in thinking that government bonds are wealth. The debt-servicing in the future entails taxes in the future and there will be no increase in the income available to households: their interest receipts will equal the extra taxes. Ricardo presented his *equivalence theorem* as a piece of arithmetic but he considered that people did not behave as if they had done the calculation. They treated government bonds as wealth providing a stream of future income from interest.

Barro (1974) hypothesised that households are rational enough to anticipate the future taxes entailed by present government borrowing. They respond by increasing their saving to realise their target of future income-after-tax. In Figure 3.1 the savings function shifts to S' (implying a reduction in present consumption due to expected future taxes). The rate of interest stays constant and the bond sales do not crowd out investment. Barro considered that a government could follow the monetary rule regardless of the size of its deficit. Bond sales would allow large deficits without inflation. The additional saving would allow investment, capital accumulation and growth to be unaffected. Government borrowing to finance government consumption expenditures simply replaces private consumption. This might be suboptimal but it is better than the misinformation generated by excessive money-creation.

The evidence of the last forty years requires careful interpretation because the periods of large government deficits were also periods of high monetary growth. The increase in the monetary base allows the banks to lend more, adding to the flow of funds provided by households. Government borrowing shifts the demand function from I to I + ΔB but new money shifts the supply function to S + ΔM. The long experiment in the United States during the 1980s, when large deficits were mainly bond-financed, did not change the habits of US households, who continued to save a low proportion of their incomes compared with other countries. Interest rates rose, although tax concessions to firms helped to maintain investment. The gap between the high demand and low domestic supply of loanable funds was met by foreign lenders. The initial effect was to appreciate the dollar and lower competitiveness. Government borrowing crowded out exports rather than investment.

There are several reasons why government bonds may be treated as wealth. People may perceive the future interest payments but not the taxes. They may consider that the bonds are financing investment expenditure which will raise future growth. The bonds may also be a convenient device for spreading income over time in a way which appears to enable the preferred consumption pattern to be realised. If they are perceived as wealth, increased bond sales raise the interest rate. Bond sales to domestic households crowd out investment; if sold to foreign households the currency appreciates and exports are crowded out.

3.2 THE BOND MARKET

The market for loanable funds is the appropriate focus of attention when investigating the effects of the flow of government borrowing on the flows of saving, investment, exports, and finance from abroad. This section considers the effects of additional government borrowing on people who are holding bonds issued in the past. If this stock of bonds is not willingly held, the market is in disequilibrium and holdings change hands until the bond price adjusts to a level which clears the market. The bond market differs from the loanable funds market in two ways. First, it refers to the total stock of bonds rather than the flow of additional bonds. Second, the suppliers and demanders are reversed. A supplier of new bonds is demanding funds; a demander of new bonds is offering funds.

Pension funds, insurance companies and other agents of households maintain portfolios of assets of which only a part is government bonds. Many of these assets are close substitutes for each other, money being the exception. The demand for government bonds will be strongly influenced by the prices of private bonds, equities and foreign financial paper. For the moment, we ignore such influences and confine our attention to the way the demand for bonds responds to three variables: nominal income, the rate of interest and the expected rate of inflation.

The nominal demand for government bonds Bd can be expressed in a way which matches the pattern of the demand for money given in Chapter 2.

$$Bd = b\,PQ \tag{3.1}$$
$$b = b\,(r, \pi^e) \tag{3.2}$$
$$+\ \ - $$

In equation (3.1) b is the demand for bonds per unit of nominal income. Equation (3.2) states that b varies with the rate of interest and the expected rate of inflation. For example, if a bond promising \$2 per annum sold for \$100 in the absence of inflation, the fixed *coupon* of \$2 gives an interest yield of 2 per cent. If the same bond sold for \$40, the rate of interest rises to 5 per cent. The rise in the rate of interest (fall in the bond price) increases the demand.

Suppose that the bond market clears when a bond with a \$2 coupon sells for \$100, but then expected inflation changes from zero to 3 per cent per annum. If the interest on the bond is to yield the same expected purchasing power as before it would have to rise to 5 per cent. The bond price would fall to \$40. (The dramatic fall is because the inflation is expected to last forever in this example.) The demand for bonds falls as expected inflation rises. Provided the nominal rate of interest rises with expected inflation, the *real rate of interest* (Rri) will remain constant. The Rri can be defined by the following approximation:

$$Rri \equiv r - \pi^e \tag{3.3}$$

This is only an approximation because expected inflation also lowers the real value of the bond. Strictly, the Rri is $(r - \pi^e)/(1 + \pi^e)$ which is less than definition (3.3). For example, if r is 12.32 per cent and π^e is 8 per cent, the Rri is $(0.1232 - 0.08)/(1 + 0.08) = 4$ per cent.

The market for bonds is illustrated in Figure 3.2. The interest rate is inversely related to the bond price: demand increases with r. The supply of bonds is B and this stock is willingly held when the interest rate is r_1. If the government wished to obtain $\$\Delta B$ from selling new bonds it would have to offer the higher interest of r_2 which drives down the price of existing government bonds. With many close substitutes in financial markets, only a small increase in interest is needed to absorb the flow ΔB into the stock held by households. The interest-elasticity of demand is high. Households' wealth increases because the increase in the number of bonds they hold outweighs the fall in the price of each bond.

The Bd function is drawn on the assumption that other things are constant. Demand would increase if nominal income increased and the function would shift to Bd' which shows households demanding a larger stock at each interest rate. The extra income has generated extra savings. In this particular example, the authorities have chosen ΔB as

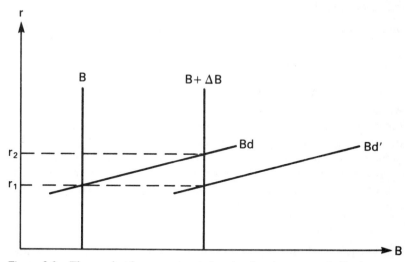

Figure 3.2 The market for government bonds when income and all other assets are constant.
B is the existing stock. Bd shows the stock which households wish to hold increasing with r. When the stock increases by ΔB, the interest rate must rise from r_1 to r_2 for the greater stock to be willingly held. Increased income shifts Bd to Bd'. The increased stock is willingly held at the initial interest rate of r_1.

that sale of new bonds which can be absorbed with no change in the rate of interest. (How would this be pictured in a diagram of the loanable funds market? In Figure 3.1, the savings function would shift from S to S' but the cause is now the rise in income, not the rise in future taxation for a given level of present income.)

3.3 BOND SENORAGE

This section considers the size of the budget deficit which can be financed by bond sales. The government increases its debt to households by ΔB during the year, this being the nominal value of the new bonds sold. However, not all of ΔB is available for spending; a part must be used to service the past debt. B is the average value of the stock of debt during the year and the interest payments on this amount to rB. Writing Def for the deficit excluding interest payments, bond sales finance this as follows

$$\text{Def} = \Delta B - rB \qquad (3.4)$$

Rewrite this as

$$\text{Def} = (\Delta B/B - r)\,B$$

and express the deficit as a ratio to nominal income

$$\frac{\text{Def}}{\text{PQ}} = (\Delta B/B - r)\,\frac{B}{\text{PQ}} \qquad (3.5)$$

$\Delta B/B$ is the rate of growth of the debt stock. In the previous section, we showed that the nominal rate of interest could remain constant provided the demand for the total bond stock grows at the same rate as nominal income PQ. Hence constant r occurs if $\Delta B/B$ is $\pi + q$. The demand for bonds per unit of nominal income is b, which will equal the supply B/PQ when the bond market clears. Writing d for the deficit as a ratio to nominal income, which is sustained for many years, equation 3.5 becomes

$$d = (\pi + q - r)\,b \qquad (3.6)$$

The Rri is $r - \pi^e$, but with d sustained for several years actual inflation will become expected and the Rri is $r - \pi$. Equation (3.6) can be rewritten as

$$d = (q - \text{Rri})\,b \qquad (3.7)$$

A sustainable deficit requires that output growth exceeds the real rate of interest. Suppose the bond stock is equal in value to half the annual flow of income b = 0.5, and the bond sales needed to maintain this ratio can be achieved by offering a real rate on bonds of 2 per cent: Rri = 0.02. With output growing at 4 per cent per annum, the deficit can be 1 per cent of national income.

$$d = (0.04 - 0.02)\ 0.5 = 1 \text{ per cent}$$

Now suppose the bond stock is 1.5 times national income and Rri of 6 per cent is required to persuade people to hold this larger proportion of government bonds in their portfolios

$$d' = (0.04 - 0.06)\ 1.5 = \textit{minus}\ 3 \text{ per cent}$$

This high value of b requires a budget surplus. The cost of servicing past debt exceeds the funds obtainable by bond sales and the difference must be met by current taxation in excess of current expenditure net of debt servicing. Alternatively, the government could obtain a command over resources by money senorage in addition to bond senorage, a combination which is considered in the next section.

3.4   THE SUSTAINABLE BUDGET DEFICIT

We now combine the bond-financed deficits of section 3.3 and the money-financed deficits of Chapter 2 to consider some of the implications of using both methods at once. Combining equations (2.17) and (3.7) the total of both money senorage and bond senorage enables the government to obtain the command over the following share of nominal income:

$$d = (\pi + q)\ k/h + (q - Rri)\ b \tag{3.8}$$

Here q is determined by the supply behaviour of firms and households and h is determined by the behaviour of the banks. A sustainable deficit must not affect q and h which can be treated as constants in equation (3.8). Three of the variables are ratios to nominal income: d for the deficit, k for the money stock and b for the bond stock. However, two of these are themselves dependent on the nominal interest rate and the inflation rate

$$k = k\ (r, \pi, \text{wealth}) \tag{3.9}$$
$$-\ -\quad\ +$$

$$b = b\ (r, \pi) \tag{3.10}$$
$$+\ -$$

A sustainable deficit implies constant inflation which is therefore expected. Hence both equations refer to actual inflation, which is also relevant to the real rate of interest.

$$Rri = r - \pi \qquad\qquad\qquad (3.11)$$

The wealth variable, in real terms, depends mainly on the growth of output q. To the extent that households also treat government bonds as wealth, some bond senorage for a given value of d reduces inflation by both reducing the growth of the money supply and increasing the growth of the demand for money. High bond sales drive the Rri above q, forcing increased reliance on money senorage.

If the wealth variable is ignored the solution to the four equations would yield constant values for r and π, hence Rri, to obtain d. The assumption is that the functions k( ) and b( ) are stable. The conclusion is that the government can obtain control over a high proportion of output either by taxing directly and keeping d small, or by running a large value of d and taxing indirectly via inflation. The limit to the value of d is the dislike of inflation. Excessive bond senorage can raise the Rri and lower investment, thereby affecting output growth and breaking the condition that the deficit is sustainable.

The deficit discussed in this section is smaller than the published figures of a government's deficits which include interest payments and expenditure on government investment. Occasional large deficits for short periods can be important stimuli to an economy following a sudden fall in aggregate demand. Sustained low deficits can be comfortably financed by a combination of bond and money senorage. Continued high deficits are either inflationary or inhibit output growth via their effects on the Rri.

3.5 INTEREST PARITY AND EXCHANGE RISK

In Chapter 2, the Purchasing Power Parity theory of exchange rate changes was presented. In its relative version (RPPP) this states that the rate of change of the exchange rate will be equal to the difference between the domestic and foreign inflation rates. The theory follows from the notion that differences in competitiveness in goods from different countries will influence the supply and demand for currencies and set in train exchange rate adjustments which push the prices of the goods towards equality when those prices are converted to the same currency. A country with relatively high inflation will have uncompetitive exports and a low demand for its currency from those wishing to buy the exports, with the result that the currency depreciates. The depreciation restores competitiveness.

With an international market for loanable funds, a government may be able to borrow at the world rate of interest and need not bid up the domestic rate r beyond the foreign rate r*. For a large borrower such as the United States, the effect may be to bid up both r and r* but the equality between them would remain if financial capital were perfectly mobile. However, once foreign lenders begin to suspect that repeated large deficits are unsustainable by bond-financing alone, they may also suspect that future deficits will be increasingly financed by money-creation. The purchasing power of the borrower's currency would then fall. If the borrower is the United States, the dollar is expected to depreciate and lenders will require a higher interest rate on US bonds to compensate them for this. Writing x for the expected rate of depreciation

$$r = r^* + x \tag{3.12}$$

For example, if the dollar is expected to depreciate against the yen by 4 per cent and the Japanese interest rate is 6 per cent, the US rate will have to be 10 per cent to attract Japanese purchasers of US bonds. If one dollar costs Y200 now, these yen spent on a US bond will be worth $1.10 in one year's time but Y212 if spent on a Japanese bond. Provided the dollar is expected to depreciate to 200/1.04 yen, the $1.10 would be worth Y212 and the two deals are equivalent.

Equation (3.12) expresses the condition known as *uncovered interest parity* to distinguish it from those deals where the buyers of foreign bonds cover themselves against exchange rate changes by dealing in the forward market for currencies. Continuing the example of the previous paragraph, a Japanese purchaser of US bonds might buy the bonds today and at the same time enter a deal to sell dollars in one year's time at a discount of 4 per cent on today's value, thereby covering himself against exchange risk. The forward exchange rate itself depends on the expected depreciation of the dollar.

Uncovered interest parity would be consistent with RPPP if this were the theory of exchange rate changes held by dealers in the international markets for bonds and currencies. The expected depreciation would then equal the difference between expected inflation rates. Using starred variables for the foreign country

$$x = \pi^e - \pi^{*e} \tag{3.13}$$

Combine (3.12) and (3.13)

$$r = r^* + \pi^e - \pi^{*e}$$
$$r - \pi^e = r^* - \pi^{*e}$$

giving $\quad Rri = Rri^*$ \hfill (3.14)

Real rates of interest in the domestic and foreign country tend to
equality. Note that this example implies that people form their
expectations by gathering and processing information in a manner
consistent with theories about economic behaviour. They hold three
hypotheses: that a budget deficit unsustainable by bond sales alone will
eventually lead to money-creation; that monetary growth causes
inflation; and that depreciation results from different inflation rates.
Expectations formed in this way are known as *rational* expectations
(compare the Adaptive Expectations Hypothesis AEH of Chapter 2,
when π^e is formed from studying past inflation rates. The AEH was
often consistent with behaviour in labour markets. Rational expectations seem more common in financial markets in the medium run of
several years).

The Rational Expectations Hypothesis leaves open which theory
about the economy people use for expectations formation. For example,
they may note that the exchange rate departed from RPPP in the past
and therefore they expect it to return to RPPP in the near future.
Writing e_{t-1} for the past actual depreciation of the exchange rate,
people might expect

$$x = \pi_{t-1} - \pi^*_{t-1} - e_{t-1} \tag{3.15}$$

In this case, the expected depreciation compensates for the past loss of
competitiveness.

Exchange rates and interest rates react rapidly as 'news' arrives about
possible changes in policy. Relevant information is incorporated into
expectations which in turn influence present prices in the international
financial markets. Rational expectation applies to such rapidly adjusting
markets where processing information is relatively costless compared
with the large value of transactions. The effect can be considerable
volatility in exchange rates and interest rates.

Volatile exchange rates in the past create uncertainty over their value
in the future. People may have an expectation about the rate of
depreciation but they hold it with less conviction than when past
exchange rates have moved on a consistent trend. If the dollar, for
example, has fluctuated widely, the foreign purchaser of US bonds will
require an uncertainty premium to compensate him for the increasing
risk that his expectation of depreciation is wrong. Uncertainty is also
present in the guesses of future policy. A large bond-financed deficit
may become money-financed, but the deficit itself may be reduced, a
possibility which reduces the expectation of inflation and a depreciation
of the currency but which further adds to the chance that the
expectation will turn out to be wrong. Both past volatility of the

exchange rate and uncertainty over future policy cause foreign purchasers of domestic bonds to require a risk premium in addition to the interest premium predicted by interest rate parity. Condition 3.12 becomes

$$r = r^* + x + \text{the risk premium} \tag{3.15}$$

3.6 GOVERNMENT BORROWING FROM FOREIGN BANKS

Preceding sections focused on bond-financed deficits. Domestic and foreign purchasers of a government's bonds are attracted by the interest offered, which is paid in the currency of that government and therefore carries an inflation risk for domestic purchasers, translated into a depreciation risk for foreign purchasers. The government's obligations to service the debt are known in terms of the nominal amount of that country's currency. Standard economic analysis allows us to explain the effects of such borrowing, although the influence of expectations makes precise prediction unlikely, particularly for the timing of changes in exchange rates when demanders of a currency come to suspect that a deficit is unsustainable by bond sales alone.

During the 1970s many governments borrowed in a quite different way. They received loans from foreign commercial banks at interest rates which varied during the life of the loan in response to changes in current rates in the world market. The behaviour of governments is often difficult for an economist to explain or predict. Commercial banks usually conform to economic principles or disappear via bankruptcy. Sometimes financial manias cause speculative bubbles which burst and are followed by financial panics, but such events are usually short-lived and have become less frequent as more Central Banks learn to control their domestic financial sectors. The debt owed by Third World countries to the commercial banks of industrialised countries has become a long-run phenomenon. It had accumulated to about $300 billion by the late 1980s, or one and a half times the magnitude of the record annual US deficits of the period. The sovereign debtors cannot service most of it, and it accumulates at current rates of interest. In the accounts of the commercial banks, it appears as an asset: as the debtor falls further behind with debt servicing, the greater becomes the debt and the faster the asset grows in the lender's account. Bank shares fell in value as stock markets realised the extent of each bank's exposure. Only in 1987 did the main banks start to write off a proportion of the debt in their accounts, while maintaining the sovereign debtors' liability to repay eventually.

This section examines the curious events which led to this accumulation of unserviceable sovereign debt. In the late 1950s, a loanable funds market developed which was not under the direct control of any Central Bank. In the 1970s, there was a sudden influx of funds to this market. During the 1980s, high real rates of interest led to an *increase* in the demand for such funds, a destabilising reaction which further raised interest rates.

This special market for loanable funds developed in 1957 when the Bank of England imposed tight restrictions on the use of sterling by foreigners. Many British banks kept their foreign clients by borrowing and lending dollars, using the banks' subsidiaries in continental Europe where there were fewer restrictions on such deals. An inter-bank trade in dollars developed. Other banks joined this market for dollars and loans, in particular the subsidiary in France of the Central Bank of the Soviet Union whose telex code is EUROBANK. The dollar earnings of Soviet trade were deposited with this bank rather than a US bank where they would have appeared unpleasantly beyond control at the height of the Cold War. When not required, these dollars were lent to the other banks where they become known as Eurodollars. This market became increasingly used by US banks which were prohibited from charging domestic borrowers interest above a maximum set by laws against usury which were legislated before expectations of inflation developed. No such laws applied in Europe.

In 1973, a workable cartel of oil producers was formed and oil prices quadrupled within a few months. Many members of the Organisation of Petroleum Exporting Countries (OPEC) had large current account surpluses of dollars, the currency in which oil is traded. In the world of Chapter 1, OPEC would have sent these funds to oil-importing countries where they could have financed the technical adjustments made profitable by the change in the relative price of a major input to production processes. In the world of the mid-1970s, such long-term investments in real capital seemed liable to sequestration by the countries suffering from the effects of the cartel. Instead, the funds were lent for short periods to the banks operating in the Eurodollar market where their ownership would remain anonymous to governments. The main demand for the funds was from developing countries wishing to borrow for long periods to finance oil imports and investment expenditures. The banks had to discover a relatively risk-free method of borrowing short from OPEC and lending long to the Third World. The problem was resolved by negotiating loans for long fixed periods as required by the borrowing countries, but at interest rates tied to current market rates, as required by the lending banks who themselves were borrowing for only short periods. The deal would be about the number of percentage points above that rate in a particular market, usually the London Inter-bank Offer Rate (LIBOR). Sovereign borrowers seemed reliable to the banks. During the 1970s, the extent of money-creation in the main industrial countries held real interest rates at low levels and LIBOR plus a few per cent seemed reasonable to the borrowers. The Euromarket started with British legislation pushing British banks to other countries. It made use of the Soviet Union's dollars. It grew with the dollars of US banks escaping legislators who considered that excessive *nominal* rates of interest constituted usury. To these were added the dollars of oil producers many of whom believed that *any* interest charge was usury. The banks acted as financial intermediaries between rich sovereign lenders wanting to lend short and poor sovereign borrowers wanting to borrow long.

In 1979, there was a second major rise in oil prices. Most governments of industrialised countries were determined to avoid a repeat of the inflation of the 1970s and responded with tight monetary policies. During the early 1980s, inflation fell more rapidly than nominal rates of interest and real rates reached historic levels. Third World debt was denominated in dollars and necessitated large trade surpluses if it was to be serviced. The debtors needed dollars for interest payments. Labour markets in industrialised countries adapted only slowly to the surprising slowdown in monetary growth and the resulting recession reduced the demand for the commodities which constituted most of the exports from the Third World. Countries which had borrowed to finance genuine investment projects were squeezed between low export demand and high interest rates. Countries whose debts were incurred to finance government consumption had no increase in the tax base from which to raise the taxes required for debt servicing. By the late 1980s, a small secondary market for Third World debt had developed, involving perhaps $5 billion of the total of over $300 billion. The debt was trading at 10–80 per cent of its book value, depending on the credibility of the governments concerned. Roberts and Remolona (1987) pointed out the dangers of this secondary market: a Third World country had an incentive to threaten to default, lower the value of its debt on the secondary market and buy back the debt at a fraction of its face value.

For most of the debt, the interest due was added to the total and generated a flow demand for dollars in the Euromarket which raised interest rates yet further. The problem of Third World debt was still unresolved in the late 1980s. It discouraged further lending to finance genuine investment and inhibited the supply-side growth which would

enable those trade surpluses to be achieved which would allow the debt
to be serviced.

Eurocurrency has now come to mean any currency which is sold in a
market outside that currency's country, not necessarily in Europe.
Euroloans are deals denominated in Eurocurrencies. Strictly, the
'banks' operating in the Euromarket are really *non-bank financial
intermediaries*. They do not take demand deposits and therefore do not
create money via the monetary base multiplier. The world stock of
dollars is controlled by the US. The flow to the Euromarket each year is
made possible by the current account surpluses which countries, mainly
Europe and Japan, have with the United States. The intermediaries
then negotiate Euroloans using these dollars. Most of the loans are now
to reliable multinationals, who prefer to deal in the Euromarket, which
confines deals to amounts usually exceeding $1 million and sometimes
over $1 billion. The size of deals and the freedom from restrictive
legislation allow the intermediaries to lend at rates of interest below
those in the US and pay more for their borrowing than the US
borrowing rate. The intermediaries are often foreign subsidiaries of
parent banks whose activities are within the control of a Central Bank.
The intermediaries' actions are monitored and subjected to controls
which can remain rather loose provided there is no recurrence of events
such as the lending to Third World countries during the 1970s.

3.7 SUMMARY

This chapter has considered some of the problems created by
governments which borrow to finance current expenditures and repeat
the process for many years. It is not about borrowing for government
investments which increase potential output growth, nor for government expenditures which provide a short-run stimulus to demand when
this lags behind the growth of potential output.

When a government borrows its own currency from residents, the
interest rate rises and investment is reduced. When it borrows its own
currency from foreigners the currency appreciates and exports become
uncompetitive. For modest levels of borrowing these effects may be too
small to be noticeable, but repeated excessive borrowing becomes
unsustainable without creating new money. Once markets suspect that
new money will be created, the nominal rate of interest rises to preserve
the real rate of interest on bonds.

A government which borrows foreign currency has to achieve trade
surpluses in later years in order to service the debt. Third World

countries specialising in commodity exports may discover that the demand generated for commodities by industrialised countries is less than was expected at the time the debts were incurred. Many countries borrowed from commercial banks at variable interest rates instead of a rate agreed at the time of the initial loan. Large debts were incurred when real interest rates were historically low during the 1970s, and the debts became unserviceable when rates became historically high in the 1980s. Low export demand combined with mounting interest rates on accumulating debt to make the debt unserviceable.

PROBLEMS FOR CHAPTER 3

1. Suppose households are aware that budget deficits financed by bond sales must be financed from future taxation and adjust their savings accordingly. What would be the effect on consumption and investment of a reduction in the government's bond-financed deficit? In practice, households behave as if they did not calculate using Ricardo's Equivalence Theorem. What in practice is likely to be the effect on consumption and investment of a reduction in the bond-financed deficit?

2. For several years, the nominal stock of government bonds has grown at the same rate as nominal income and the ratio of the two is steady at 0.7. The growth rate of real income is 3 per cent and the real rate of interest is 2 per cent. What is the proportion of nominal income which the government can obtain by a bond-financed deficit?

3. If the government of your country were borrowing at a rate of interest which exceeded the growth rate of real output, would you expect it to reduce its budget deficit or create money? Why?

4. Show that uncovered interest parity combined with the expectation of relative purchasing power parity will lead to equal real rates of interest between countries.

5. Explain why government borrowing to finance government investment can lead to a stock of debt which is easily serviced.

6. Why do some sovereign borrowers seek to borrow more when the rate of interest rises?

7. You have surveyed a panel of foreign exchange dealers and discover that on average they expect currency A to depreciate against the yen by 10 per cent, with two-thirds of the panel expecting a depreciation in the range of 9–11 per cent. For currency B, the average expectancy is also of a 10 per cent

depreciation, but to include two-thirds of the panel the range must be 5–15 per cent. The Japanese rate of interest is 3 per cent. What rate of interest might Japanese lenders require from bonds denominated in currency A? and in currency B?

8. Show that a government which borrows its own currency can always service its debt, but a government which borrows a foreign currency must achieve a surplus on the current account of its balance of payments.

9. How would you judge whether a sovereign borrower is reliable?

10. In your country, do households treat government bonds as wealth?

FURTHER READING

Taylor (1979) examines crowding out and shows that its effects were difficult to capture with the econometric models of the late 1970s. Dumas (1985) discusses some of the effects on economic growth.

Ricardo's Equivalence Theorem is in his 'The Funding System', reprinted in volume IV of the Sraffa (1951–55) edition. Buchanan (1958) compares domestic and foreign borrowing by governments.

Chapter 9 of Chick (1983) examines some of the confusions found in the literature on the determination of the rate of interest.

The sustainable budget deficit is analysed in Miller and Sargent (1984). This article with others in the controversy is reproduced in the readings edited by Havrilesky (1985). Hamilton and Flavin (1986) and Evans (1987) report empirical findings on the effects of the US budget deficits of the 1980s.

We have followed Williamson (1983) in treating uncovered interest parity as the important macroeconomic relation.

Lever and Huhne (1985) provide a readable account of Third World debt. Stewart (1986) discusses the difficulties created for debt servicing by the US deficit. Chapter 10 of Hallwood and MacDonald (1986) gives an introduction to the Eurocurrency system; Hogan and Pearce (1982) provide a more detailed account. Thomas and Wickens (1987) suggest the curious effects which the debt had on the value of the dollar. Guttentag and Herring (1986) point out the myopia affecting the decisions of large banks which might be expected to be more cautious.

PART III
The Short Run

4. Quantities and the Interest Rate

This chapter examines the behaviour of firms and households during the period immediately following a dramatic reduction in aggregate demand. The monetary contraction in the United States during the early 1930s is an example of such an event. The effect on other countries, however, was a loss of export orders and a wave of pessimism resulting in cancelled orders for investment goods. Aggregate demand is not only influenced by money and the appropriate policies to counter a demand contraction are not always or not primarily monetary policies.

The increased understanding of behaviour when economic activity is constrained by too little expenditure has enabled governments to apply policies which reduce the likelihood of such situations developing. Data are now promptly gathered and monitored to reveal whether aggregate demand is growing more slowly than aggregate supply. When this is the case governments can put into effect moderate versions of those policies originally designed to counter dramatic demand shocks.

For most of the postwar decades both the body of theory about aggregate demand and the quality of demand data advanced more rapidly than the theory and data about aggregate supply. Expenditure was often stimulated even when it was not constraining income. Policy-makers in the 1980s became disillusioned with the management of aggregate demand. There is an argument that by ignoring demand management they are making insufficient use of past discoveries. Keynesian theories inspired much of the classificatory systems of aggregate economic statistics. This chapter gives highly simplified versions of the equations which form the basis for the demand side of modern econometric models of a national economy. A further simplification is the assumption that output can be expanded without significant effects on the price level. The behaviour of firms and households keeps output below its natural level in the short run; policy can stimulate the economy to hasten the adjustment process. This result would follow from the sluggish adjustment of nominal wages discussed in Chapter 2, but there is much more to Keynesian economics than its appreciation that relative prices are often out of equilibrium and slow to adjust.

What causes a shortage of aggregate demand? Usually it is some
event such as a reduction in exports. Firms do not react by immediately
reducing prices. Instead, investment plans are cancelled, expenditure is
further reduced and the process feeds on itself. Keynes emphasised the
psychological aspects when an epidemic of pessimism runs through
business. Once expectations of future profit have been affected, income
(output, aggregate supply) is constrained by expenditure (aggregate
demand). Changes in income then dominate all other variables in
importance. The fall in income reduces consumption and further affects
demand.

In its milder form a demand shortage can appear if past investment
has raised present potential output but firms have not yet expanded
their markets. Current investment is postponed. Initially, workers may
not be sacked but recruitment is reduced and voluntary quits are not
replaced. Firms employ more labour than they need for the actual
output produced, expecting orders to increase soon. The expected cost
of firing workers now, then hiring and training in a few months' time
when orders pick up, outweighs the cost of *hoarding labour* during the
interim. When firms have already incurred the cost of past investment
but some of the equipment is not yet in use, and when hoarded labour is
being paid, output can be expanded with little increase in average costs.
A diagram in Q, P space would show the aggregate supply function as
almost horizontal over the relevant range. A long and unpleasant
adjustment period can be avoided if a demand stimulus is applied by
governments before the idle equipment deteriorates, the hoarded
labour is sacked and some firms cease trading.

Demand management requires careful assessment of the natural level
of output and the natural rate of unemployment. Although some
policies such as tax cuts provide an immediate effect, others such as
infrastructure investment require a highly efficient bureaucracy if their
timing is to be as planned. The behaviour of firms, households, banks
and the foreign sector has to be forecast with sufficient accuracy to
enable any demand shortage to be met by properly timed stimuli. In
most industrialised countries in the 1980s, policy-makers are wary of
economists' ability to spot occasions when economies can be expanded
without being overstimulated. Expansionary demand policies are held
in reserve to deal with dramatic and obvious demand shocks, leaving the
behaviour of firms and households to provide the growth in aggregate
demand during most years. However, the improvements in forecasting
techniques and the awareness of the dangers of extreme policy changes
have made gentle experiments in returning to demand management
feasible.

This chapter examines the effects of expenditure on income – of orders on output; of aggregate demand on aggregate supply. It refers either to the short run immediately following a demand shock, or to those periods of a year or two when the natural level of output has expanded beyond actual output. The chapter confines itself to an economy on a fixed exchange rate. This allows attention to be focused on one relative price set by the sector where prices adjust rapidly, the rate of interest determined by the financial-and-monetary sector. In the next chapter variations in a second relative price are also considered: the price of foreign exchange which is also rapidly determined, again by financial sectors in the domestic and foreign economies.

4.1 THE BALANCE OF PAYMENTS CONSTRAINT

In the short run, the domestic and foreign price levels are the result of events in the past. We can consider businessmen being reluctant to lower output prices when their wage costs are fixed and unable to raise them when they are short of orders. If the nominal exchange rate E is fixed, competitiveness as measured by EP^*/P is also constant. With no change in foreign income, exports X are constant.

With the relevant relative prices constant, the main influence on imports Z is income. Writing Q for income or output,

$$Z = zQ \tag{4.1}$$

where z is the *propensity to import*. Q may be considered as the value added within the domestic economy with firms' total sales being $Q + Z = (1 + z)Q$. Alternatively, the value-added can be considered distributed as income to households who then spend a proportion of this on imports.

The current account consists of the receipts for exports, the payments for imports and the payments to foreign countries of dividends, interest and profit Dip incurred by past surpluses on the capital account. (Dip is negative if there had been past outflows of funds on the capital account.) The current account is in deficit if Dip + Z exceeds X. With prices constant, the deficit increases with imports, which increase with income.

$$\text{Current a/c deficit} = \text{Dip} - X + zQ \tag{4.2}$$

The capital account records the flow of funds into the country to purchase financial paper. In a world of mobile financial capital this flow responds to the rate of interest in the domestic economy but in the short run capital is not perfectly mobile. A large inflow requires a differential between the domestic rate r and the foreign rate r*. Taking the foreign rate as fixed, the inflow of funds on the capital account is

$$F = -F_o + fr \qquad (4.3)$$

If the domestic rate were zero, there would be a large outflow of funds as domestic households purchase foreign bonds.

Balance of payments equilibrium occurs when the capital account surplus equals the current account deficit.

$$-F_o + fr = Dip - X + z Q$$

Rearranging

$$r = \frac{1}{f}[F_o + Dip - X] + \frac{z}{f} Q \qquad (4.4)$$

This relation is derived geometrically in Figure 4.1 where it is the line labelled BP. It is a locus showing those combinations of r and Q which bring balance of payments equilibrium. The upward slope signifies that

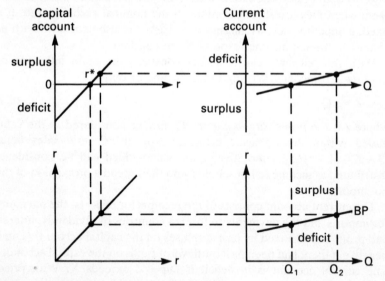

Figure 4.1   Balance of payments equilibrium.
Top left. The surplus on the capital account increases with r. When r is below r* funds flow out of the country.
Top right. The current account deficit increases with Q.
Bottom left. A 45° line to turn the r-axis.
Bottom right. The locus of combinations of Q and r which bring balance of payments equilibrium. Above the BP locus there is a surplus on the balance of payments.

imports increase with Q and cause a current account deficit but equilibrium can be preserved by an appropriate rise in the rate of interest to create a capital account surplus. The economy might be at any combination of r and Q. At a point above the BP locus the interest rate is high enough to generate a capital account surplus in excess of any current account deficit caused by the value of Q at that point.

If the balance of payments is in surplus, foreign countries settle their accounts by providing gold or foreign currencies to the Central Bank. There is an increase ΔR in the foreign reserves held in the domestic economy. *The balance of payments identity* is

$$F + X - Z - Dip \equiv \Delta R \tag{4.5}$$

If ΔR is positive, the assets of the Central Bank have increased. The foreign purchasers of bonds or exports have provided reserves in exchange for new domestic currency created by the Bank, hence the Bank's liabilities have increased. The new money is spent on domestic bonds or exports and finds its way into the domestic economy where it increases the high-powered money stock and hence the money supply. We shall see that this rise in the money supply has a short-run equilibrating effect which acts via the rate of interest.

4.2 THE GOODS SECTOR

Recall from Chapter 1 the definitions of the components of aggregate demand and the way households plan to dispose of their income

$$Ad \equiv C + I + G + X - Z \tag{4.6}$$
$$Q \equiv C + S + T \tag{4.7}$$

In a world of flexible prices Q causes Ad, but in a world where the only flexible price is the rate of interest, income is constrained by expenditure and Ad causes Q. The market is in equilibrium when

$$Q = Ad \tag{4.8}$$

Households decide how to spend their *disposable income* $Q - T$, where T is a policy variable which we treat as exogenous. In a world where Q is determined by firms and households responding to flexible prices, the split between C and S is determined by the rate of interest, but when Q is determined by aggregate demand the effect of variations in Q dominate the effects of r. Both C and S respond more to changes in Q than to changes in r. In the short run of constrained demand, the functional relationships can be written as

either $C = c(Q - T)$ (4.9)
or $S = s(Q - T)$ (4.10)

The parameter c is known as the *propensity to consume* and s is the *propensity to save*. Since $s = (1 - c)$ only one of these parameters needs to be discovered by empirical work.

Spending power flows from firms to households in the form of income. Provided households spend on consumption, firms' sales are maintained. They would also be maintained if households sent their savings to the market for loanable funds and some firms used the funds to finance investment expenditures with other firms. However, some of the savings may flow abroad and another part may simply be used to hold more money. If the rate of interest has just fallen, households will demand a greater money stock than before. Of the total stock of money in existence, more is wanted to be held by each household in idle balances (the liquidity ratio k has increased; the velocity at which money circulates through the economy has decreased). Spending falls while these 'idle' balances are being built up. In the short run, 'savings' may not be a flow of loanable funds to finance investment. Instead S is defined as that part of income after tax which is not spent on consumption. It is a withdrawal from the circular flow of spending power.

Taxation is also a withdrawal. The government taxes to finance its expenditures but the government's budget is not always balanced. If T exceeds G, more spending power is being removed from the economy than the government's expenditure on goods and services.

The third withdrawal is imports Z because this expenditure is not on the value added by domestic firms. The greater are imports the smaller is the proportion of households' spending which generates orders for domestic production. Of the three withdrawals, T is determined by policy but S and Z increase with income. Using equations (4.1) and (4.10),

$S + T + Z = s(Q - T) + T + zQ$
or $S + T + Z = (1 - s)T + (s + z)Q$ (4.11)

If taxes are raised by one unit expenditure falls by $1 - s = c$ of a unit because c is the proportion which would have been spent by households if this spending power had not been removed. If income increases by one unit some of the increase is spent on domestic production but a proportion $s + z$ is not. For example, if $s = 0.1$ and $z = 0.3$ each increase in Q by one unit results in an increase in expenditure of only 0.6 of a unit with the remainder being a leakage from the circular flow of spending power.

These leakages are balanced by three injections into the flow of spending power. In the short run none of these injections depends upon income. Government expenditure is determined by the authorities. Exports depend upon foreign income when the exchange rate is fixed; they are exogenous to a model explaining the behaviour of domestic firms and households. Investment depends partly on business optimism and partly on the rate of interest r. A rise in r reduces the number of investment projects which appear profitable, hence

$$I = I_o - br \tag{4.12}$$

where I_o is taken as constant and b shows the response of investment to changes in r.

With G and X exogenous, the main influences on the injections into the flow of spending is the rate of interest

$$I + G + X = I_o + G + X - br \tag{4.13}$$

The goods market is in equilibrium when the leakages are equal to the injections.

$$S + T + Z = I + G + X \tag{4.14}$$

Algebraically, this is simply another way of stating that $Q = Ad$ and follows from equations (4.6), (4.7) and (4.8). We met a similar condition in Chapter 1 where price adjustments assured both that the condition was met *and* that income would then be at its natural level. In the short run when aggregate demand constrains income, price adjustment is too sluggish to bring about the latter result. The only price which responds rapidly is the rate of interest. Equation (4.14) is an equilibrium in the sense that what is produced is sold (or income equals expenditure) but there is a range of incomes at which this may occur. Using (4.11), which expresses withdrawals as a function of income, and (4.13), which expresses injections as a function of the rate of interest, condition (4.14) becomes

$$(1 - s) T + (s + z) Q = I_o + G + X - br$$
$$\text{or} \quad r = \frac{1}{b} [I_o + G + X - (1 - s) T] - \frac{(s + z) Q}{b \cdot} \tag{4.15}$$

where all the terms are treated as constants except r and Q. Equation (4.15) shows the combinations of these two variables which will bring equilibrium in the goods sector. The locus of these equilibria is illustrated in the bottom right diagram of Figure 4.2. The remaining diagrams show how the locus can be derived geometrically. The locus is

conventionally labelled IS because an economy with negligible government and foreign trade would be in equilibrium when I = S.

The IS locus slopes down because an increase in income is insufficient
by itself to generate an equal increase in expenditure. Consumption
increases but the propensity to consume is less than unity; the
difference is savings. Only part of consumption expenditure is on
domestically produced output; the remainder is on imports. However,
an appropriate fall in the rate of interest would cause investment
expenditure to increase by the same amount as the extra savings and
imports. All of the extra output which generated the extra income
would then be sold. Firms would maintain the higher level of output
without finding that unsold stocks are accumulating.

The locus is a guideline to show where the goods sector would move if
it were not already on the locus. We might observe a combination of Q
and r which was off the locus but such an observation would be only

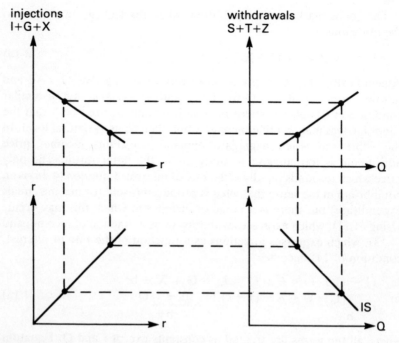

Figure 4.2 Goods market equilibrium.
Top left. Injections fall as r increases.
Top right. Withdrawals increase with Q.
Bottom left. The 45° line showing r = r.
Bottom right. The locus of equilibrium combinations of Q and r.

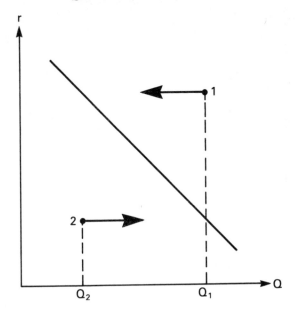

Figure 4.3 Disequilibria in the goods market.
At point 1 the rate of interest is too high for the output Q_1 to be purchased. There is an excess supply of goods. Income exceeds expenditure and firms cut back production.
At point 2 expenditure exceeds income. Firms respond to the excess demand by increasing output.

temporary. Figure 4.3 shows two such combinations and the directions of movement which would occur in such disequilibria.

Equilibrium in the goods sector can be preserved if the rate of interest falls when income increases. Balance of payments equilibrium entails a rise in the rate of interest when income increases, otherwise foreign reserves would change. The goods sector and the foreign sector are jointly in equilibrium at only one combination of Q and r, the point where the IS and BP loci intersect in Figure 4.4. The next section shows how the actions of the monetary authorities combine with the behaviour of firms and households to bring about this equilibrium.

4.3 THE MONETARY SECTOR

In the short run the monetary sector behaves differently from the description given in Chapter 2 which referred to behaviour in the

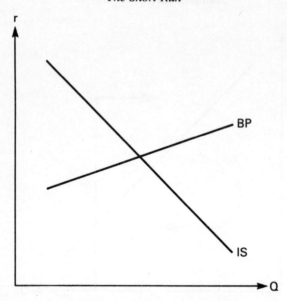

Figure 4.4   When the exchange rate is fixed, income and the rate of interest are determined by the interaction of the goods and foreign sectors.

medium run of two or more years: when people find themselves holding too much money they increase their expenditures on goods, provided they have time to make this adjustment. In the short run, changes in the stock of money and in the demand for money have their initial effects in financial markets. The participants in such markets react to an excess supply of money by buying financial paper or by offering loans. When the money supply falls, banks and other financial intermediaries react immediately by selling bonds in the attempt to obtain more money. The short-run impact of monetary changes is in financial markets. The goods market is affected by the financial sector but this relates mainly to investment expenditure.

In Chapter 2, the demand for money was shown to depend on four variables: nominal income, the rate of interest, expected inflation and wealth. When real income is constrained by expenditure in the short run and the rate of interest is the only price which adjusts rapidly, attention can be confined to the effects of these two variables on the demand for money:

$$Md = Md\,(Q, r) \qquad\qquad\qquad\qquad\qquad (4.16)$$
$$+, -$$

The money supply is a multiple of the monetary base. The behaviour of the commercial banks reinforced by rules imposed by the Central Bank ensure that this multiple is roughly constant

$$M = h\,H \tag{4.17}$$

The monetary sector is in equilibrium when the stock is willingly held:

$$M = Md \tag{4.18}$$

This short-run equilibrium is brought about by the interaction of the money and bond markets. An increase in income causes more money to be demanded because people wish to make more transactions. They hold stocks of bonds which can be easily traded in financial markets. Some households sell bonds but the total bond stock is fixed and the effect is to raise the rate of interest. The interest on bonds is the opportunity cost of holding money and an increase encourages firms and households to adjust the timing of their receipts and expenditures, thereby reducing the demand for money.

Figure 4.5 illustrates this sequence in the left-hand diagram. The money supply is shown as constant at M. When income is Q_1 the demand for money is the relation labelled Md (Q_1) which increases as the rate of interest falls. Equilibrium is at r_1. An increase in income shifts the demand function and creates an excess demand for money if the rate of interest stays at r_1. People react by reducing their demand for bonds and the bond stock is no longer willingly held. The excess supply of bonds drives down the bond price and raises the rate of interest. This reduces the demand for money, a movement up the new Md (Q_2) function, until equilibrium is restored at the higher interest rate r_2. There is now no excess demand for money. Bond sales cease and the rate of interest remains constant.

(In the long run, rises in real income with a constant money supply drive down the price level instead of raising the rate of interest. Some of the extra income flows to the market for loanable funds where it keeps down the rate of interest, countering the effect of increases in investment intentions of firms responding to the growth in income. This happened in Britain during some decades of the nineteenth century. In the short run, stock adjustments in the money and bond markets are more important than the changes in flows of loanable funds. Nominal wage contracts and other contracts for inputs inhibit firms from rapidly lowering output prices when aggregate demand constrains output. If all prices have time to adjust the sequence runs from income growth to savings growth to a lower rate of interest. With negligible price adjustments the sequence is from income growth to a rise in the demand for money which leads to a higher rate of interest.)

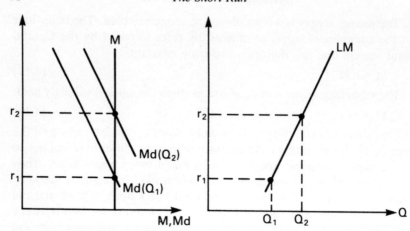

Figure 4.5 Equilibria in the monetary sector.
Left. The money supply is M. When income is Q_1 the demand for money is Md (Q_1) which increases as the rate of interest falls; the equilibrium interest rate is r_1. An increase in income to Q_2 raises the interest rate to r_2.
Right. With a fixed money supply, equilibrium is preserved if the increase in Md due to increasing income is countered by the fall in Md due to increases in the rate of interest.

The demand for money matches the fixed money supply provided the increased demand caused by higher income is countered by a higher rate of interest. The diagram on the right of Figure 4.5 shows the locus of combinations of r and Q which result in monetary equilibrium. The demand for money is often called 'liquidity preference', and the locus is conventionally labelled LM to convey that liquidity preference L equals the money supply M at any point on the locus.

The IS locus shows those combinations of Q and r which bring income into equality with expenditure and the LM locus shows points of monetary equilibrium. Both sectors are in equilibrium where the two loci cross. Figure 4.6 gives examples of disequilibrium combinations and the directions of change of Q and r which eliminate these disequilibria. Point 1 lies above the LM locus implying a rate of interest which has reduced the demand for money to a level which is less than the money stock. The excess supply of money leads households to buy bonds and the interest rate falls. Point 1 is also above the IS locus, implying that the high interest rate has reduced investment expenditure and aggregate demand is less than output. The excess supply of goods causes firms to reduce output to a level which can be sold. From point 1 the movement is south-westwards. The government holds tax revenue, its expenditure

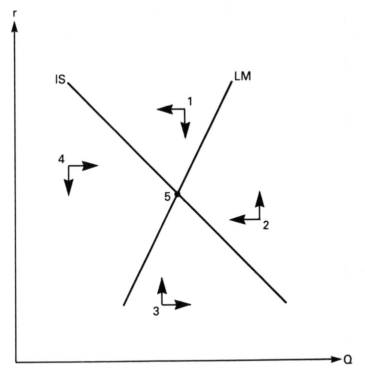

Figure 4.6   Moves to domestic equilibrium.
At point 1 there would be an excess supply of money and r would fall; the excess supply of goods would cause income to fall.
At point 2 the excess demand for money raises r and income exceeds expenditure leading to a reduction in Q.
At point 3 r is too low for monetary equilibrium and Q too low for goods market equilibrium.
At point 4 there are excess demands for both money and goods. Q and r change until domestic equilibrium is reached at *point 5*.

and the money supply constant. Exports are assumed constant as a result of the fixed exchange rate. The behaviour of firms and households causes the monetary and goods sectors to interact and bring the economy to the equilibrium values of income and the rate of interest. However, this domestic equilibrium may not be consistent with the balance of payments constraint set by the fixed exchange rate.

Figure 4.7 illustrates a domestic equilibrium combined with a balance of payments surplus. The low level of income Q_1 generates a low expenditure on imports. The high rate of interest r_1 makes domestic

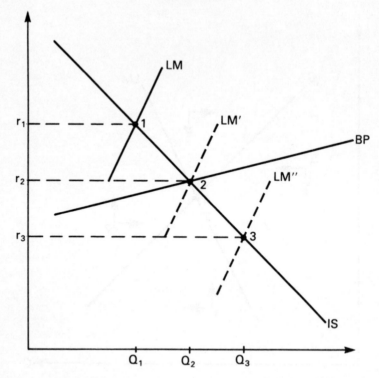

Figure 4.7   When the exchange rate is fixed, the monetary sector adjusts to bring balance of payments equilibrium.
Point 1 shows internal equilibrium but a balance of payments surplus. The money supply would increase, shifting LM to LM'.
Point 2 shows internal equilibrium coinciding with balance of payments equilibrium.
At *point 3* the high income generates high imports and the low interest rate generates a deficit on the capital account. The money supply would fall shifting LM″ to LM'.

bonds attractive to foreign purchasers and receipts of foreign exchange exceed import expenditure. With the IS and BP loci fixed, the monetary sector would need to shift to LM' to ensure that the domestic equilibrium coincided with balance of payments equilibrium. In the next section this shift is shown to be the result of the monetary authorities' actions to preserve the fixed exchange rate.

4.4 MONETARY CHANGES AND THE BALANCE OF PAYMENTS

The accounts of the Central Bank show the high-powered money stock H as a liability backed by reserves of foreign exchange R and domestic assets D. As in section 2.1, the accounting identity is

$$H \equiv R + D \tag{4.19}$$

With a fixed exchange rate the Bank cannot control H for more than a few months. Over a period of a year or two, H is determined by the goods and foreign sectors.

When bond dealers and exporters are receiving more foreign exchange than is demanded by importers, the surplus is deposited with the commercial banks who deposit it in turn with the Central Bank. The Bank credits the commercial banks with the domestic equivalent or provides domestic currency in exchange, thereby increasing H. The Bank could bring about a corresponding reduction in H by selling part of its bond holdings to households via an open market operation. In Figure 4.7 the effect would be to hold the economy at point 1. When increases in foreign reserves are countered by open-market operations, the process is known as *sterilising the surplus* on the balance of payments. It is a policy which might be adopted if the authorities considered that the surplus was due to a seasonal surge in exports. (From equation (4.4) the algebra of the BP locus shows that a rise in exports results in a lowering of the locus. In Figure 4.7 the authorities consider that the locus which is drawn is only seasonal. They have incorrectly estimated that the annual flows will result in a locus through point 1.) If the policy is continued for more than a few months, bond and currency dealers note the rise in reserves and begin to suspect that the fixed exchange rate cannot be maintained. The currency may be revalued to become more valuable in terms of other currencies. Since there is no chance of a devaluation while the country accumulates foreign reserves, speculators cannot lose. Exporters from the country rush to convert their foreign earnings into domestic currency before the revaluation occurs, and importers delay payment for as long as possible in the hope that the revaluation will enable them to pay less domestic currency per unit of foreign currency. These *leads and lags* by traders reinforce the actions of speculators. The excess demand for the currency feeds on itself and the exchange rate cannot remain fixed.

A regime of fixed exchange rates requires the monetary authorities to stop sterilising surpluses as soon as these are realised to be more than seasonal. The increase in foreign reserves then results in an increase in the money supply. For each rate of interest monetary equilibrium can be maintained at a higher level of income than before. The LM locus shifts to the right. Figure 4.8 shows the changes in the equilibrium combinations of Q and r.

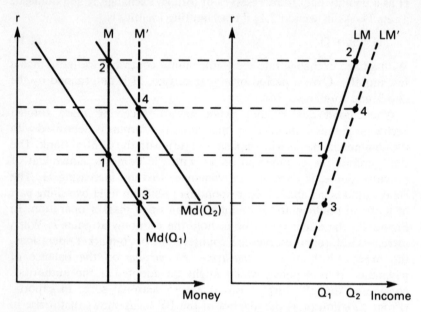

Figure 4.8   An increase in the money supply shifts the LM locus.
Left. When the money supply is M, an increase in income from Q_1 to Q_2 shifts the demand function, and equilibrium moves from point 1 to point 2. For a money supply of M', the two equilibria are point 3 for Q_1 and point 4 for Q_2.
Right. The corresponding LM loci.

As the money supply increases, the rate of interest falls and encourages investment expenditure. Returning to Figure 4.7, the domestic economy moves down the IS locus from point 1. The increase in investment adds to expenditure on domestic value-added and firms respond by increasing output. Income increases and generates more expenditure on imports. The fall in the rate of interest reduces the foreign demand for bonds. The balance of payments moves to equilibrium. The change in foreign reserves ceases and the money supply remains constant.

What happens if the authorities expand the money supply further and lower the rate of interest to r_3 in Figure 4.7? The extra increase in investment raises expenditure and income, which causes a rise in imports and a deficit on the current account. The lower interest rate causes a deficit on the capital account and there is a large overall deficit on the balance of payments. The money supply can be maintained at this level if the drain of foreign reserves is countered by open market operations to buy bonds from households with new money. This *sterilisation of the deficit* could occur until there are no foreign reserves left. However, the foreign exchange market will anticipate a devaluation of the currency long before this. Now the leads and lags operate in the reverse direction to an anticipated revaluation. Importers buy foreign exchange earlier than they would if they expected the exchange rate to remain constant. Exporters hold on to their foreign exchange earnings in case the domestic currency is devalued. During the period of fixed exchange rates in the 1950s and 1960s, sterilising deficits was possible for a few weeks rather than months. Central Banks engaged in the practice to maintain stability in the monetary sector during unusual peaks in imports, when the foreign exchange market realised that the deficit on the balance of payments was only a very short-run phenomenon. Over a period of one or two years, fixed exchange rates can be maintained only if sterilising deficits for a few weeks is followed by sterilising surpluses for a few weeks. On average, the two practices have to cancel out. The authorities cannot control the money stock, taking its average for the year, if they wish to maintain fixed exchange rates. They can control the blend of foreign and domestic assets backing the monetary base but not the total.

4.5　EXPANSIONARY POLICIES WITH FIXED EXCHANGE RATES

Suppose there is an overall equilibrium in the goods and monetary sectors and on the balance of payments. Unemployment is above its natural rate, and surveys of firms reveal that some labour is being hoarded and there is idle equipment. The behaviour of firms and households combined with present government policy is generating insufficient aggregate demand. An expansionary policy would stimulate output with a negligible rise in the price level. The government can increase its expenditure on goods and services or reduce taxes. In Figure 4.9, the effect is to shift the IS locus to the right. (Referring to the algebra of the locus in equation (4.15), an increase in G or a reduction in T would raise the locus, which is more easily pictured as a rightward shift.)

If the money supply stayed constant, the increase in expenditure

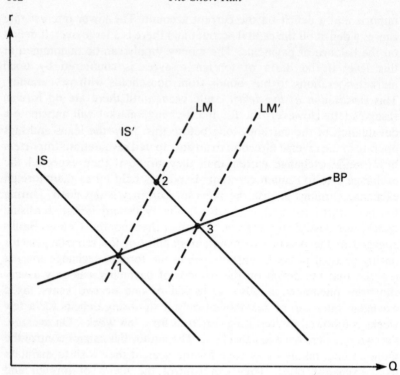

Figure 4.9   A fiscal expansion shifts IS to IS' and the internal equilibrium from point 1 to point 2.
At point 2 the high rate of interest causes a surplus on the capital account and the money supply increases. The monetary sector shifts from LM to LM' and the new internal and external equilibrium is at point 3.

would generate extra income and force a rise in the rate of interest. Figure 4.9 shows the LM locus more steeply sloped than the BP locus. With the low interest-elasticity of demand for money, the rise in r needed to keep the demand for money constant is proportionately greater than the increase in Q. The gentle slope to the BP locus reflects the responsiveness of international financial capital to changes in the domestic rate of interest. As imports increase with Q and cause a current account deficit, only a small increase in r is required to generate a corresponding capital account surplus and preserve balance of payments equilibrium. The fiscal expansion moves the domestic economy from point 1 to point 2, which is above the BP locus and therefore associated with a balance of payments surplus. The money supply increases and reinforces the effects of the fiscal policy, moving the economy to point 3.

The policy increases the government's budget deficit but it also increases income. If the reserves were adequate before the expansion, the monetary authorities could increase the monetary base via open market operations instead of leaving the increase to the rise in reserves. In effect, the increased deficit is then financed by both money and bonds. The policy also increases the current account deficit. Balance of payments equilibrium is preserved by the inflow of funds to buy financial paper which must be serviced in the future. In the following period the flow of dividends, interest and profit to other countries will be greater. Unless exports increase, a higher rate of interest will be required for each level of income. (The algebra of the BP locus is given in equation (4.4), which shows the locus shifting up when Dip increases but down when X increases.)

When there is a severe shortage of aggregate demand, firms are pessimistic about the profitability of investment. The IS locus takes this pessimism as given and treats investment as increasing only if the rate of interest falls. Any increase in the orders received by firms during the present period will reduce pessimism about the future. In the next period the IS locus shifts to the right because the behaviour of firms has changed: they invest more at each rate of interest. The budget deficit can then be reduced. By the third period, aggregate demand may have caught up with the natural level of output, but by then the investment has been plugged into the processes of production and the capacity to produce is itself expanding. When attempting to cure a major shortage of expenditure the authorities are justified in expanding any component of aggregate demand initially. Investment becomes increasingly important as the economy approaches supply constraints.

When demand is expected to constrain output for only a short period, the expansion of government expenditure can itself be on investment such as infrastructure. Project appraisal takes into account the low social costs of using unemployed or hoarded labour and adjusts market prices accordingly in the accounting calculations. An efficient bureaucracy can use forecasts of aggregate demand to discover those projects which become worthwhile when there are idle resources although they would not be if the economy were at its natural level of output. When current account deficits are increasing, the emphasis can be on those projects which reduce exporters' costs or encourage improvements in export quality.

During the late 1960s and the 1970s many policy-makers treated Keynesian economics as a substitute for microeconomics. The analytical framework came to be associated with mounting budget deficits and current account deficits. Investment is the crucial link between the present and the future. It enables a cure for a present shortage of aggregate demand to remove a future shortage of aggregate supply. Output growth raises the tax base and reduces the problem of servicing past budget deficits. Export growth reduces the current account deficit. The next section gives illustrations of the impact on income of a demand expansion when activity is constrained by a shortage of expenditure.

4.6   INCOME MULTIPLIERS

If firms decide to invest less, the immediate effect is a fall in orders given to other firms. With expenditure constraining output, firms produce less and pay households less income. Consumption now falls and leads to a further reduction in orders and income. When prices respond sluggishly, all the adjustment occurs in quantities. The initial deviation from the natural level of output is amplified rather than corrected. Economic behaviour in the aggregate can result in a rapid reduction in income. The corrective actions of the price mechanism are often long-run and may come into operation only after the early fall in income has been exacerbated by the ensuing quantity adjustments. The realisation that such adjustments can occur led to the modern systems of national accounts which enable expenditure flows to be monitored. Rapid policy responses can reverse the process.

Income multipliers calculate the effects on income of an exogenous change in expenditure. They provide numerical approximations which are relevant in the short run of one or two years, although they are capturing a dynamic process. For example, a fall in investment by £1 billion results in an immediate fall in income by that amount. If households save 20 per cent of their income and spend 30 per cent on imports, they reduce their orders to domestic firms by £0.5 billion. This expenditure reduction leads to a further fall in income of £0.5 billion and the next round of expenditure falls by £0.25 billion. The process is an infinite series:

$$1 + 0.5 + 0.25 + 0.125 + \ldots$$

which eventually sums to 2. Most of the process occurs in the early stages. As an approximation of the short-run effect, the initial change in expenditure caused a fall in income twice as great. The multiplier is 2.

The IS and BP loci can be used to derive the algebra of multipliers, but this can be simplified by assuming that financial capital is perfectly

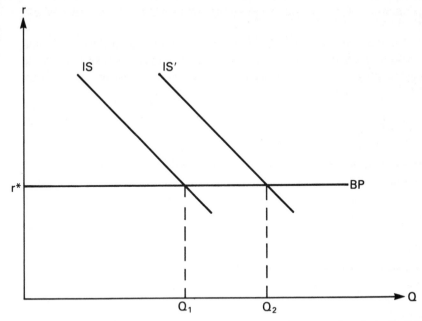

Figure 4.10 When financial capital is perfectly mobile across frontiers, the BP locus is horizontal and the rate of interest is the world rate r*.

mobile across frontiers. The economy can lend or borrow any amount at the world rate of interest. The BP locus is a horizontal line moored at this rate, as illustrated in Figure 4.10. With the rate of interest constant, equation 4.15 giving the algebra of the IS locus can be rearranged to

$$Q = \frac{1}{s + z} [I + G + X - (1 - s) T] \qquad (4.20)$$

where s and z are the propensities to save and import and all the other terms are exogenous, including investment which is now determined by the world interest rate.

If economic behaviour reduces I or X by £1 billion, the change in income is

$$\Delta Q = \frac{1}{s + z} \qquad (4.21)$$

In the case of exports, this is known as the *foreign trade multiplier*. The impact of export orders is highest if the economy has a low propensity to import. If $s + z = 0.2 + 0.3$, the multiplier is 2. With a low import propensity of 0.1 but the same savings propensity the multiplier would be 3.33.

An increase in G by £1 billion would raise income by the same amount as an increase in exports in this example because the mobile capital prevents any crowding out of investment. However, a reduction of taxation by £1 billion increases income by only

$$\Delta Q = \frac{(1-s)}{s+z} \tag{4.22}$$

When households are left with more income after tax they save some of the increase and this limits the rise in expenditure and income.

A government which is reluctant to increase its budget deficit can provide a stimulus to demand by increasing taxation and spending all the extra revenue. If both G and T increase by one unit, the *balanced budget multiplier* is

$$\Delta Q = \frac{1}{s+z} - \frac{1-s}{s+z} = \frac{s}{s+z} \tag{4.23}$$

These approximations exaggerate the size of the multiplier if financial capital is not perfectly mobile. Balance of payments equilibrium then entails a rise in the rate of interest as income expands, but this rise affects investment expenditure and moderates the expansion of income. (The effect of an increase in exports is ambiguous. With imperfect capital mobility the IS locus shifts up and the BP locus shifts down, possibly by enough to lower the rate of interest. The increase in investment would then reinforce the effect of the increase in exports.)

The reader is advised to plod through the following simple algebra, treating it as a checklist on which variables influence others and which cause the IS, LM and BP loci to shift.

Exercise with fixed exchange rates

The equations describe an economy where government expenditure and taxation are negligible, the exchange rate is fixed, and income is determined by expenditure.

(1) Ad = C + I + X − Z
(2)   C = 0.8 Q
(3)   I = 23.4 − 0.1 r
(4)   X = 27
(5)   Z = 0.3 Q

(6)　　Q = Ad
(7)　　F = −1.8 + 1.2 r
(8)　　X + F − Z = 0
(9)　Md = 0.3 Q + 10.4 − 0.1 r
(10)　　M = 2H
(11)　　M = Md

i.　Derive the IS locus by plugging equations (2)–(6) into (1) and expressing r in terms of Q.

ii.　Derive the BP locus by plugging (4), (5) and (7) into (8). Use IS and BP to discover the equilibrium values of r and Q. What are the values of C and I?

iii.　What is the value of the trade deficit? What is the value of the capital account surplus? In this example, what must be the value of dividends, interest and profits flowing abroad?

iv.　Use equations (9), (10) and (11) to derive the LM locus, expressing r in terms of Q and H. What is the value of H? (Note that H is endogenous to this system of equations.)

v.　What are the propensities to import, to consume and to save? What is the value of the foreign trade multiplier?

vi.　Replace equation (4) by

(4′) X = 28

Derive the new equations IS′ for the goods sector and BP′ for the balance of payments. What are the new values of r and Q? (Calculate to two decimal places.) Sketch the shifts in the two loci. What is the new value of I? Why is the increase in income greater than predicted by the foreign trade multiplier?

Numerical Answers:
(ii)　r = 4 per cent, Q = 100, C = 80, I = 23.
(iii)　Z − X = 3, F = 3, Dip = 0.
(iv)　H = 20.
(v)　z = 0.3, c = 0.8, s = 0.2, ftm = 2.
(vi)　r = 3.69 per cent, Q = 102.06, I = 23.03.
The ftm predicts Q = 2 if X = 1.
However the fall in r causes a rise in I and this ΔI must also be multiplied to find its impact on Q.

4.7 SUMMARY

Financial markets adjust rapidly. Goods markets adjust prices more slowly than quantities when there is a shortage of aggregate demand. Some of the implications of this behaviour can be found by studying its effect on just two variables: income and the rate of interest. The analysis reveals the types of policy which are effective when exchange rates are fixed and other price adjustments are too slow to be relevant in the short run. The focus is on the demand side of the goods market. The algebra reveals the importance of observing data on the propensities to save and import, and the responsiveness to the rate of interest of investment, the demand for money and international capital flows.

PROBLEMS FOR CHAPTER 4

1.   Give examples of government expenditure for this year which could encourage business investment next year when the government expenditure could then be reduced.
2.   Give examples of government investment expenditure this year which would increase the capacity to produce next year.
3.   Give examples of government policies which would increase export quality or lower export costs while preserving the fixed exchange rate and keeping to the General Agreement on Tariffs and Trade.
4.   Why does expenditure increase when both government expenditure and taxation are increased?
5.   A frugal and very open economy has a savings propensity of 0.4 and an import propensity of 0.7. What is the value of its balanced budget multiplier?
6.   During the 1950s, international flows of capital were not very responsive to interest rate differentials and the demand for money was thought to be highly responsive to interest rate changes. (The BP locus had a steeper slope than the LM locus.) Show that in such a world a fiscal expansion must be associated with a monetary contraction if the fixed exchange rate is to be preserved.

FURTHER READING

See Chapter 5, p. 126.

5. Quantities and the Exchange Rate

The authorities can manage a country's monetary sector in a way which fixes the exchange rate. Most of the main trading nations adopted this policy during the era of the Gold Standard until 1914 and the decades of the Dollar Standard in the 1950s and 1960s. In the 1980s the European Monetary System is almost a Deutschemark Standard. A country operating within a regime of fixed exchange rates may decide to devalue its currency, a once-only rise in the domestic price of foreign exchange which is expected to discourage imports and encourage exports. The early sections of this chapter discuss some of the conditions which ensure that a devaluation has the intended effects. The implication is that policy determines the exchange rate and economic behaviour determines the money supply once the exchange rate is set. In a model describing behaviour, the money supply is endogenous.

When countries prefer to control their money supplies rather than the exchange rate, behaviour provides the link from the policy-determined money supply to the exchange rate. The analytical framework is the same but the moves from cause to effect involve climbing through it in a different direction. The later sections of the chapter show the important differences between monetary and fiscal policies under regimes of floating rates compared with fixed rates.

5.1 DEVALUATION

When the authorities stimulate expenditure they increase the deficit on the current account. This deficit may prove unsustainable and the only remaining policy is to change the exchange rate. In Chapter 1, the real exchange rate EP^*/P was used as an index of competitiveness. When demand is depressed in the short run, variations in P^* and P can be assumed to be minor. A rise in the price of foreign exchange E will then cause a rise in the competitiveness of exports. It will also enable domestic production to compete with imports. The devaluation of the domestic currency raises the price of foreign currency. If the rate of interest stayed constant, the effect on income would be a multiple of the increased exports ΔX and the reduction in imports ΔZ.

$$\Delta Q = \frac{1}{s + z}(\Delta X + \Delta Z) \tag{5.1}$$

The rise in exports and fall in imports enable a current account balance to be achieved at a higher level of income than before. When there is imperfect capital mobility, balance of payments equilibrium can be maintained with a lower rate of interest for each level of income. The BP locus shifts down. Figure 5.1 illustrates the effects of a devaluation, raising the price of foreign exchange from E_1 to E_2. In this example the new equilibrium is at a lower rate of interest; the effects of higher exports and lower imports are reinforced by more investment.

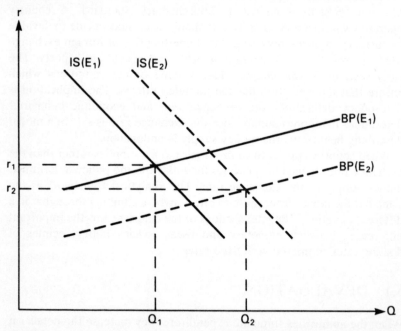

Figure 5.1 A devaluation raises the price of foreign exchange from E_1 to E_2. The IS locus shifts to the right and the BP locus shifts down. In this example, the rate of interest has fallen.

5.2 THE MARSHALL–LERNER CONDITIONS

Most industrialised countries produce and consume approximately similar bundles of goods. If one such country devalues the foreign demanders of it exports and the domestic demanders of imports switch expenditure from or to similar goods so that the elasticities of response to exchange rate changes are high. Some countries produce specialised exports which have a low elasticity of demand. A devaluation may increase sales only slightly and receipts measured in foreign currency would fall although the devaluation ensures that receipts in domestic currency increase. If the country has a low elasticity of demand for imports, import volume falls proportionately less than the rise in the import price. The devaluation will result in more import expenditure when measured in domestic currency and this could exceed the increase in export receipts. The devaluation could worsen the current account.

Imports are affected by both the exchange rate and income. The objective of a devaluation is to generate a larger trade surplus with current income than is desired after income has expanded. This section investigates the conditions under which a devaluation increases the trade surplus for a given level of income. Provided the conditions are met, income can then be expanded and the extra imports need not entail extra borrowing from abroad.

Economists estimate the responsiveness of exports and imports to exchange rate changes by studying the effects of past devaluations in the same or other countries and by estimating the price-elasticities of demand for individual goods. By comparing proportionate changes, the units of measurement cancel out: elasticities are simply numbers. In what follows, the elasticities of the volumes of exports and imports in response to changes in the exchange rate are assumed known. The effect of a devaluation on the trade surplus can be discovered by expressing the surplus as a function of the elasticities. The main thrust of the argument can be preserved and the algebra much reduced by making some simplifying assumptions.

With expenditure constraining income in both the home and foreign economies, price level changes are insignificant. We set the domestic and foreign price indexes P and P^* both at unity. X is both the volume and value of exports. Import volume is measured in units which make EZ the value of imports where E is the price of foreign exchange expressed in domestic currency. Before the devaluation the trade surplus TS is assumed to be zero:

$$\text{Initially } TS = X - EZ = 0 \qquad (5.2)$$

implying that $Z = X/E$. Equation (5.2) is manipulated to incorporate the known elasticities. Using the Greek letter eta η for elasticity, we define:

$$\eta x \equiv \frac{E}{X} \frac{\Delta X}{\Delta E} \qquad (5.3)$$

$$\eta_Z \equiv (-)\frac{E}{Z}\frac{\Delta Z}{\Delta E} \tag{5.4}$$

The increase in the price of foreign exchange lowers import volume by ΔZ. Since elasticities are easier to discuss as positive numbers, a minus sign is included in the definition to counter the negative value of ΔZ.

The effect of the devaluation on the trade surplus is straightforward in the case of exports: it is ΔX. For imports there are two effects: the change in volume ΔZ increases TS by $E \bullet \Delta Z$ (and since ΔZ is negative the increase is expressed as $-E \bullet \Delta Z$), but the increase in the price of foreign exchange by ΔE reduces TS by $\Delta E \bullet Z$. It is this latter effect which could endanger the desired impact of the devaluation; the increased cost of imports could outweigh both the reduction in import volume and the rise in export volume. After the devaluation,

$$TS = \Delta X - E \bullet \Delta Z - Z \bullet \Delta E \tag{5.5}$$

and the algebraic problem is to convert this expression to incorporate the elasticities.

$$TS = \Delta E \left(\frac{\Delta X}{\Delta E} - \frac{E}{\Delta E} \bullet \Delta Z - Z \right)$$

$$= \Delta E \bullet \frac{X}{E}\left(\frac{E}{X}\frac{\Delta X}{\Delta E} - \frac{E}{X}\frac{E}{\Delta E} \Delta Z - \frac{E}{X}Z \right) \tag{5.6}$$

but equation (5.2) allows us to use the approximation $Z = X/E$.

$$TS = X \bullet \frac{\Delta E}{E}\left(\frac{E}{X}\frac{\Delta X}{\Delta E} - \frac{1}{Z}\frac{E}{\Delta E} \Delta Z - \frac{Z}{Z} \right)$$

$$= X \bullet \frac{\Delta E}{E}\left(\eta_X + \eta_Z - 1 \right) \tag{5.7}$$

This is the *Marshall–Lerner condition*. It states that the trade surplus generated by a devaluation will be positive if the sum of the elasticities of demand for exports and imports is greater than unity. $\Delta E/E$ is the proportional extent of the devaluation. Knowledge of this, and the elasticities, and the value of exports before the devaluation enables us to predict the size of the trade surplus. This, combined with information about dividend, interest and profit flows, gives the current account surplus before the expansion of income.

In terms of Figure 5.1, the authorities may wish to expand income from Q_1 to Q_2 but have a current account balance at the higher level of income. Servicing past borrowing requires a trade surplus for current account balance. The trade surplus generated by the devaluation with income held at Q_1 must be greater than this to allow for the extra imports generated by the extra income. Knowledge of the elasticities and the initial export flows then allows the extent of the required devaluation $\Delta E/E$ to be calculated.

(The Marshall–Lerner condition for a successful devaluation takes foreign and domestic price levels as constant. Firms do not require a higher price to persuade them to produce more. Over the relevant range of output, the supply elasticities of both imports and exports are assumed to be infinite. When income is not constrained by expenditure, firms have to switch resources towards exports from other production. The supply elasticities are finite and the authorities may have to take action which reduces the total expenditure generated within the domestic economy. Removing a current account deficit under such circumstances is considered in a later chapter.)

5.3 PROBLEMS OF DEVALUATION

A regime of fixed exchange rates creates an element of certainty in international markets for goods and finance. Devaluations have to be rare if the system is to survive. A devaluing country usually engages in a round of rapid and secret negotiations with other countries before the devaluation to explain its case and minimise the risk of setting off competitive devaluations by other countries.

During the months following a devaluation, export volumes may show little change. Those exports which were contracted at a price denominated in the foreign currency will maintain the same sales volume although their value in domestic currency rises by the full extent of the rise in the price of foreign exchange. Exports priced in the exporter's currency will yield no increase in foreign exchange until the demand expands. The demand elasticity for exports may appear very low if the quantity response is measured only three months after the devaluation but can rise as much as sixfold if two years is allowed for the adjustment. (For example, US exports in the early 1970s showed a short-run price-elasticity of only 0.3 if the quantity response is measured three months after the price change, but 1.8 if the response is measured two years later.) Measured in domestic currency, the rise in export earnings can initially be far less than the increase in the price of foreign exchange. Import demand is also price-inelastic in the short run while customers search for cheaper domestic substitutes. Total expendi-

ture on imports may rise for a few months by almost the full extent of
the rise in the price of foreign currency.

Figure 5.2 shows the time-path of the trade account following a
devaluation. Initially, the small deficit is accentuated. It starts to
improve after about six months, turns into a small surplus after a year
and most of the effects have worked through after two years. This J-
shaped adjustment path implies an initial drain of foreign reserves if the
new exchange rate is to be held. When reserves are low, foreign Central
Banks or the International Monetary Fund may provide loans to carry
the country over the adjustment period. The alternative is a large rise in
the domestic rate of interest which will reduce the beneficial effects of
the devaluation. International approval of a devaluation is particularly
important when the country has few reserves of foreign exchange and
has to rely on official loans.

5.4   FLOATING EXCHANGE RATES

Each Central Bank may prefer to control its country's money supply
rather than the exchange rate. It can refuse to change its assets by

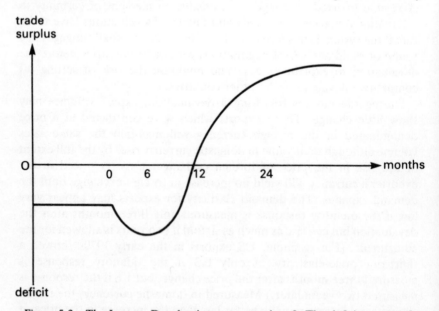

Figure 5.2   The J-curve. Devaluation occurs at time 0. The deficit worsens for
the next six months, moves to surplus after twelve months and the main effects
have worked through after two years.

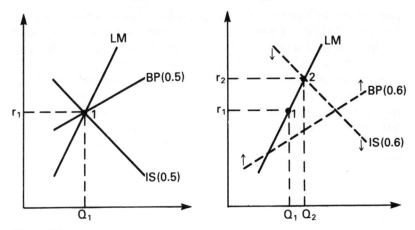

Figure 5.3
Left. Equilibrium is at point 1 when the money supply is fixed and the floating exchange rate settles at 0.5 units of domestic currency per unit of foreign currency.
Right. The domestic currency is undervalued when the price of foreign exchange increases to 0.6. Domestic equilibrium is at point 2 which lies above BP (0.6) signifying that the domestic currency is in excess demand. As the exchange rate falls back to 0.5, the BP locus rises and the IS locus fall until they intersect at point 1.

selling or buying foreign exchange. Instead the price of foreign currency is left to be determined in the foreign exchange market. Importers, exporters and dealers in financial paper influence the supply and demand for currencies. The price of foreign exchange in terms of domestic currency changes until the foreign exchange market is in equilibrium, with each rise in the price leading to a reduction in imports and an increase in exports. With domestic and foreign price levels constant, a rise in the price of foreign exchange is also a rise in the index of competitiveness. Imports are influenced by both the exchange rate and income. Domestic financial paper is in greater foreign demand at higher domestic rates of interest. An equilibrium level of the exchange rate will stay constant if a rise in income, causing increased imports which increase the supply of the domestic currency in the foreign exchange market, is matched by an appropriate rise in the rate of interest to cause an equal increase in the demand for the currency.

Figure 5.3 pictures an economy where the domestic currency is the £. The foreign currency is the dollar and the equilibrium exchange rate E is £0.5 per \$. The BP locus shows those combinations of Q and r which would preserve this equilibrium. Points above BP (0.5) show an excess demand for the currency. (In the previous sections such points would result in a balance of payments surplus. The economic activity which would cause a surplus with fixed exchange rates now causes a fall in the price of foreign exchange.) The IS (0.5) locus shows equilibrium in the goods sector when imports and exports have adjusted to the exchange rate E = 0.5. The LM locus is fixed by the authorities who are able to control the money supply when they give up control of the exchange rate. Domestic equilibrium is determined by the goods and monetary sectors but this combination of Q and r must result in an equilibrium price of foreign exchange.

5.5   FISCAL EXPANSION WITH FLOATING RATES

This section examines the effects of an increase in government expenditure when the money supply stays constant. In Figure 5.4, the increased orders from government would shift the goods sector from IS (0.5) to IS' (0.5) if the exchange rate stayed constant. A rise in the rate of interest is required to maintain monetary equilibrium, but this makes domestic financial paper more attractive to foreigners who offer foreign exchange for the domestic currency. The price of foreign exchange falls. The impact of the fiscal expansion is moderated by the two price changes: the interest rate and the exchange rate. Investment and exports fall, imports rise. However, there must be a net expansion of income because this was what triggered the rise in the rate of interest (the movement up LM) which in turn caused the fall in competitiveness.

After repeated fiscal expansions the accumulated effect of bond-financed deficits may further moderate the effect on income. A proportion of the bonds are bought by domestic rather than foreign households. Wealth increases and this raises the demand for money for given income and given rate of interest. The LM locus shifts to the left.

5.6   MONETARY EXPANSION WITH FLOATING RATES

An increase in the money supply has a major effect upon income provided foreign financial capital is responsive to a rise in the domestic rate of interest. In terms of Figure 5.5, this condition is shown by the BP locus having a slope which is less steep than the LM locus. The monetary expansion shifts LM to LM' and lowers the rate of interest. Domestic financial paper becomes less attractive to foreigners and the

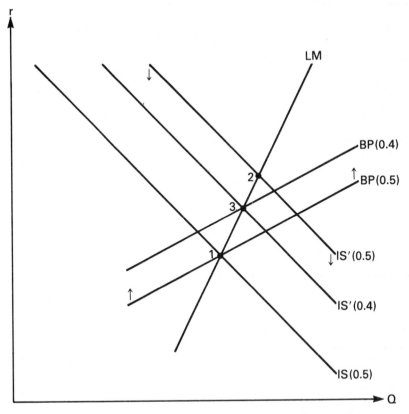

Figure 5.4 A fiscal expansion when the exchange rate floats and the money supply is fixed.
Point 1 shows the initial equilibrium with the exchange rate at 0.5. The fiscal expansion would shift the goods sector to IS′ (0.5) if there were no change in the exchange rate.
Point 2 is above BP (0.5) showing that the currency is undervalued due to the high rate of interest.
The price of foreign exchange falls to 0.4 to give the new equilibrium at *point 3*. The effects of the expansion have been moderated by the appreciation of the currency.

currency depreciates. The rise in competitiveness raises exports and lowers imports. The final effect upon the rate of interest and hence investment is ambiguous. In Figure 5.5 there is a fall in the interest rate at the new equilibrium exchange rate. However, the trade surplus leads to an unambiguous effect on income.

Section 4.5 showed that a pure monetary expansion was not possible

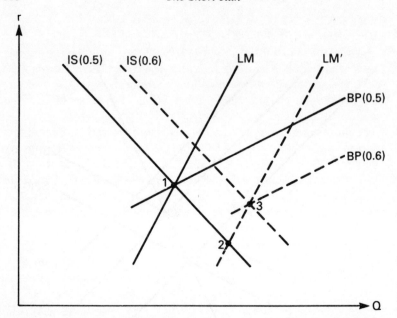

Figure 5.5   The effects of monetary expansion are reinforced by depreciation.
Point 1 is the initial equilibrium with the exchange rate at 0.5. Monetary
expansion shifts LM to LM'.
    With no change in the exchange rate, the economy would be at *point 2* but this
is below BP (0.5) showing that there is an excess supply of the currency. The
depreciation raises the price of foreign exchange to 0.6 and the new equilibrium
is at point 3.

with fixed exchange rates but a fiscal expansion generated an increase in
income both from the rise in government expenditure and the
subsequent rise in the money supply as the reserves increased. With
floating exchange rates, a fiscal expansion has only minor effects on
income because the fall in competitiveness moderates the effect of the
increased government expenditure. A monetary expansion has major
effects on income when the exchange rate floats, the monetary effect
being reinforced by the increase in competitiveness.

Exercise on Floating Exchange Rates

1. In an open economy with no supply constraints, the equilibria in
    the goods, monetary and foreign sectors are described by the
    following equations.
    IS: $100r = 900 + 200E - 5Q$

LM: $100r = -2000 + 25Q$

BP: $100r = 250 - 100E + 3Q$

Q is real income, r the per cent rate of interest and E is the sterling price of one dollar (sterling is the domestic currency). Combine IS with LM to derive an expression for Q in terms of E. Use LM and BP to obtain a second equation expressing Q in terms of E. What are the equilibrium values of Q, E and r?

2. The authorities use open-market operations to shift the monetary sector to LM': $100r = -2100 + 25Q$. What are the new equilibrium values of Q, E and r? Use IS and LM' to discover what would be the values of Q and r if E did not alter. Sketch in Q, r space the shifts of the three loci. Why does the price of foreign currency rise?

3. Starting with the situation described in question 1, what would be the effects upon Q, r and E of a fiscal expansion which leaves the LM locus fixed but shifts the IS locus to

IS': $100r = 1000 + 200E - 5Q$

Use the LM and IS' loci to discover what would be the values of Q and r if E stayed the same as in question 1. Sketch in Q, r space the shifts in the loci. Why does the price of foreign currency fall?

Numerical answers

1. $Q = 100$, $E = £0.5$ per $, $r = 5$ per cent.
2. $Q = 104.05$, $E = 0.608$, $r = 5.013$.
3. $Q = 101.35$, $E = 0.204$, $r = 5.34$.

5.7 MONETARY POLICY AND UNCERTAINTY

When the exchange rate is freely floating, the authorities are able to choose the blend of new money and new bonds which they use to finance the budget deficit. The preceding sections assumed that the authorities chose a monetary target leaving bond sales to fill any gap in the deficit. The public's holdings of bonds were assumed to have no influence on the demand for money. Open-market operations change the money supply and it was this change which was assumed to influence the rate of interest. Although this is the main effect, open-market operations can have a subsidiary effect on the demand for money which reinforces the effect on the money supply. Using new money to purchase bonds from the public both increases the monetary base and reduces the demand for money by reducing the public's holdings of non-monetary assets. The extent of this latter effect is difficult to forecast.

In the short run, following an increase in the monetary base, the commercial banks may hold more base money than they need to meet the Central Bank's rules or ensure banking prudence. They have not yet made the loans which result in firms and households increasing their deposits. When the commercial banks are not 'loaned up' to the full extent, the money supply is less than the rules permit. The relationship is the imprecise one of 'less than or equal to'

$$M \leq hH$$

When the rules themselves are changing, as during the 1980s when financial deregulation occurred in many countries, the value of the parameter h increases. The link between the monetary base H and the money supply M becomes imprecise in the other direction. The authorities may consider that control of H is irrelevant except within a wide range. Instead the Bank may choose to control the rate of interest, buying bonds from the public if it is too high and selling bonds from the Bank's stock of domestic assets when the rate seems too low.

Figure 5.6 shows uncertainty about the demand for money and the money supply. The monetary sector may be anywhere between LM_1 and LM_2 and the authorities have only a vague notion of its most likely position although the quantity of base money is constant and known. If one were to ask the experts at the Bank to bet on where the true position of the locus lay, the odds would not change much between LM_1 and LM_2. We are dealing here with uncertainty rather than riskiness to which a subjective probability can be attached. The goods sector however is sufficiently stable for the authorities to know the position of the IS locus. The target income is Q_2 and this target can be achieved by using open market operations to keep the rate of interest at $\bar{r}$. If the authorities choose to control the monetary base rather than the rate of interest, income might be anywhere in the range Q_1 to Q_3. When the goods sector is stable but the monetary sector is not, controlling the rate of interest enables the income target to be achieved.

When the Central Bank imposes strict and constant rules on the commercial banks and the banks lend up to their limit, the money supply is a predictable multiple of the base. When the demand for money is a stable function of a few easily monitored variables, the LM locus is known to the authorities provided the monetary base H is fixed. The goods sector may be unpredictable because investment intentions or export markets are volatile. Figure 5.7 shows the known LM locus and the limits to the range of possible IS loci. If the income target is Q_3, monetary base control will result in actual income in the narrow range of Q_2 to Q_4. The stable monetary sector pushes the uncertainty into a wide range of possible rates of interest which encourage investment if income

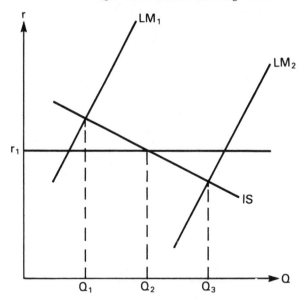

Figure 5.6 The goods sector is known to be represented by IS. There is uncertainty about the position of the monetary sector which may be anywhere between LM_1 and LM_2 although the monetary base is fixed. Fixing the base leads to a range of possible incomes from Q_1 to Q_3. Fixing the interest rate at $\bar{r}$ allows the target income of Q_2 to be achieved. Here the IS locus takes into account variations in the exchange rate, as shown below.

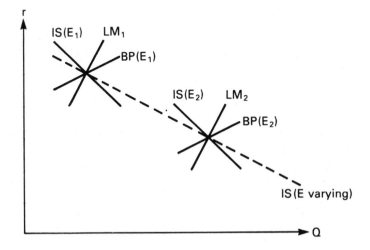

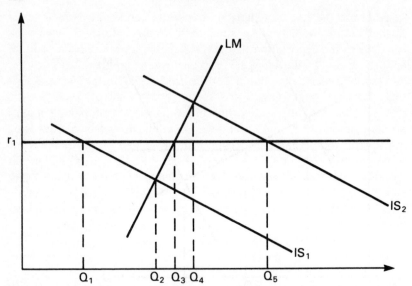

Figure 5.7 The goods sector is within the range IS_1 to IS_2 but its precise position is unknown. Target income is Q_3. The monetary sector is predictably on LM if the base is controlled and the range of possible incomes is Q_2 to Q_4. If the interest rate is controlled at r_1 income may be anywhere in the wider range Q_1 to Q_5.

is below target and discourage it if income is beyond target. If the authorities chose to control the rate of interest rather than the base, income might be anywhere within the wide range of Q_1 to Q_5. When the monetary sector is stable but the goods sector is not, monetary base control is more likely to result in the income target being achieved.

5.8 MANAGED FLOATS AND THE NEED FOR RESERVES

A *free float* occurs when the authorities avoid any interference in currency markets. There would be no need for foreign reserves and the monetary base could be backed entirely by domestic assets. In practice, the supply and demand for a currency can vary widely from day to day with resulting variations in exchange rates. Some dealers are influenced by their notion of the month-to-month equilibrium exchange rate and some will speculate when actual exchange rates depart from this notion. This is stabilising speculation which keeps the actual rate near its equilibrium trend. Destabilising speculation occurs when a dealer suspects that the actual exchange rate is off its trend but will depart even further before the corrective adjustment occurs. He buys overvalued currency in the expectation that it will become more overvalued and if enough dealers do the same the prophecy is self-fulfilling. The currency moves into a speculative bubble. When the bubble bursts the destabilising speculators make losses and such events ought to weed out the species. Unfortunately, the worthy stabilising speculator making modest profits from month to month and the destabilising speculator out for a quick profit but eventually caught with a big loss are both the same person at different times of day, with different currencies. The various moods are not specific to individuals. Speculators survive and may move an exchange rate towards or away from equilibrium. Most commercial banks avoid speculation and confine their dealing to that which allows their accounts in each currency to be balanced at the end of each day. With most deals done by commercial banks and speculators moving a currency in unpredicted directions, day to day fluctuations can be large.

When a Central Bank considers that its currency is overvalued it can take corrective action by simply creating money and using it to buy foreign exchange. If the currency seems undervalued a few weeks later the process is reversed. The equilibrium value may change gently from month to month but the actions of the Bank iron out the extreme day-to-day fluctuations. This is known as a *managed float*.

The world moved to a regime of floating rates between 1969, when the US dollar ceased to be tied to gold, and 1972, when the last of the main currencies, sterling, ceased to be tied to the dollar. At that time it was thought that quite small reserves would be sufficient to manage a float, where 'small' is relative to a country's import bill. In practice, large reserves are required to cushion an exchange rate from fluctuations. Anticipation of a depreciating US dollar has led Central Banks to add the yen and the Deutschemark to the currencies favoured for reserves. The facilities provided by the supranational International Monetary Fund have also been extended.

Multinational firms consider that floats are under-managed and respond by holding a variety of currencies. This private demand for different monies combines with Central Banks' demands for reserves to cause fluctuations in each country's demand for money. When reserves were mainly US dollars, foreign exchange deals in another country's currency were usually for that country's exports or financial paper and currency rapidly returned to circulation within its home country. The demand for a stock of money to be held came from that country's firms and households. If the US dollar is expected to depreciate, other countries and large firms prefer to hold a blend of currencies combining dollars with Deutschemark and yen. While this reshuffling is in process, it affects both the foreign exchange market and each country's domestic money market. The need for reserves is to enable managed floats which prevent extreme day-to-day fluctuations. When Central Banks change their view of the optimal blend of reserves, the flow demand for currencies changes in the foreign exchange market.

Multinational firms place deposits with commercial banks to provide their stock of monies kept for transactions purposes. These deposits are blended according to the currency of the expected transactions, but the blend will be changed if exchange rates are expected to change. The effect is to compound those of the changes in Central Banks' blends of reserves. The holding of a given blend of monies, whether by multinationals for transactions or Central Banks for managed floats, reduces the volatility of exchange rates. A change in the owners' view of the optimal blend exacerbates volatility. Such changes of view are less frequent than the extreme day-to-day variations in the supplies and demands for currencies which would occur with a free float. The stability enabled by the holding of stocks outweighs the volatility generated during periods when the stocks are adjusted.

When the authorities hold the exchange rate out of equilibrium it is known as *dirty floating*. The more usual dirty float is when a newly industrialised country holds its currency below its equilibrium value while it develops its export markets. The country is usually borrowing from abroad for investment and has surpluses on both the current and capital accounts of its balance of payments. Its Central Bank supplies its currency to the foreign exchange market by buying foreign currencies. The rise in the monetary base is prevented by sterilising it via open market operations, selling bonds to its domestic residents and withdrawing the receipts from circulation. Strict exchange controls are required to prevent speculators from anticipating an appreciation.

An overvalued currency is difficult to maintain by a dirty float rather than a restrictive monetary policy. The motive is usually to provide imports which are cheap in terms of the domestic currency. For a short period, the loss of reserves can be sterilised by purchasing bonds from domestic residents. If the loss of reserves is to be avoided and a restrictive monetary policy is not desired, the only action open to the authorities is to ration foreign exchange.

The need for reserves arises from the attempts by Central Banks to reduce exchange rate fluctuations. These attempts have been only partially successful and the unpredictability of exchange rates has led to unpredictability of the goods sectors in most countries. Changes in the blend of reserves held by foreign Central Banks can cause fluctuations in the foreign demand for domestic money and can lead to unpredictability in the monetary sector.

5.9 SUMMARY

This chapter continued the study of an economy during those periods when income is constrained by expenditure. The period of analysis is the short run of a year or two which is relevant to policies which can influence expenditure. We assumed that the price level and the wage rate were inherited from past periods and focused our attention on two endogenous prices, the rate of interest and the exchange rate. In the short run, the money market has closer links with the bond market than the goods market. Monetary changes influence the rate of interest which then affects investment and the foreign sector.

The analysis was made manageable by dividing the economy into three sectors: goods, money and foreign. Changing the exchange rate regime from fixed to floating causes major changes in behaviour and policy options. The following table shows which variables are determined by the interaction of behaviour and policy (endogenous variables) and which are decided outside the IS–LM–BP model by the policy-makers.

Regime	Sector	Endogenous	Policy
Fixed E	IS	Q, r	G, T
	LM	Q, r, H	E
	BP	Q, r	
Floating E	IS	Q, r, E	G, T
	LM	Q, r	H
	BP	Q, r, E	

The components of aggregate demand are determined by the endogenous and policy variables: C by Q and T, I by r, X by E, Z by Q and E.

The chapter used simple algebra to show how the demand side of an economy can be treated mathematically. Econometric models of a national economy are elaborations of such methods, sometimes carried to wondrous extremes. The final sections introduced some of the problems of uncertainty which face both policy-makers and the households and firms who are policy-takers.

PROBLEMS FOR CHAPTER 5

1. An economy has a floating exchange rate and income is constrained by expenditure. The authorities reduce taxes and finance the budget deficit by bond sales. International capital is responsive to interest rate changes. What are the effects of the fiscal expansion on income, exports and investment (a) if the demand for money is not affected by wealth? (b) if increased bond holdings raise the demand for money?

2. Show that the authorities can control the exchange rate or the money supply, but not both.

3. In a world where most exchange rates are fixed, why is it advisable for the authorities in one country to obtain the agreement of other countries before devaluing?

4. A country has a fixed exchange rate. It trades in a world where supply elasticities are high and only demand constrains output. Imports and exports are both 100. The elasticities in response to a change in the price of foreign exchange are 1.8 for exports and 0.9 for imports. What is the trade surplus for constant income if there is a 10 per cent devaluation?

5 The authorities consider that their models give accurate predictions of the behaviour of the goods sector. They deregulate the monetary sector and are unsure of the effects. Would you advise them to control the monetary base or the rate of interest? (Assume that inflation is unlikely.)

FURTHER READING

Stewart (1986) provides a highly readable account of the main features of Keynesian economics. Gordon (1987) is a detailed introductory textbook with an early emphasis on international aspects in this edition. Helpful summaries of IS–LM–BP are in Chapter 8 of Dennis (1981); and Chapter 6 of Llewellyn (1980).

Williamson (1983, pp. 146–56) gives the full Marshall–Lerner conditions including supply elasticities. Mathematical economists may like to attempt the early article by Bickerdike (1920) which was too difficult for the economists of the time and was ignored. The present text adopts the exposition in Rivera-Batiz (1985).

The importance of capital mobility was emphasised by Fleming (1962) and Mundell (1963). The graphical analysis is due to Wrightsman (1970).

6. Quantities and the Price Level

This chapter extends the study of the short run to include those situations when changes in the price level are significant. The first section shows the effects of such changes on aggregate demand. The second shows how a change in the price level may be initiated by events on either the demand side or the supply side of the goods market. In Chapter 2, the emphasis was on the authorities' initiating monetary expansion and the suppliers of goods and labour reacting to the authorities by raising prices and wages. This chapter explains why the authorities sometimes react to supply-side events, attempting to avoid short-run falls in output by pursuing accommodating fiscal and monetary policies. Our understanding of inflation, repeated rises in the price level, can be enhanced by considering the institutional characteristics of a country which led the authorities to react in this way. The final section shows why the growth in the main component of aggregate demand, consumption, is reduced by inflation. The chapter shows that accurate forecasts of economic aggregates from year to year require more detailed knowledge of the components of demand and the behaviour of institutions than implied by the medium-run approximations of the monetarists.

6.1 THE AGGREGATE DEMAND FUNCTION

In Chapter 2, the money supply was treated as the cause of nominal income PQ: for a given money supply, a rise in P implies a fall in Q of the same proportion. This theory is often a helpful approximation for the medium run of two or more years, but it implies that an excess demand for money entails an excess supply of goods, both being eliminated by a fall in the price level. In the short run, this close link between the money and goods markets does not hold. The close links are within financial markets: money, bonds and foreign exchange. An excess demand for money is matched by an excess supply of bonds which drives up the rate of interest. This reduces investment but it also increases the attractiveness of domestic bonds to foreigners, and lowers the price of foreign exchange. Imports rise and exports fall. The link is indirect from an excess demand for money to some components of aggregate demand via the rate of interest and the exchange rate.

The *aggregate demand function* is the short-run relation between the volume of expenditure and the price level, with fiscal policy and the money supply held constant. Its purpose is to provide an analytical framework which allows consideration of price-level changes which are not only the result of money supply changes. The derivation of the function starts by considering the effect of a rise in the price level on the demand for money. Writing this to include all the main independent variables:

$$Md = k\,PQ \tag{6.1}$$

where $k = k\,(r, \pi^e, \text{wealth})$
$\qquad\quad -\ -\quad\ +$

The elasticities of demand with respect to both P and Q are approximately unity. The liquidity ratio k falls with the rate of interest, r, and expected inflation π^e but rises if wealth increases. A once-only rise in the price level increases Md proportionately. If the rise is expected to be once only, π^e is unaffected. Firms and households attempt to obtain more money by selling bonds which drives up the rate of interest and lowers investment. (In an IS–LM diagram the LM locus shifts to the left, the increased demand for money having the same effect as a reduced supply. There is a movement along the IS locus.)

The rise in the rate of interest increases foreign demand for the currency and the price of foreign exchange falls. Export competitiveness declines because the real exchange rate EP*/P has been affected both by the fall in E and the rise in P. Exports fall and imports increase. (The IS locus now shifts to the left. The analysis is the same as Chapter 5 when the money supply falls but with competitiveness decreased by the changes in both E and P. The final effect on the rate of interest is ambiguous; it could fall and cause a small rise in investment to moderate the large increase in the trade deficit. The analysis assumes that the fall in business optimism does not occur until the next period.)

The aggregate demand function is labelled Ad in Figure 6.1. It is drawn as a straight line to avoid confusion with the monetarist's approximation to an aggregate demand function which is the rectangular hyperbola PQ = constant. Deriving the function requires knowledge of six elasticities to discover the effect of P on investment, exports and imports.

1. The elasticity of Md in response to P, which is approximately unity.

2. The interest-elasticity of Md. This is usually well below unity. The responsiveness of r to a change in Md is the inverse of this and is therefore large.
3. The interest-elasticity of investment. In practice the elasticities are estimated for different sectors. Expenditure on new housing is elastic, on industrial building less so, and on manufacturing equipment the elasticity is low.
4. The interest-elasticity of foreign demand for domestic bonds. As international financial markets have become more integrated, this elasticity has increased with corresponding larger impact on the demand for the domestic currency.
5. The elasticity of exports to changes in the real exchange rate.
6. The elasticity of imports to changes in the real exchange rate.

These elasticities are standard parameters in an econometric model of an economy. Their net effect is summarised by the downward slope of the Ad function in the left diagram of Figure 6.1. The function would shift to the right if there were changes in economic behaviour such as an increase in business optimism causing more investment, or an increase in the propensity to consume, or increased foreign income which led to greater export demand. Policy-makers can shift the function to the right by expanding the monetary base or increasing government expenditure or reducing taxes.

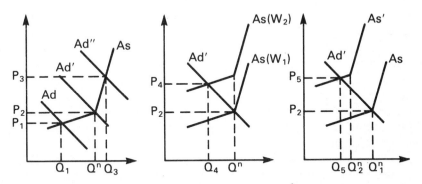

Figure 6.1 Left. A demand-pull rise in the price level is small when demand shifts from Ad to Ad', but large when demand moves to Ad" and increases output beyond Q^n.
Centre. With no change in the natural level of output, a rise in the nominal wage raises the price level and lowers actual output.
Right. A supply shock raises P and lowers both actual output and the natural level of output.

6.2   A RISE IN THE PRICE LEVEL

Output prices are sometimes pulled up by increased expenditure and sometimes pushed up by increased costs. This section considers how to distinguish between the two types of price rise. Each rise is treated as an isolated event to avoid confusion with inflation, a sustained series of rises in the price level, which is considered in a later section.

Suppose there is a bond-financed increase in government expenditure with only minor wealth effects on the demand for money. Aggregate demand increases for each price level, shown in Figure 6.1 as the shift from Ad to Ad'. Firms and households are managing with the same money holdings as before. Nominal income has increased but the increased rate of interest has lowered the liquidity ratio; money is circulating through the economy at greater velocity. If the economy were producing below its actual output, the price rise is small (in the last two chapters it was treated as insignificant). The rise is larger if the demand expansion is carried beyond the economy's natural level of output. Small shifts of the Ad function can be achieved without monetary expansion. Whatever the cause of a *demand-pull* rise in the price level, there is an associated rise in output in the short run.

A *cost-push* price rise is usually caused by a round of wage increases in excess of the rise in labour productivity. In the short run, excessive wage claims can sometimes seem exogenous to any model of economic behaviour even when variables such as expected inflation are included. An extreme example is the 1968 wage increases in most European countries which were triggered by strikes and riots. More frequently, wage increases are pushed by unions which emphasise notions of 'fairness' and attempt to preserve wage differentials with a group whose skills were in excess demand and received large increases from employers for microeconomic reasons. The centre diagram of Figure 6.1 pictures an increase in the general level of wages as a vertical shift in the aggregate supply function. Provided there has been no increase in the natural level of output, a cost-push price rise is associated with a fall in actual output.

A *supply shock* is a dramatic change in supply conditions. The industrial unrest in Europe in 1968 affected labour supply. The oil price rises of 1974 and 1979 are most conveniently analysed by considering their effects on the stock of capital. During the preceding two decades oil prices had been falling relative to other prices. Buildings and equipment were designed to use this cheap input: oil and capital-in-place were complements. The formation of a workable cartel of oil producers in 1974 enabled them to impose a fourfold increase in the price of oil. The main short-run option for saving oil was to leave the more oil-intensive equipment idle. In the short run, the effect of the oil price rise was similar to a fall in the amount of capital: a rise in output prices combined with a fall in both the actual and natural levels of output. The right-hand diagram of Figure 6.1 illustrates the north-west shift in the aggregate supply function.

6.3 RULES VERSUS DISCRETION

The monetary rule is that the money supply should be expanded at the same rate as the expected natural growth rate of output. It is a medium-run and cautious policy which relies on monetary base control and a close link between the base and the money supply. Its object is to use the monetary base as a controllable *instrument* to hit the nominal income *target*.

In the short run, the authorities may prefer to use both fiscal and monetary policy to achieve the target of a constant growth of nominal income. Price-makers in the economy are then constrained by the expectation that higher prices will be associated with less output. A nominal income target leaves the authorities with some discretion to react to events by varying the blend of fiscal and monetary policy. For example, a monetary expansion in line with the monetary rule might be neutralised by a loss of export orders. An additional monetary expansion combined with increased government expenditure could maintain output growth and a constant price level.

Demand management can also be used in the short run to maintain the natural level of output regardless of what happens to the price level. An excessive rise in nominal wages can be matched by an appropriate demand expansion to increase output prices and keep down real wage growth in line with productivity growth. The demand managers react to decisions in the labour market. *Ex post*, the wage negotiators seem to have been prescient in fixing the high nominal wage. The authorities have validated the wage increase by ensuring a price increase. This is known as a *validated cost-push* rise in the price level as shown in Figure 6.2. The next round of wage negotiations is less constrained by the expectation that workers will be priced out of jobs by high wages. Repeated validations lead to inflation.

Discretionary demand management involves two types of decision. First, by how much should nominal income be expanded? Validated cost-push results if nominal income is always expanded by the amount needed to hit the real income target, regardless of the behaviour of

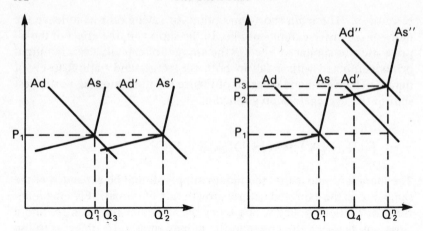

Figure 6.2 Left. When nominal wages increase in line with productivity, aggregate supply shifts from As to As'. A 'demand rule' analogous to the monetary rule ensures that actual output increases from Q_1^n to Q_2^n. With no shift in the aggregate demand function, output would increase only to Q_3.
Right. When nominal wages increase more rapidly than productivity, aggregate supply shifts to As". With a 'demand rule' output would be only Q_4 and the associated unemployment would put downward pressure on the next round of wage negotiations. If the authorities validate the wage increase by moving demand to Ad", output is at its natural level and there is no feedback to the wage negotiators.

nominal wages. Many advocates of demand management consider that the authorities should develop a reputation for engineering a constant growth of nominal income to create a predictable environment for wage negotiators. The authorities would then counter demand shocks but avoid both demand-pull and validated cost-push. Other demand managers consider that conditions vary each year and discretion should be used to vary the growth of nominal income, with labour market behaviour controlled by a separate policy package involving implicit or explicit agreements between wage-setters and the authorities.

The second use of discretion in demand management comes after the nominal income target has been decided. How can it be achieved? Discretion can be used to select whatever combination of fiscal and monetary instruments seem most appropriate for the particular time. There is now increasing agreement that to treat a monetary *instrument* as if it were itself a target is to make the tail wag the dog. The effects of monetary expansion can be predicted only approximately. The response of policy-makers is to design policy within the constraints imposed by setting a wide range of permissible monetary growth rates.

If nominal income growth is to be 6 per cent, the policy package may involve monetary growth in the 3–9 per cent range. The wide range takes into account both the unpredictability of the monetary sector's behaviour and the possible need for the monetary authorities to vary the monetary base, for example to manage the exchange rate.

6.4 INFLATION

Inflation is defined as repeated rises in the price level. It is caused by the interaction of demand-pull and cost-push, with the former dominating in some periods and the latter in others. The interaction depends upon expectations which are not directly observable although one can often make an informed judgement about which group is the more surprised: the authorities about the behaviour of the labour market or the wage negotiators about the extent of current inflation. Empirically, the demand-pull element cannot be repeatedly generated by balanced budget expansions or bond-financed expansions; the associated increases in taxes or interest rates would choke the increase in demand. Inflations require budget deficits to be financed by new money. If the price rises are not initiated by the authorities they must be accommodated by increases in the money supply, otherwise the rate of interest would rise and cut off the expansion of aggregate demand: hence Friedman's famous dictum: 'Inflation is always and everywhere a monetary phenomenon.' Distinguishing demand-pull from cost-push involves discovering whether the authorities are initiating events or reacting to them. Sometimes the evidence is sufficiently clear to make this distinction.

During the late 1960s, a series of monetary expansions occurred in the United States. Output was at or above its natural level and unemployment below its natural rate. The evidence was consistent with monetary demand-pull. Other countries also expanded their money supplies to preserve the fixed exchange rate with the dollar. The result was world-wide inflation. Countries with electorates averse to inflation were the first to break the link with the dollar in 1971 and allow their currencies to appreciate.

In the United Kingdom during the 1960s there was a different sequence. Large wage increases surprised the authorities who responded with fiscal expansions to validate the cost-push. The competitiveness of British exports fell as British inflation exceeded world inflation. The 1967 devaluation of sterling was forced on the authorities by a run from the pound. The rise in import costs increased the cost of living and led to a further round of wage increases which were only partly validated. Unemployment rose and output stagnated in keeping with the hypothesis of cost-push.

In most countries for much of the 1970s inflation rates exceeded the nominal rate of interest, implying rapid monetary growth. (Switzerland was the only country with stable prices and Swiss banks were able to charge foreign depositors: the charge was less than the expected loss of purchasing power of foreign currencies.) Monetary demand-pull occurred during 1972–73, exacerbated in the United Kingdom by deregulation which allowed the money supply to expand more rapidly than the base.

In 1973, there was a sudden depletion of fishing grounds in the Pacific, crop failures in the Soviet Union and an Arab-Israeli war which encouraged the formation of an oil cartel. None of these events was caused by monetary growth. They raised the prices of fish, grain and oil relative to other prices and wages. These supply shocks caused an immediate fall in labour productivity. In the United States, monetary growth lowered real wages because the labour market displayed only *nominal wage resistance*. In most European countries, the attempt to use demand policy to accommodate to the supply shock was met by *real wage resistance* and unemployment increased. Cost-push was initiated by the supply shocks and exacerbated by wage increases to dominate demand-pull. The combination of inflation, low or negative output growth and rising unemployment became known as *stagflation*. It implies changing conditions on the supply side of the economy. If wage-setters are aiming for the equilibrium rate of increase of nominal wages, they have to form expectations about both the inflation of output prices and the growth of labour productivity. An excess supply of labour would result if either of these expectations were too high.

The problem of reducing inflation is that of minimising unemployment during the slowdown of monetary growth. The problem is exacerbated if monetary constraints are applied when there is a fall in labour productivity which is unperceived by the labour market. This was the situation in 1979 when the second oil price shock occurred. Oil prices doubled, but most governments decided not to accommodate the shock by demand expansion. How labour markets absorbed the new policies varied from country to country. In South Korea, manual workers accepted wage cuts of 6 per cent, partly because the explanations of employers were made more believable by cuts in managerial salaries of 10 per cent. In West Germany, the announcements of a believable Central Bank enabled wage-setters to form correct anticipations about the slowdown in output prices, though not the productivity slowdown. In France, a closely regulated monetary sector was able to meet the steady reductions in monetary targets, and an incomes policy was imposed to prevent excessive wage increases during the period when inflationary expectations fell in response to the falls in actual inflation. In the United States, the information about falling inflation was transmitted via a rise in short-term unemployment leading to a rapid fall in nominal wage growth.

The record rise in unemployment during 1980 and 1981 occurred in the United Kingdom. There were three reasons for this. First, wage-setting was dominated by strong unions who held expectations of high inflation. Second, North Sea oil production increased and the rise in oil exports caused an appreciation of the currency and a fall in competitiveness. (Chapter 7 considers events of this type in more detail.) Third, the growth in the money supply was 6 per cent below the growth in the price level in 1981, a sudden slowdown in monetary growth which was caused by the dramatic rise in the nominal rate of interest controlled by the authorities. Unlike the British labour market, financial markets anticipated falling inflation. The rise in nominal interest coincided with a fall in expected inflation and the real interest rate rose, adding further to the appreciation of sterling. Non-oil exports fell and imports particularly of manufactures increased. The intention of the authorities was to allow monetary growth to fall gently, thereby avoiding excessive surprises for the labour market. The sudden fall occurred because the authorities were focusing on a broad definition of money.

We have defined 'the' money supply as currency in circulation plus demand deposits, the M1 definition. Its growth can be reduced either by reducing the growth of the monetary base or by raising the rate of interest and reducing the demand for M1. The British authorities considered that the apposite definition of money was M3, which is M1 plus various interest-bearing time deposits. Under some circumstances the demand for M3 can rise with the rate of interest. The vain attempt to control the demand for this broad money involved repeated rises in the rate of interest which rapidly shrank the growth in demand for M1. With the British money stocks demand-determined, they are best considered as indicators of policy rather than as instruments. The cause was the rise in the rate of interest; the main effect was the appreciation of sterling.

To summarise, controlling inflation involves controlling the money stock. In economies with reserve requirements, monetary base control is effective. If the money stock is demand-determined, interest rates can be used as instruments but the appropriate measure of money must then be carefully monitored. Expectations of inflation can be reduced in line with actuality if the pronouncements of the authorities are believable.

Incomes policies can be used for short periods while actual inflation falls and lowers expectations formed adaptively. Either process encourages contracted nominal prices or wages to stay near their equilibrium ratio to the general level of output prices. In economies where unemployment has a rapid effect on nominal wage increases, monetary policy is transmitted to the goods and labour markets via temporary unemployment. The long-term unemployment prevalent in Europe during the 1980s is partly due to real wage resistance following the productivity slowdown caused by supply shocks.

6.5   CONSUMPTION, INCOME AND INFLATION

The demand for money increases with the price level but falls with expected inflation. This latter influence is small except during hyperinflations, usually defined as price rises exceeding 50 per cent a month, but it is an understandable reaction: people run to the shops to spend their money before its purchasing power falls. The stock of *real money* M/P which they wish to hold is reduced when expected inflation is very high. By the same reasoning their flow of real consumption expenditures should rise with expected inflation. Consumption should be more than that predicted by income during times of high inflation. This is not what happened. The inflation of the 1970s fell far short of hyperinflation in most countries, but was certainly noticeable. The evidence points to a strong negative influence of inflation on consumption. Before examining this influence, the evidence of the effect of real income on real consumption is considered for periods when inflation is not significant.

In Chapter 4, current consumption was treated as a simple function of current disposable income. Writing Y for real disposable income

$$C = C(Y) \qquad\qquad (6.2)$$

where C ( ) is the notation for the consumption function. When consumption is hypothesised to depend only on current disposable income, this is known as the Absolute Income Hypothesis (AIH). The simplest form of the AIH is that C is proportionate to Y. In this case, the growth of C and Y are at the same rate.

$$c = y \qquad\qquad (6.3)$$

Here c is the per cent per annum change in real consumption expenditure and y is the per cent per annum change in real disposable income.

An alternative hypothesis is due to Milton Friedman. If there is an unusual fall in current income which is expected to be temporary, households maintain their consumption by drawing on savings. An unusual rise is treated as a windfall and mainly saved. Households form a notion of permanent income, and actual income is divided into permanent and temporary components. These latter may be positive or negative but have a negligible effect on consumption. In a sense, permanent income is their expected income. If the expectations are formed adaptively consumption is determined mainly by observable past incomes. Current income is influential only to the extent that it changes permanent income. Combining the algebra of the permanent income and the adaptive expectations hypotheses, the prediction is that:

c increases when y increases
but c decreases if Δy is positive

$$c = c (y, \Delta y) \qquad (6.4)$$
$$+ \quad -$$

where Δy is the percentage point change in income growth between the current and preceding quarter and c ( ) is the function relating the growth of consumption to the independent variables.

A modification to equation (6.4) results from the notion that households will be more inclined to consume this year if they saved a high proportion of their income the previous year. Writing $(S/Y)_{-1}$ for last year's savings ratio, consumption growth would be greater if this ratio increased. For the period when inflation was low and its variability small, the following equation fitted the evidence well. Real consumption growth seemed to be explained by real income growth, its change, and the savings ratio.

$$c = 0.5\, y - 0.2\, \Delta y + 0.1\, (S/Y)_{-1} \qquad (6.5)$$

where the numbers are the parameters estimated from UK data for the 1950s and 1960s.

This equation supports a combination of the absolute and permanent income hypotheses, with the latter having the most strength. The implication is that the short-run propensity to consume is small and therefore the multipliers are smaller than the examples given in Chapter 4. Suppose a tax cut raises the growth of disposable income from 2 per cent last quarter to 4 per cent this quarter (expressing the quarterly growths as the increase over the corresponding quarter of the previous year). With $y = 4$ and $\Delta y = 2$, c is only 1.6 with a small modification for last year's savings ratio. If equation 6.2 had been true c would have been 4. The main impact of the tax cut works through to consumption only when y has become steady. However, the multipliers are still there.

With Q–T growing at the rate y, the fall in T still causes increased consumption, more orders to firms, with an ensuing increase in Q depending on the import propensity.

Equation 6.5 gave poor predictions of consumption growth during the high and variable inflation of the 1970s and the falling inflation of the 1980s. If expectations about inflation are formed adaptively households are surprised by actual inflation unless it is constant for several years. With imprecise knowledge of the general price level in a particular week, households interpret each individual price rise as a change in that good's relative price and shop around in the attempt to find a substitute at a price which is expected. Consumption is postponed while learning proceeds. The growth of consumption expenditure is less when there is inflation and much less when inflation is increasing. Equation (6.5) is extended to include the inflation rate over the previous year π and its percentage point change between the current quarter and previous quarter $\Delta \pi$.

$$c = 0.5\,y - 0.2\,\Delta y + 0.1\,(S/Y)_{-1} - 0.1\pi - 0.3\,\Delta \pi \qquad (6.6)$$

Equations such as (6.6) fit the evidence far better than (6.4). They hold for the last four decades. Modern consumption functions show that consumption grows with income but at a slower rate. This rate is further reduced if income is accelerating in the current period, with much of the surprising increase in income being saved. However, if this had also happened one year previously, the rise in the savings ratio then will raise current consumption growth. Inflation and particularly its increase lowers consumption growth. Falling inflation raises consumption growth above the rate predicted by the real variables y, Δy and S/Y.

6.6   SUMMARY

This chapter removed the simplifying assumption of Chapters 4 and 5 that the price level is constant. It showed that the explanation of aggregate demand in the short run is more complicated than implied by the medium-run approximation given in Chapter 2, where the aggregate demand function was simply a rectangular hyperbola in Q, P space whose position was fixed by the money supply.

Chapters 4 and 5 examined the short-run determination of and effects of changes in two relative prices, the rate of interest and the exchange rate. For consistency, this chapter ought to follow with the third important relative price, the real wage. Instead, it examined the price level but noted that nominal wages sometimes appear to be exogenous to a model of economic behaviour in the short run. The result is that we can distinguish the causes of price level changes between cost-push and demand-pull. With cost-push, the real wage rises above equilibrium, output falls below its natural level and unemployment rises above its natural rate. With demand-pull, the reverse applies. Inflation is always associated with monetary growth and in that sense it always involves demand-pull. However, inflation is the interaction of cost-push and demand-pull, complicated by unobservable expectations. The policy problem is to minimise unemployment while inflation is reduced. The choice of policy depends upon discovering whether demand-pull or cost-push dominates, how forward-looking expectations can be given enough reliability to reduce the dependence on adaptive expectations, and how the institutional structure of each economy influences the response to policy.

Many short-run problems involve institutional customs, expectations which change too slowly or which suddenly move to extremes, and policy-makers who take a monocausal view of events. Discussion of such problems is often aided by setting them in an analytical framework which is widely recognised amongst economists. Inertia or slowly changing expectations can be revealed by time-series data. Shocks can be simulated by changing the appropriate parameters. The basic framework is the algebra behind the three sectors which interact to determine the aggregate demand function, and the supply behaviour of firms and households which determines the aggregate supply function. Extending the table at the end of the previous chapter for floating exchange rates, we could reduce the many behavioural equations (known as *structural equations* which express a dependent variable in terms of the variables which cause it to change) to four summary equations (*reduced forms*).

Sector	Endogenous variables	Policy variables
IS	Q, r, E, P	G, T
LM	Q, r, P	H
BP	Q, r, E, P	–
Aggregate supply	Q, P	?

Neoclassical adjustment endogenises the nominal wage W to allow the third relative price W/P to clear the labour market. Simple Keynesian algebra treats W as exogenous and r as the link between the monetary and goods sectors. The combination of Keynesian demand analysis, neoclassical supply analysis but exogenous wages is sometimes called the *neoclassical synthesis*. Note that the equations treat as constants people's expectations about investment opportunities, inflation, exchange-rate appreciation and the growth of labour productivity. They form a very convenient table of contents but are only a part of the explanations of economic events.

This concludes Part III of the book. Its analysis can be described as Keynesian because of the emphases on aggregate demand and the short run. This last chapter has shown that Keynesians are aware of the problems of fluctuations and also study the supply side of an economy. A sufficiently partial selection of policy recommendations can build a caricature of a Keynesian: expand demand, the budget deficit and the current account deficit, then legislate for an incomes policy when all goes wrong. Such caricatures can be easily manufactured for any group of economists: that the Neoclassicists of Chapter 1 believe in instantaneous price adjustment; that the Monetarists of Chapter 2 believe that only money matters; that the balanced budgeteers of Chapter 3 believe that budget deficits should never be allowed. Sometimes such caricatures seem applicable to politicians when single-mindedness is their only weapon for breaking government inertia. The right balance of policies between fiscal and monetary, demand-side and supply-side, the short run and the medium run, is still a matter of debate but the limits of the debate amongst economists are set by the empirical work inspired by the many theoretical contributions to our understanding of aggregate economic behaviour.

PROBLEMS FOR CHAPTER 6

1. What information about elasticities is required to discover the effect of a rise in the price level on the quantity of expenditure?
2. Last year actual output was at its natural level. This year the expansion of the money supply is exactly countered by a fall in investment and the aggregate demand function is unchanged. Last year's investment has caused an increase in this year's natural level of output. Nominal wage increases are in line with increased productivity: the wage-setters expect a constant price level. What happens to this year's P and Q relative to last year's?
3. How would you distinguish between inflation which is initiated by the monetary authorities and that initiated by wage-setters?
4. An economy is at its natural level of output. The government then expands the monetary base and imposes a wage freeze. What

happens to output and the price level? (Note that the steep section of the As function implies recontracting, which is now illegal. Are households or firms rationing employment?)

5. The following estimates have been made:

$Y^P_{t-1} = 100$, which was last year's permanent income
$Y_{t-1} = 100$, which was last year's actual (or absolute income)
$Y_t = 104$, which is this year's actual income

This year's permanent income is estimated as follows;

$$Y^P_t = Y^P_{t-1} + 0.6 (Y_t - Y^P_{t-1})$$

What is the percentage growth in consumption between $t-1$ and t if the following version of the absolute income hypothesis is true?

$$C_t = 0.8 Y_t$$

What is the percentage growth in consumption if the following permanent income hypothesis is true?

$$C_t = 0.8 Y^P_t$$

6. Why might a household spend more on consumption goods if it expected an increase in inflation? Why do households spend less on consumption goods when actual inflation increases?

7. Which of the following are not relative prices: the rate of interest, the exchange rate, the price level, the nominal wage?

8. In your economy, do nominal wages usually increase in line with the sum of productivity increases and the rise in output prices? Can the difference be explained by differences between actual and expected inflation?

9. In your economy, what is the relative importance of 'news', compared to past trends, in influencing prices in (a) the foreign exchange market, (b) the stock market, (c) the bond market, (d) the labour market (where prices are wages), and (e) the goods market?

FURTHER READING

Hicks (1974) provides an early warning against excessive criticism of Keynesian economics. Okun (1981) emphasises the importance of implicit contracts, custom and institutions for our understanding of economic behaviour. Part IV of Gordon (1987) provides a clear introduction to the standard analysis of inflation. Hillier (1986) gives a more advanced theoretical exposition of the short run and the medium run with an interesting emphasis on the government's budget. Davidson et al. (1978) provide a fundamental contribution to the econometrics of the consumption function. Serre and Cobham (1985) and Cobham and Serre (1985) provide an account of French monetary institutions and the successful combination of monetary and incomes policies.

Norton (1982) analyses the deterioration of economic performance during the 1970s with cross-country comparisons of the main economies.

Part III has assumed simple behavioural relations to explain consumption and investment. This simplicity has the benefit of clarifying the interaction between the goods, monetary and foreign sectors. The cost is the neglect of many important discoveries about consumption and investment behaviour. A good introduction to these discoveries is in Dornbusch and Fischer (1983): chapter 6 on consumption, wealth and lags and chapter 7 on investment spending.

PART IV
Adjustment

7. Tradeables and Non-Tradeables

This chapter makes an important distinction between two types of output. In primary and secondary industries, most of the output can be exported or substituted for imports: agriculture, fishing, mineral extraction and manufacturing produce goods which are internationally tradeable. Many servicing industries and much of the output of the construction industry add value in a form which cannot be moved across national boundaries. The practical categorisation is not always clear-cut and there are some obvious exceptions to classifying all services as non-tradeable. In the Standard Industrial Classification, services include tourism, computer software and the value-added by the provision of insurance and banking services, each of which can make a major contribution to exports. However, the conceptual distinction between tradeables and non-tradeables is clear. Analysis which incorporates this distinction explains many puzzles and leads to important policy conclusions.

7.1 TWO METHODS OF DISAGGREGATING OUTPUT

We start with the standard analysis of the gains from trade when all output is tradeable and then discover the modifications which are required when some output is non-tradeable. In Figure 7.1, the left-hand diagram pictures the demand decisions of an economy where expenditure is on two types of goods. Q^1 is the quantity of primary goods such as food and Q^2 is the quantity of secondary goods such as manufactures. The prices of these goods are P^1 and P^2. Income is spent entirely on these goods, hence the weighted sum $P^1Q^1 + P^2Q^2$ varies with income. The three straight lines show three different levels of income. Each line has a slope of $-P^2/P^1$. For a given income, the community can choose its blend of expenditures anywhere on the line corresponding to that income.

The three short curves are community indifference curves. Those to the north-east represent more utility than those near the origin. Given a

145

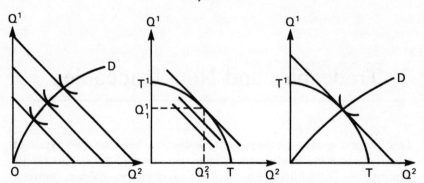

Figure 7.1 Left. As income increases but relative prices remain constant, the blend of Q^1 and Q^2 demanded is given by the curve D.
Centre. The production possibility frontier is T'T. The value of output is maximised when Q_1^1 and Q_1^2 are produced.
Right. Relative prices are given by the slope of the tangent common to both T'T and the highest achievable indifference curve.

particular income and a particular price ratio, the community will choose that combination of Q^1 and Q^2 which yields most utility, represented by the point of tangency between the curve and the income line. Of the infinite number of possible incomes and indifference curves, three are shown. As income expands from zero at the origin, the community chooses the series of points on the curve D. Given the price ratio P^2/P^1, D shows the chosen blend of Q^1 and Q^2 changing as income expands. The D curve is drawn with a decreasing slope to signify that manufactures have a greater income-elasticity of demand than food.

The centre diagram of Figure 7.1 shows the production possibility frontier T'T. The resources in the economy will be fully used if production is on the curve, and firms can move along the curve by transferring resources from the production of one output to the other. With resources given, firms in the aggregate will choose that point on the curve which maximises revenue $P^1Q^1 + P^2Q^2$. Three revenue lines are drawn, each with a slope of $-P^2/P^1$. Revenue is maximised when the blend of output is Q_1^1 and Q_1^2. Firms have determined the supply of output and the amount of income available to the community given the ratio P^2/P^1.

Both the demand decision and the supply decision were taken on the assumption that the relative price was given. If the economy were planned by authorities who had full information about preferences, resources and technology, prices would be irrelevant and the authorities could instruct firms to produce where the highest indifference curve touches T'T, as shown in the right-hand diagram of Figure 7.1. The community's satisfaction would then be maximised subject to the constraint of the production possibilities. Alternatively, supply and demand in the markets for the two goods will force an equilibrium price ratio which gives the same result. The equilibrium price ratio is the slope of the line through the point of tangency of T'T and the highest possible indifference curve.

When the economy is opened to world trade, the relative price is imposed by the large international market. We assume that the world values food more highly relative to manufactures than does the domestic economy. The price line becomes less steep and domestic producers raise their production of food from Q_1^1 to Q_2^1 in the left-hand diagram of Figure 7.2, thereby maximising their revenue. There has been no change in the tastes of the domestic community, whose indifference map stays the same as before. However, the price changes cause changes in the blend of the two goods which is demanded. The right-hand diagram of Figure 7.2 shows the changes in choice brought about by the changed price ratio, assuming that income has been adjusted to maintain indifference. The D curve no longer shows how the pattern of expenditure changes with income. The new relation between the blend of the two goods and income is shown by D' which is relevant to the new, lower ratio of P^2/P^1.

The change in the price ratio has caused domestic producers to transfer resources from manufacturing to food, and production is what

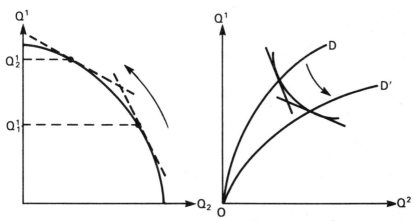

Figure 7.2 Left. An exogenous increase in P^1 relative to P^2 results in an increase in the production of Q^1, given the resources available to firms.
Right. An exogenous rise in P^1 relative to P^2 results in a decrease in the demand for Q^1, when utility is held constant.

determines income. In Figure 7.3, food production has risen from Q_1^1 to Q_2^1. Firms cannot sell all this production in the domestic market, but they can export food which the world market values more highly than the domestic market, and they can import manufactures which are valued less highly in the world market. They export $Q_2^1 - Q_3^1$ of food and import $Q_3^2 - Q_2^2$ of manufactures.

The line marked G'G shows the maximum revenue for firms. It is also the income line for the community, which can choose its blend of expenditure anywhere along it, trading exports for imports to arrive at the point where D' cuts G'G. This result is possible because both types of output are tradeable. The community could have chosen any point along G'G, including the point where the old D curve cuts the income line. At this point, more food can be purchased than Q_1^1 and more manufactures than Q_1^2 which is clearly an improvement over the position with no international trade. If the community chooses some other point on G'G this must be because it is an even greater improvement. Hence there are 'gains from trade'.

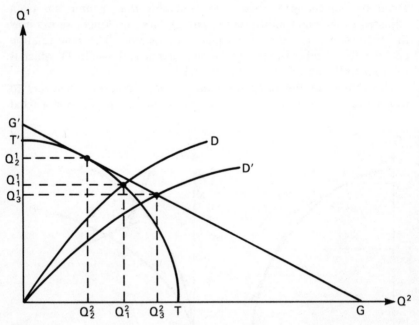

Figure 7.3 International trade imposes the relative prices which determine the slope of G'G. Domestic firms produce on T'T and supply Q_2^1 and Q_2^2. Demand is where D' cuts G'G, at Q_3^1 and Q_3^2. Exports of $Q_2^1 - Q_3^1$ are exchanged for imports of $Q_3^2 - Q_2^2$. With no international trade, both production and demand would be Q_1^1 and Q_1^2.

During the last half-century, non-tradeables have become a significant part of output and expenditure. Much of this production is in
response to the expenditure by governments acting as the agent of
households: motorways, social services, defence, health services. Some
of it is produced in response to the direct demand from firms and
households: local wholesalers and servicing organisations, retail distribution, catering. If the domestic economy is to be in equilibrium, the
pattern of prices, indirect taxes and wages has to be such that the blend
of non-tradeable and tradeable output conforms to the blend which is
demanded. By definition, any disparity between the supply of and
demand for non-tradeables cannot be corrected via the foreign sector.

Figure 7.4 shows an economy's output classified into tradeables Q^T
and non-tradeables Q^N. The pattern of prices has resulted in equilibrium with production at point B on the production possibility curve, and
demand also at point B on the curve D. The D curve has a decreasing
slope to denote the higher income-elasticity of demand for non-
tradeables than tradeables although recent empirical work reveals only

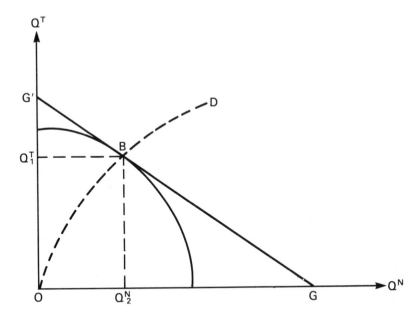

Figure 7.4 The bold curve shows the production possibilities when output is a
blend of tradeables Q^T and non-tradeables Q^N. The curve D shows the blend of
Q^T and Q^N demanded for each level of income. G'G is the tangent at B and has
a slope of minus P^N/P^T. Equilibrium is at B with Q_1^T and Q_2^N both supplied and
demanded.

a small difference between the two elasticities. The slope of G'G is given by the relative price; it is $-P^N/P^T$, where P^N and P^T are price indices for the two types of output.

Total output can be measured in non-tradeable equivalents, when it is the distance OG. Of this distance, the actual production of non-tradeables is the distance OQ_2^N. The production of tradeables Q_1^T is equivalent in value to the distance between Q_2^N and G. This follows because the slope of G'G is P^N/P^T which equals the distance OQ_1^T divided by the distance $Q_2^N G$. Hence $Q_2^N G$ is OQ_1^T times P^T/P^N.

The main feature of Figure 7.4 is that it is analogous to the closed economy of Figure 7.1 rather than the open economy of Figure 7.3. The equilibrium is achieved by changes in prices within the economy. The price of tradeables is determined by the world economy and the fixed exchange rate, hence the internal adjustments needed to clear both markets involve changes in the price of non-tradeables. The importance of this ratio P^N/P^T becomes apparent in the next section, where the case of the sterling devaluation of 1967 is used to illustrate the dynamics behind the static analysis of tradeable and non-tradeable supply and demand.

7.2 ABSORPTION AND SWITCHING

The expenditure on goods by the residents of the domestic economy is $C + I + G$, which is known as *domestic absorption*. It is the total demand in the domestic marketplace. Each of the three components has an import content. Expenditure on domestically-produced goods is the result of both home and foreign demand; it is $C + I + G + X - Z$ and it is this expenditure which, *ex post*, is the same as income. When absorption exceeds income, imports must exceed exports. This gap must be met by either an inflow of financial funds or a loss of reserves.

During 1967, the British reserves fell rapidly. Absorption exceeded income but the raised interest rate was insufficient to entice a capital inflow. The international currency market had already come to suspect that a devaluation would occur and the gap between domestic and foreign interest rates was insufficient to cover the expected devaluation. In spite of a positive interest rate differential, funds flowed out of the country.

The analysis that follows allows balance of payments disequilibria to be described. Its conclusion is that a combination of policies is required to bring about both balance of payments equilibrium and equilibrium in the markets for tradeables and non-tradeables. The two policies are to reduce absorption and change the price of tradeables relative to non-tradeables. This important analysis is due to Corden (1977). Many of its features are also relevant to an economy with floating exchange rates.

Consider first the blend of outputs that are supplied in the domestic economy, the volume ratio Q^T/Q^N. Suppose there is an increase in P^T caused by a rise in the price of foreign exchange, but P^N stays constant. The volume ratio will change as firms find Q^T more profitable to produce than Q^N. Q^T includes production for export markets and the foreign exchange obtained from these sales converts into a greater quantity of domestic currency. The price of those tradeables produced for domestic sales will tend to rise in sympathy with those for exports. If the economy stays on its production possibility curve, domestic income derives from domestic production which consists of more tradeables and less non-tradeables than before.

Domestic absorption need not be the same as domestic income. In the short run, it can be raised above income by borrowing from abroad, or selling reserves of foreign exchange. Absorption determines the value of tradeables and non-tradeables demanded in total but it does not determine the blend which is demanded. The volume ratio Q^T/Q^N which is demanded will fall when P^T rises. The amount of Q^T which is demanded by the domestic economy includes imports but excludes exports. If P^T rises both imports and domestically produced tradeables become more expensive relative to non-tradeables with the result that less tradeables and more non-tradeables are demanded than before, for a given level of absorption.

Domestic production of Q^T includes exports but domestic demand for Q^T includes imports. Domestic income is generated by the production of both Q^T and Q^N. Domestic absorption is composed of expenditures on both Q^T and Q^N. By definition, equilibrium in the non-tradeables sector must be the result of the domestic supply of Q^N being the same as the domestic demand for Q^N. If the supply of tradeables is to be equal to the demand for tradeables, exports must equal imports and income must equal absorption.

In previous chapters, we discussed the various short-run expedients which enable the authorities to hold absorption above income. Here we are considering a situation where such policies are ineffective so that imports must be brought to equal exports by ensuring that absorption is no greater than income. However, we now have the additional problem of the supply of and demand for non-tradeables. We have to find a policy which ensures that the ratio Q^T/Q^N which is supplied is the same as the ratio which is demanded.

In Figure 7.5 the line G'G has a slope of minus P^N/P^T and this price

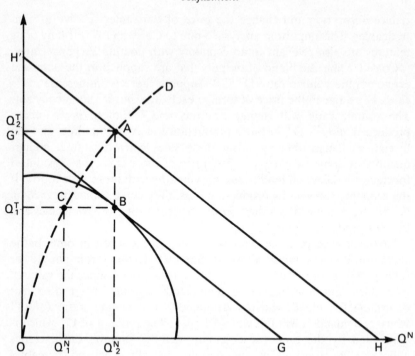

Figure 7.5 The D curve shows the blends of Q^N and Q^T demanded at each level of absorption. H'H shows the absorption possibilities given P^N/P^T and point A gives the blend actually demanded. Point B is on the production possibility frontier and is the most profitable blend of output given P^N/P^T, represented by the slope of G'G. Measured in terms of Q^N, income is OG and absorption OH. The supply of and demand for non-tradeables are both Q_2^N. The demand for tradeables is Q_2^T but the supply is only Q_1^T.

If a reduction in absorption were used to bring the tradeables sector to equilibrium, absorption would fall to point C but here the supply of non-tradeables Q_2^N exceeds the demand Q_1^N.

ratio persuades firms to produce at point B. The production becomes income, which is equal to the distance OG when measured in terms of non-tradeables. However absorption is at point A, showing the economy absorbing more than it produces. Absorption consists of Q_2^N of non-tradeables and Q_2^T of tradeables. The excess of imports over exports is $Q_2^T - Q_1^T$. Measured in non-tradeables, this gap is the distance GH. At point A, the non-tradeable sector is in equilibrium. A is on the curve D which shows the demand for the two types of output, and A is vertically above the point B which shows the production of the two outputs. Q_2^N is both supplied and demanded.

What happens if aggregate demand is managed so that absorption is reduced without changing the ratio P^N/P^T? Absorption moves down the curve D until the point C is reached. At C, the demand for and supply of tradeables are both Q_1^T. However the demand for non-tradeables is now only Q_1^N which is less than the supply Q_2^N. There is an excess supply of non-tradeables. If relative prices do not change, output and employment in the non-tradeable sector will fall. The attempt to bring about balance of payments equilibrium has created disequilibrium in the non-tradeables sector because relative prices have not changed.

The ratio of price indices P^N/P^T can be lowered by subsidising exports and the production of tradeables and taxing imports and the production of non-tradeables. A simpler method is to devalue the currency, raising the price of foreign exchange. Firms then shift production towards exports and import substitutes and away from the production of non-tradeables. In Figure 7.6, production moves from point B, the point at which the old price line was tangential, to point J where the new price line K'K is tangential. There is a change in the blend of Q^N and Q^T which is supplied, with a greater proportion of output being tradeable.

The change in relative prices has the opposite effect on the blend of goods and services which are demanded at each level of absorption. The curve D swings in a clockwise direction, representing an increasing demand for non-tradeables at each absorption level in response to the fall in P^N/P^T. The devaluation changes OD to OD' because tradeables are more expensive, measured in the domestic currency.

An accurate devaluation results in firms moving counter-clockwise from B to J along the production possibility curve, with demand moving clockwise from D to the curve D' so that the point J shows supply and demand equal in both sectors. However, the devaluation alone is not able to move the economy to point J. The change in relative prices has not eliminated the excess of absorption over income.

Income (or production, or supplies of Q^N and Q^T) is at J, which is on K'K, the price line with a slope equal to the new, lower ratio of P^N/P^T. Measured in non-tradeable equivalents, income is the distance OK. Absorption (or expenditure in the domestic market, or demands for Q^N and Q^T) is now at A' on D'. At A', the decline in reserves has been reduced but not halted: the fall each period in the stock of reserves is equal in value to the flow of non-tradeables given by the distance KL. For balance of payments equilibrium, the devaluation must be accompanied by a fall in absorption which moves the demands for Q^N and Q^T from point A' to point J.

Sterling was devalued in November 1967. During 1968 both govern-

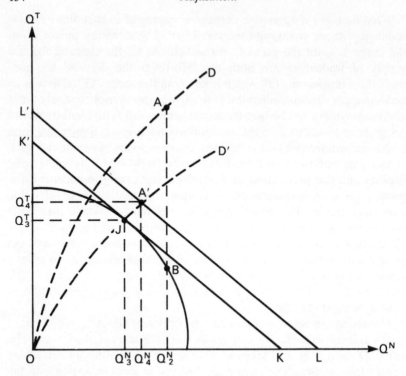

Figure 7.6 Devaluation moves the point of most profitable production from B to J. The locus of demand shifts from D to D'. The increased cost of imports has reduced absorption from A on D to A' on D' but a further reduction is required. At A' there are excess demands for both non-tradeables and tradeables. Point A' cannot be an equilibrium. Policy must be used to reduce absorption from L'L to K'K, thereby eliminating the excess demands for non-tradeables $Q_4^N - Q_3^N$ and tradeables $Q_4^T - Q_3^T$.

ment expenditure and taxation increased; however the economy did not attain point J, in spite of the budget surplus. The resulting excess demand for non-tradeables drove up P^N thereby modifying the effects of the devaluation. Absorption was further reduced in 1969 but by then inflation had become embedded in people's expectations.

The conditions under which a devaluation leads to increasing the reserves of foreign exchange were given in Chapter 5. They are more complicated when the supply elasticities are finite. (Curiously, they appeared in the early article by Bickerdike (1920).) Usually the elasticity conditions are met, but the approach was criticised for concentrating solely on the markets for exports and imports and for assuming equilibrium before and after the devaluation.

The work of Alexander (1952) showed that a drain on the reserves could be halted by reducing absorption. This theory was applied by the International Monetary Fund in its advice to recipients of loans, guided by the further work of Polak (1957), and the absorption approach proved effective. A debate developed about the relative merits of reducing absorption *or* devaluing as a cure for balance of payments disequilibrium. A devaluation is a change in relative prices which switches production towards exports and import substitutes and switches demand from imports. Such switching would also be achieved by appropriate taxes and subsidies. The controversy is therefore known as the *absorption versus switching* debate. Johnson (1957) argued that some disequilibria require both quantity changes and price changes. Introducing non-tradeables into the analysis emphasises Johnson's conclusion. A continuing deficit on the balance of payments can be eliminated and the economy held at full employment only if a reduction in absorption is accompanied by a devaluation. Both policies have to be applied simultaneously.

7.3 THE STRUCTURALIST THEORY OF INFLATION

Neoclassical economics predicts that wages for the same type of worker will tend towards equality regardless of the type of industry or firm in which such workers are employed. Efficient or inefficient firms and declining or expanding industries cause disequilibria in the short run, but in the long run equal skills and work will receive equal pay. In the short run, the same type of worker may receive the same pay for reasons other than the long-run market forces of neoclassical economics. Wage differentials become established for a variety of reasons and in the long run the neoclassical reasons may be the most important, but once such differentials are established they become accepted as fair. Notions of fairness contribute to, and in turn are reinforced by, the social structure. In the short run, it may be considered wrong for one worker to undercut the wage of another, similar worker, and wrong for an employer to pay different rates to different workers of similar skills. Theories of wages which emphasise the social pressure towards equal pay for equal services are known as *structuralist* theories. They were used by Scandinavian economists to explain the inflation which occurred in many small economies during the period of fixed exchange rates.

The Scandinavian countries had rapid export growth, strong currencies and no symptoms within the balance of payments of an excessive expansion of aggregate demand. Yet their inflation rates were higher than the world rate. This puzzling phenomenon led to a theory of inflation which took a structuralist view of money wage increases, distinguished between the tradeables and non-tradeables sectors, and noted that productivity rose most rapidly in the tradeables sector.

P, P^T and P^N are the price indices for all output, tradeable output and non-tradeable output, respectively. The rates of change of these price levels are written π, π^T and π^N. The problem is to explain π, the overall inflation rate within a particular economy. However, π is a weighted average of the inflation rates in the two sectors:

$$\pi = (1-a)\pi^T + a\pi^N \tag{7.1}$$

where a is the proportion of total output which is non-tradeable.

The tradeables sector is competitive. Its firms are price-takers and its inflation rate π^T is the world rate. Labour productivity increases rapidly in this sector, partly because of competitive pressures and partly because there were more opportunities for technical change in the production of agricultural and manufactured goods during the 1960s. Output per person employed in producing tradeables increases at a rate t. The money wage is determined competitively, rising at a rate which ensures that the real wage stays in line with the marginal product of labour. Writing w^T for the rate of increase of the money wage in the tradeables sector:

$$w^T = \pi^T + t \tag{7.2}$$

Both the variables on the right are exogenous; π^T comes from the world market and t is supply-determined.

If the link from the tradeables to the non-tradeables sector were only via market adjustments, some years might elapse before the many adjustments had taken place. However, structural pressures ensure that money wages in the non-tradeables sector rise at the same rate as w^T, hence any proportionate wage differentials between the two sectors are preserved.

$$w^N = w^T \tag{7.3}$$

The non-tradeables sector is not subject to competitive pressures in the short run. Firms preserve their profit margins by applying a proportionate mark-up over unit labour costs, which rise with money wages but fall as productivity increases. Once this mark-up is determined, π^N is caused by w^N and n, the increase in labour productivity in the non-tradeables sector.

$$\pi^N \ w^N - n \tag{7.4}$$

which from (7.3)

$$= w^T - n$$

and from (7.2)

$$= \pi^T + t - n$$

The lower productivity growth in the non-tradeables sector results in π^N exceeding π^T. When π^T becomes positive via demand-pull in the world economy, π^N is the result of cost-push in one sector of the domestic economy.

Combining this equation with (7.1) gives

$$\pi = (1 - a) \ \pi^T + a \ (\pi^T + t - n)$$

or $\quad \pi = \pi^T + a \ (t - n) \tag{7.5}$

Since t is greater than n, the inflation in the country's general price index π is greater than the world rate π^T. It depends upon π^T, the proportion of total output which is non-tradeable and the difference between productivity growth in the two sectors.

This and the previous section dealt with two problems which arose under the period of fixed exchange rates. When an economy is losing reserves, a reduction in absorption corrects the balance of payments disequilibrium but also creates excess supply in the market for non-tradeable output, with associated unemployment or labour hoarding. When absorption exceeds income, a devaluation is insufficient by itself to cure the balance of payments disequilibrium: both a devaluation and a reduction in absorption are required. The analysis resolves the theoretical controversy of the absorption *vs.* switching debate and explains the disappointing results of the 1967 devaluation of sterling.

The distinction between tradeables and non-tradeables also explains why an economy with a strong balance of payments but close social links between the labour markets in the two sectors could have an inflation rate which exceeds the world rate.

The non-tradeables sector has two uncompetitive aspects. Its workers are able to maintain the same increases in money wages as in the tradeables sector despite lower productivity growth. Its firms are able to use mark-up pricing policies in spite of a higher rate of increase in unit labour costs. However, non-tradeables such as health, education and welfare services have a high income-elasticity of demand. Health services in particular have an extremely low price-elasticity of demand. The magnitudes of these two elasticities enabled the non-tradeables sector to grow even faster than the tradeables sector (a increased during the 1960s).

7.4   THE EFFECT OF OIL PRICE RISES ON OIL IMPORTERS

The quadrupling of the price of crude oil in the winter of 1973–4 was followed by a fall in labour productivity. During the following decade productivity grew again but at a much slower rate than in the two decades preceding 1973. Studies of individual industries by Berndt and Wood (1979) for the United States and by Kilpatrick and Naisbitt (1984) for Britain have revealed oil, capital and labour are used to produce output in a different manner from that which was thought before 1974. (Strictly, their studies refer to 'energy'. However, the rise in the oil price also led to rises in the prices of substitute fuels.) The old view was that oil would be substituted for either existing capital or labour. It now appears that the stock of capital equipment is designed to operate with specific amounts of oil: saving oil involves leaving capital idle. Oil and capital are complements and there are two relevant factors of production: a composite of oil-and-capital and labour. The old view of considering three factors as independent variables which cause output does not explain the changes in productivity which occurred between the periods up to and after 1974. A short-hand for this is to say that much capital equipment became obsolete after 1974, as if there were a fall in the amount of capital. Tradeables have more capital-intensive technologies than non-tradeables. The effect of the oil price rise was to reduce the supply of tradeables by more than the supply of non-tradeables. In Figure 7.7, this is shown by the movement of the production possibility curve inward from the continuous curve to the dashed curve. The contraction of production possibilities is more marked for tradeables than non-tradeables. At point 1 in Figure 7.7, the economy is shown at its equilibrium before the supply shock of the oil price rise. Because this point is on the production possibility curve it shows the quantities of non-tradeables Q^N and tradeables Q^T which could be supplied. The income line tangential to point 1 has a slope of minus P^N/P^T; this price ratio provides the signals and incentives for firms to move to this point and generate this income. The curve OD shows the blends of Q^N and Q^T which would be demanded at each level of absorption, given the price ratio P^N/P^T. Since point 1 is on OD, these amounts of Q^N and Q^T are both demanded and supplied. Income equals absorption and P^N/P^T is at its equilibrium value.

The supply shock of the oil price rise shrank the production possibilities to the dashed curve. For each level of Q^N, the attainable production of Q^T is less, and the slope of the production possibility curve is also less than before the shock. If P^N/P^T stayed constant,

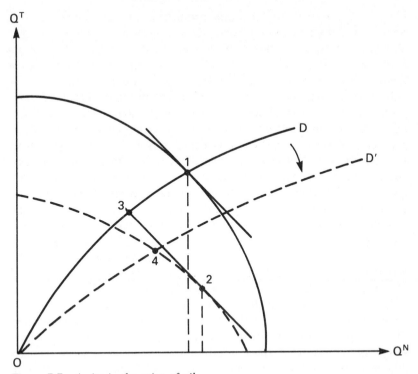

Figure 7.7 A rise in the price of oil.
Point 1. Equilibrium before the supply shock. Income equals absorption. Both tradeables and non-tradeables markets clear. The shock causes capital obsolescence which lowers production possibilities to the dashed curve, a shrinkage which is more marked for Q^T than Q^N.

Point 2 shows the amounts of Q^N and Q^T which firms would wish to supply if P^N/P^T stayed the same as at point 1, but this price ratio leaves unchanged the blends of demands for each level of absorption, which stay along OD.

If the income of point 2 were spent, absorption would be at *point 3*. There would be excess supply of Q^N and excess demand for Q^T. When P^N/P^T falls, demands move clockwise to OD′. Supplies move counter-clockwise around the new production possibility curve from point 2 to point 4.

Provided absorption is adjusted to income, *point 4* is where both markets clear. Note that point 4 may be anywhere on the new production possibilities to the left of point 2. Non-tradeable output could fall or rise following the oil price rise. Tradeable output unambiguously falls.

production would move to point 2 but the income from this production would generate demands at point 3. These two points denote disequilibria in both markets: for Q^N the supply at 2 exceeds the demand at 3, and for Q^T the supply at 2 falls short of the demand at 3.

Borrowing from abroad (from OPEC) could raise absorption above income, but with P^N/P^T constant production of non-tradeables is at point 2, and the demand for non-tradeables would equal supply only if absorption moved out along OD beyond point 1 to a point vertically above point 2. The borrowing would have to be massive indeed to cover the combination of increased absorption and reduced income.

If income is to equal absorption, both the tradeables and non-tradeables markets must clear: π^N must be less than π^T so that P^N/P^T falls. The income line which was tangential at point 2 now swivels counter-clockwise around the production possibility curve. The curve showing the blend of demands swivels clockwise from OD. The new equilibrium is at a point such as 4. When the adjustments are completed, less tradeables are both supplied and demanded (point 4 is unambiguously lower than point 1). There is ambiguity about the amount of non-tradeables supplied and demanded (Q^N at 4 may be more or less than Q^N at 1). However, the ratio Q^N/Q^T has increased. Since Q^N is mainly services and Q^T is produced by those sectors of the economy which are loosely termed 'industry', this change in the blend of outputs is sometimes called *deindustrialisation*.

The extent of the difficulties experienced by oil importers after 1974 depended upon the speed with which P^N/P^T fell to its new equilibrium. P^N is the price index of outputs which are labour-intensive and where suppliers are insulated from international competition; it is strongly influenced by the money wage index W. Tradeables are subject to strong international pressure and their domestic price P^T depends upon the price of foreign exchange E and the foreign price of tradeables P*. Hence the following approximation applies:

$$P^N/P^T = W/EP^* \tag{7.6}$$

In a small open economy the monetary authorities can change E but cannot influence P*.

During the 1920s, a resistance to cuts in money wages developed in most industrialised countries. During the 1970s most European labour markets insisted that money wages should rise in line with prices. This real wage resistance meant that increases in EP* caused increases in W. During the two decades prior to 1974, real wages had risen in line with the record increases in labour productivity. When productivity declined following the 1974 shock, real wages stayed constant. (In Britain real wages rose, but the early and mid-1970s were periods of confusingly erratic demand policies and on-off attempts at wage controls.)

The United States is different from Europe in two respects. First, the labour market displays resistance to money wage cuts but not real wage cuts. Second, the economy is large enough to influence the world price of tradeables. The supply shock was followed by no rise in money wages for a year, but monetary policy accommodated a rise in P^T which in turn affected P^*.

Black (1979) and McCallum (1983) have shown how the institutional characteristics of an economy influence its speed of response to a supply shock. The decisions of an independent and consistent Central Bank will be taken as given by the wage negotiators, as in West Germany. Labour markets may consist of strong unions, strong employers' organisations and a strong social consensus (Germany and Sweden) or little consensus (Britain). They may have little unionisation but react rapidly to disequilibria once these have appeared (the United States). One cannot make predictions about the speed of response to a supply shock which are generally applicable to all economies. Within each economy institutions change very slowly, and the consistent institutional characteristics allow some predictability.

7.5 THE DUTCH DISEASE

This section considers the effects on an industrialised country of oil extraction in amounts large enough to change it from being an oil importer to an oil exporter. As Krueger (1983) points out, it was ironic that oil importers blamed the oil price rises of 1974 and 1979 for rises in unemployment and inflation, whereas the oil-exporting industrialised countries also experienced stagflation. The Dutch disease occurs when the exploitation of a natural resource is accompanied by a fall in the output of manufacturing industry. It was first noticed when the Netherlands began extracting natural gas from the North Sea during the 1960s. An extreme form of the disease occurred in Britain in the early 1980s, when the rapid increase in the extraction of North Sea oil was accompanied by a dramatic fall in manufacturing employment and the redundant workers were unable to find jobs in other sectors.

The cause of the disease is simple. Oil exports cause the currency to appreciate and domestically-produced manufactures are priced out of foreign markets. The fall in the price of foreign exchange leads to import penetration into the domestic market for manufactures. By 1983, imports of manufactured goods into Britain exceeded exports for the first time since the Industrial Revolution.

There are two very different policies which the authorities can pursue following the significant exploitation of oil finds. They can accept the decline in manufacturing output and ensure that the lost employment is used to produce non-tradeables, or they can maintain manufacturing

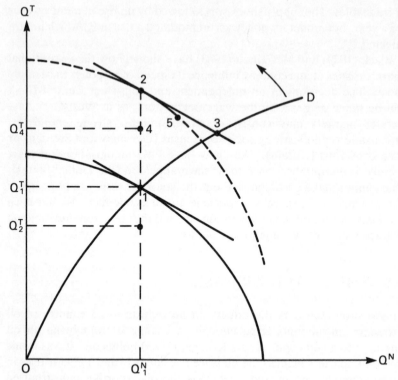

Figure 7.8   Oil production in an industrialised economy when all income is absorbed.

Point 1. Equilibrium before oil extraction.

Point 2. The notional supplies of Q^N and Q^T when Q^T includes both oil and manufactures but P^N/P^T stays the same as at point 1.

Point 3. The notional demands for Q^N and Q^T if the income at point 2 were achieved and expended.

Point 4 shows the actual output of Q^N and Q^T. Only Q_1^N is supplied, although the demand for non-tradeables is greater (at point 3). The demand for tradeables is only Q_4^T although firms could supply more (at point 2). These disequilibria raise P^N/P^T and the blends of demands shift counter-clockwise from OD. The most profitable blend of supplies shifts clockwise from point 2.

At point 5, both markets clear when income equals absorption.

output and employment near to its pre-oil level. (There are few jobs in oil extraction once the plumbing is completed.) Which policy is the better depends upon the length of time during which oil adds significantly to the output of tradeables.

We first consider the case where an economy starts producing oil and is expected to continue producing it for several decades. There are two tradeable outputs, oil and manufacturing and there is also non-tradeable output. In Figure 7.8 the pre-oil production possibilities are shown by the continuous curve drawn concave to the origin. Equilibrium occurred when Q_1^T of manufactures and Q_1^N of non-tradeables were produced; OD passes through point 1 and income equalled absorption. Oil production increases the supply of tradeables but uses negligible capital and labour and does not reduce the supply of non-tradeables. The production possibilities shift vertically upwards to the dashed curve. If P^N/P^T remained constant firms would wish to supply outputs at point 2, which is vertically above point 1. However, the income generated by this output would result in demands at point 3. The demand for Q^N exceeds the supply (point 3 is to the right of 2) and the supply of Q^T exceeds the demand (point 2 is higher than point 3). Actual production will occur at whichever is the smaller of supply and demand, at point 4 which is inside the production possibility curve. Manufacturing output is only Q_2^T. Oil output is $Q_4^T - Q_2^T$. With P^N/P^T unchanged, the oil output has resulted in a fall in manufacturing output but non-tradeable output has stayed constant at Q_1^N. There is no alternative employment for those whose manufacturing jobs are lost.

An increase in P^N/P^T eliminates both the excess demand for non-tradeables and the excess supply of tradeables. The curve OD moves counter-clockwise, and the most profitable production blend moves clockwise along the dashed production possibility curve. There is some point such as point 5 where both the tradeables and non-tradeables markets are in equilibrium. Income equals absorption and both capital and labour are fully employed. The notional supplies of Q^N and Q^T move from point 2, the notional demands from point 3 and actual outputs from point 4. When tradeables include both oil and manufactures, equilibrium results in non-tradeable output increasing above its pre-oil level (point 5 is to the right of point 1) and manufacturing output falls (it is the point on the old production possibility curve vertically below point 5).

P^N/P^T rises if W increases faster than EP*. During the initial stages of oil production the currency appreciates: E falls. There is little difficulty in bringing about the rise in P^N/P^T. Indeed, the British problem for much of the postwar period was to discourage such rises. If changes in the price of foreign exchange and money wages are too imprecise, the switching policy can be supplemented by appropriate taxes and subsidies on the outputs of the two sectors. When the oil deposits are exhausted, the switching is put into reverse. The economy moves from point 5 in Figure 7.8 back to point 1.

There is some danger in treating the ratio P^N/P^T as if it were a magic wand: wave it one way and non-tradeables expand; wave it the other way and manufactures expand. Using unfavourable relative prices to close manufacturing firms is a much simpler and faster process than using favourable relative prices to generate new firms. During the rise in oil output, the expansion of non-tradeables may lag behind the contraction of manufacturing and unemployment develops during the adjustment period. When oil production (or the oil price) declines, the re-expansion of manufacturing may be particularly difficult. The production and marketing of manufactures benefits more than other sectors from *learning by doing*: that build-up of complementarities, expertise and liaison between research, marketing and production departments which depends more on the total stock of a firm's past production than on the current flow of output. By the end of the period of oil production, the fruits of this process have been lost to domestic producers and gained by those oil importing economies which traded their manufactures for oil. Re-entering the international market for manufactures with products which are competitive in price and quality could be a difficult process. Van Wijnbergen (1984) has emphasised that the choice of policy to accompany oil extraction depends upon both the time which the oil will last and the extent of learning-by-doing.

When the period of significant oil production is expected to be short (a decade, say) manufacturing will complete its contraction and immediately find that the time for re-expansion has arrived. The contraction can be avoided or at least moderated by an appropriate policy to influence *both* P^N/P^T *and* absorption. In the long run, a graph of income would show the period of oil production as a high but short-lived blip. The policy involves keeping absorption well below income during the blip. Oil's contribution to income is used to buy foreign bonds and claims on the future profits of foreign firms. Absorption is then allowed to rise above non-oil income as interest and profits from abroad flow into the economy.

In Figure 7.9, point 5 is the same as in Figure 7.8. It shows the appropriate policy if the oil is to last for many decades. The alternative policy is to hold P^N/P^T at its pre-oil equilibrium value. Production and income are at point 2 which is vertically above point 1. (The oil production led to a vertical shift in the production possibility curve, hence the slopes are the same at points 1 and 2.) Absorption, however, is only at point 1, its pre-oil level. The difference between income and absorption is an outflow of funds to buy foreign financial paper. The extra supply of sterling to buy foreign bonds exactly matches the extra demand for sterling by foreigners buying oil. E is constant, as is $P^T = EP^*$. As the flow of interest and profit payments from abroad

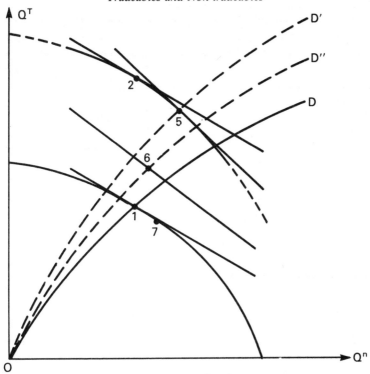

Figure 7.9   Oil extraction lasts for only a decade.

Point 1 shows the equilibrium before oil production.

Point 5 is on the production possibility curve which includes oil as tradeable output. P^N/P^T is greater than at point 1, and OD′ gives the blends of demands for this larger price ratio. At point 5 there is equilibrium when income equals absorption. Q^N is greater than at point 1. Manufacturing output is at the point on the old production curve vertically below point 5.

At point 2, the supplies of non-tradeables and manufactures are the same as at point 1 because P^N/P^T is the same at both points. However this price ratio causes the blends of demands shown by OD. If absorption is at point 1 but income is at point 2, all the income from oil can be invested abroad. The accumulation of foreign assets eventually results in a flow of interest payments from abroad which enables absorption to rise above non-oil income.

At point 6 absorption exceeds non-oil income by the amount of the interest flow. The slope of the line at point 6 is greater than at points 1 and 2 but less than at point 5. This P^N/P^T brings about the blends of demands shown by OD″. Point 6 is maintainable after the domestic oil deposits are exhausted.

Point 7 shows the domestically generated income associated with the absorption at point 6. Point 7 must be vertically below point 6: the supply of non-tradeables must equal the demand for them. However, the demand for tradeables (at point 6) can exceed their domestic production (at point 7). The flow of interest payments from abroad finances the excess of imports over exports. National income exceeds domestic income.

slowly increases, absorption can rise above income. This gap can be held permanently, unlike the temporary increase if all oil income had been expended on absorption during the short period of oil production. Instead of both income and absorption moving from point 1 to point 5 and then back to point 1, absorption slowly moves from point 1 to point 6 and stays there.

Point 6 is the post-oil equilibrium. There is a small rise in P^N/P^T. (The slope of the absorption line at 6 is greater than at point 2 but less than at point 5.) This rise shifts the income line from point 1 to point 7, vertically below point 6. (It must be here because the demand for non-tradeables must equal the supply.) More tradeables are demanded than are produced in the domestic economy, but the difference is paid for by the interest payments from abroad, whose value is equal to the vertical distance between points 6 and 7.

There are three methods which the authorities can use to prevent a fall in the sterling price of foreign exchange, an appreciation of sterling. First, they can use new high-powered money to buy foreign currency and build up the reserves. Second, they can use new money to buy foreign long-term bonds. Both these methods involve direct activity in the international currency market. The third method involves open-market operations, introducing the new money into the domestic economy by purchasing existing government bonds. This method drives down the domestic interest rate and encourages private purchases of foreign bonds, which now have a more attractive yield than domestic bonds. The action in the international currency market is by the private sector and the authorities' influence is indirect. Each method has advantages in particular circumstances.

During the initial period of increasing oil extraction, sterling became a petro-currency and a useful part of the blend of currencies held as reserves by foreign Central Banks. As these Banks built up their stocks to the desired level, there was a temporary excess demand for sterling. There was also much destabilising speculation which caused the foreign-currency value of sterling to overshoot. The behaviour of foreign Central Banks *en masse* is not very predictable and that of speculators is notoriously unpredictable. Hence any policy to hold down the value of sterling in the short run must be easily reversible at the time when Central Banks cease to build up their holdings of sterling or when the speculative bubble bursts. The appropriate policy for preventing the initial over-appreciation of sterling is to buy foreign currencies with new money. Once Central Banks' portfolios are readjusted, or market sentiment swings away from sterling, depreciation can be avoided by selling foreign reserves and reducing the monetary base.

The remaining two methods of avoiding appreciation by increasing the supply of sterling have long-term effects. The government can use new money to buy foreign bonds. In future years, interest payments from abroad increase government revenue and allow reduced taxation, enabling absorption to rise above non-oil income. The bond purchases cease when the oil income stops, but the interest payments continue.

The third method is for the government to buy back its own debt from domestic bond-holders. The resulting fall in the domestic rate of interest causes British residents to buy foreign bonds and shares. In future years, households receive less interest from domestic bonds but also pay less taxes to finance the interest. These two flows of transfer payments cancel out in their macroeconomic effects. However, households now have foreign assets which yield a continuing flow of interest from abroad, and enable absorption to rise above non-oil income. This method is appealing to those who are concerned about the size of the national debt and to those who consider that the management of a portfolio of foreign assets is more efficient when inspired by the profit motive as when held by the private sector.

Maintaining P^N/P^T constant in spite of oil extraction becomes more difficult when wages rise faster than the foreign price of tradeables. In this case the price of foreign exchange must rise. New high-powered money has to enter the international currency market at a faster rate than required just to counter the oil exports. The monetary authorities have to respond both to the oil market and the labour market. The process would be easier if Britain were a country where wage setting responds to the monetary authorities so that there would be a clear sequence of responses from oil production to money and from money to wages.

Government services form an appreciable part of the non-tradeables sector and government is able to ration the supply of such services. Other non-tradeables such as construction are financed by government but produced by the private sector, and government can limit the demand for these. If the electorate decides that the government sector is too large, the expansion of the non-tradeables sector is inhibited. If the electorate also wants lower inflation, monetary expansion will be cautious. Finally, if the labour market increases wages rapidly there will be a rise in P^N/P^T, little increase in non-tradeable output and insufficient monetary expansion to reverse the rise in the price ratio. This is the worst of all worlds and is the reason for the more rapid rise in unemployment in Britain than in other industrialised countries during the early 1980s.

PROBLEMS FOR CHAPTER 7

1. Why do countries engage in international trade?
2. Distinguish between total expenditure in the domestic economy and expenditure on the output of domestic industry.
3. What policies would you recommend if you observed:
   (a) an excess demand for tradeables and equilibrium in the market for non-tradeables?
   (b) excess demands for both tradeables and non-tradeables?
   (c) an excess supply of non-tradeables and equilibrium in the market for tradeables?
4. One-third of an economy's output is not tradeable. Labour productivity in the tradeables sector grows at 4 per cent per annum and in the non-tradeables sector at 1 per cent. The world inflation rate is 3 per cent per annum. If the balance of payments remains in equilibrium, what would you expect to be the rate of increase in the general price level in that country?
5. Why did the output of non-tradeables grow more rapidly than tradeable output in many countries during the 1960s?
6. A country's capital stock increases and raises the production possibilities for tradeables by more than non-tradeables. If income equals absorption both before and after the change, what happens to the price ratio P^N/P^T?
7. Under what circumstances would oil extraction raise total income but lower employment?

FURTHER READING

Corden (1977) discusses the effects of the rise in oil prices. The effect on tradeables of oil extraction and monetary policy is analysed in Corden (1981), Corden and Neary (1982) and Bean (1987). Theories of inflation, including the structuralist, are compared in the survey article of Frisch (1977).

8 Adjustments and Misperceptions

Financial markets usually act as shock-absorbers between the vagaries of governments' policies and the productive activities of firms and households. They adjust rapidly and participants form expectations in a forward-looking way with prices changing in response to 'news'. Expectations have to be both forward-looking and unbiased if they are to be rational, since rational people would spot a consistent bias and correct for it. Tests for the rationality of expectations are extremely difficult to devise, but some tests show that behaviour in financial markets usually conforms to the predictions of economic models. Interest rates and exchange rates move roughly in line with predictions; the errors seem random, without a pattern from which more could be learnt.

However, there are times when problems originate in financial markets. Currencies over-adjust to events or move into speculative bubbles. Lenders become myopic about the possibility that sovereign borrowers will default on debt servicing or that firms with low current profits are investing for high profit in the longer run.

This chapter investigates some of the problems which arise when different markets adjust at different speeds. It starts with an early example of expectations formation from Keynes' *General Theory of Employment, Interest and Money* which shows how wrong adjustment in financial markets can push the markets for goods and labour into disequilibrium.

The second section gives an illustration of the exciting theoretical developments of the early 1970s when a group of economists introduced the rational expectations hypothesis to macroeconomic theory and also combined this development with the assumption that markets always clear. Fluctuations in output and employment were explained by misperceptions which shifted supply and demand in each market. This revived interest in expectations-formation and the types of event which could cause misperceptions. Its importance lies in the subsequent research programme carried out by the economics profession rather than in the explanatory power of the early theories, which was only slight.

The fourth and fifth sections investigate the effect on exchange rates of rapid adjustment in the markets for financial assets (domestic and foreign bonds and money) combined with slow adjustment in import and export volumes. These sections explain part of the gyrations in exchange rates which have occurred since the end of the regime of fixed rates.

The final sections show how a dramatic shock can have permanently harmful effects on the suppliers of goods and labour. A period of low output results in a fall in the natural level of output in subsequent periods. High unemployment for several years causes a subsequent rise in the natural rate of unemployment. These sections illustrate the importance of discovering workable stabilisation policies and avoiding the extreme experiments in which so many individual countries indulged during the past two decades.

8.1   THE SPECULATIVE DEMAND FOR MONEY

When interest rates have stayed within a narrow range for many years, a sudden fall below this range could surprise households. They might expect the low rate to be temporary. The associated high bond price would also be seen as temporary. A bond purchase now is expected to result in a capital loss. Households 'save' by building up their money-holdings instead of sending a flow of money to the loanable funds market to be spent by firms on investment. When money is held because the alternative is expected to lead to a capital loss, there is a *speculative demand for money*. The demand would disappear if interest rates returned to their familiar range, or if they stayed low for long enough to become expected. The implication is that expectations are formed adaptively, at least as applied to an unusually low rate of interest. While the speculative demand is present, firms are deprived of funds. The reduction in their supply prevents the rate of interest from falling even lower and investment expenditure is discouraged. With aggregate demand constraining output, income falls and total saving is reduced. When the speculative demand for money disappears, the supply of loanable funds now remains low because income is low.

This sequence is illustrated in Figure 8.1. The initial equilibrium is at point 1. A major shock to business confidence shifts the demand for funds from I to I'. With no speculative demand for money, there would be a movement down the supply function to point 3, where the large fall in the rate of interest would limit the decline in investment from I_1 to I_3 and a rise in consumption would also occur to leave aggregate demand

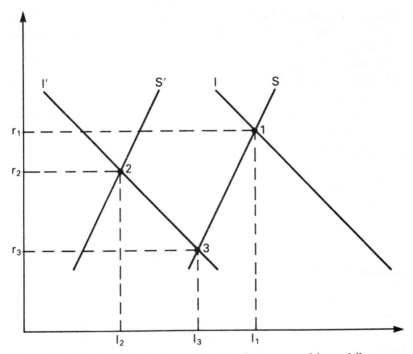

Figure 8.1   The loanable funds market when business confidence falls.
Point 1 is the initial equilibrium. The S function is both the supply function and
the savings function for a given income. The investment schedule then shifts to
I'.

In a Neoclassical world the new equilibrium would be *point 3* and the fall in
investment to I_3 would be matched by increased consumption as households
save less. However, households consider any interest rate below r_2 is so unusual
that it will be temporary.

The supply of loanable funds shifts to S' and some savings are used to build up
money holdings. Investment falls to I_2 and expenditure constrains income. S'
becomes the savings function at the lower level of income and equilibrium stays
at *point 2*.

as before. Only the blend of aggregate demand would change. Output
and employment would remain at their natural levels.

The speculative demand for money prevents this fall in the rate of
interest. If r_2 is already unusually low, funds are withheld from the
market. The supply function shifts from S to S'. If saving is defined as
non-consumption, S' is no longer a savings function while the
speculative demand persists. Once households have built up their
money stocks to the desired higher level, all savings again flow to the
market but by now the flow is less because income is less. Point 2 was a

temporary equilibrium because of the fear of a capital loss on bond purchases; it becomes a more permanent equilibrium because of the fall in income.

Throughout the process the loanable funds market cleared but output and employment fell. There is now an excess supply of labour, implying to the Neoclassicist the need for a fall in the real wage. The demand shock lowers output prices and raises the real wage. It also triggers the multiplier process which further reduces output and employment. With both unemployment and real wages rising, the Neoclassical view seems confirmed.

If the speculative demand for money remained high, the economy could return to full equilibrium by reducing prices so that the transactions demand for money fell. However, this entails a reduction in nominal wages if firms are to stay in business with lower prices. Workers refuse to recontract between the annual round of wage negotiations. Each firm's workforce senses that a wage-cut will certainly reduce living standards but is unlikely to enable the firm to lower its prices by enough to raise sales when the shortage of demand is general. By refusing to recontract, there is a sense in which workers are voluntarily increasing unemployment. However, if the loanable funds market had adjusted in the complete Neoclassical sense and with a constant money supply, the original nominal wage and price level would remain appropriate. Why enter into the painful process of reducing wages and prices when the required extent of the reductions is unknown, only to put the process into reverse when aggregate demand returns to equilibrium? Far better to expand the money supply to meet the speculative demand, however great, and then reverse the expansion once this demand diminishes. If international confidence in the currency would be threatened by a massive monetary expansion, a second-best solution is to use fiscal policy to replace the lost investment orders by government expenditure.

A more general approach to the impact of a demand shock on employment involves treating the demand for labour as derived from the demand for goods. However, there are also times when employment is reduced because the real wage rises above the marginal product of labour at its market clearing value. Excess supply of labour may be the result of either too little aggregate demand or too high a real wage. Figure 8.2 illustrates the case envisaged by some interpreters of Keynes. Point 1 shows Neoclassical equilibrium. Employment is constrained by aggregate demand to N_3. Point 2 shows that the demand shock lowered P and raised W/P but nonetheless the real wage is not constraining employment. An expansion of aggregate demand would both shift the

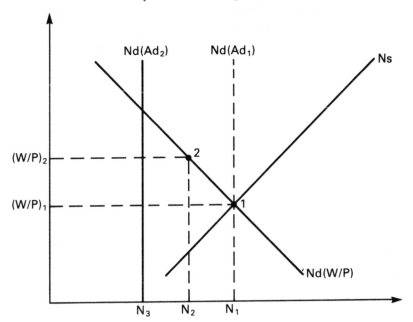

Figure 8.2 Point 1 shows a cleared labour market where the demand for labour is a function of the real wage Nd (W/P$_1$) and income generates expenditure to ensure that the demand for N$_1$ workers is also that derived from the demand for output Nd (Ad$_1$). If an aggregate demand shortage constrains employment to N$_3$, lowering the real wage from (W/P)$_2$ does not increase employment.

Nd (Ad) function *and* raise the price level to return the labour market to point 1 where both Nd (Ad) and Nd (W/P) coincide.

The econometric evidence hardly supports the appearance of a sudden speculative demand for money. Low interest rates normally lead to only a small increase in desired money-holdings, implying that people adjust their transactions in response to the lower return on bonds but do not treat unusually low interest rates as a signal for expecting capital losses on bond purchases. The weak evidence may be because the speculative demand is too short-lived to show in the data or because households do not develop adaptively their expectations of what are 'usual' rates of interest.

8.2 RATIONAL EXPECTATIONS EQUILIBRIUM WITH MISPERCEPTIONS

The rational expectations hypothesis (REH) was introduced to economics by Muth (1961): since expectations are informed predictions of future events they are essentially the same as the predictions of the relevant economic theory. In the early 1970s, several economists extended the hypothesis to the study of aggregate economic behaviour. One group of these, the *New Neoclassicists*, combined the REH with the hypothesis that all markets are always in equilibrium: the economy does not move *towards* the position predicted by the Old Neoclassicists of Chapter 1; it is *at* that position. Unlike the monetarist model of Chapter 2, even the labour market always clears. The value of the approach is that it forces the analyst to investigate exogenous events which might influence supply and demand. With disequilibria assumed away, any fluctuations in output and employment must be explained by shifts in the relevant supply and demand functions initiated by the events, including changes in the perceptions of the market participants. This section gives two examples of rational expectations equilibrium theory, the first when the perceptions are correct and the second when there are misperceptions.

Suppose we observe a large rise in the nominal wage and an insignificant change in the price level, followed by reduced employment. The effect was predictable from the cause. Even its extent was approximately known. Unions and employers' organisations have their own research departments with access to data and other research findings. They are the agents of firms and households and are paid to disseminate informed predictions. The media have experts at tailoring information to the particular requirements of their readers, viewers and listeners. Given this information, households must be gambling. With a unit elasticity of labour demand to the real wage, a five per cent real wage increase has a 19 in 20 chance of increasing living standards and a 1 in 20 chance of unemployment. They instruct their agents in the wage negotiations accordingly and the labour supply function shifts up the demand function. Who is to become unemployed is not known before the event. If a worker does become unemployed, his gamble failed but a failed gamble is not a symptom of disequilibrium. The researcher seeking to explain the supply shift is led first to the data on unemployment benefit; a rise in this reduces the cost of a failed gamble.

An interesting example of the approach is in Benjamin and Kochin (1979) who noted the close correlation between British unemployment in the interwar period and the wider availability of unemployment benefit. The timing of events is also consistent with the view that rising unemployment caused public sympathy for those caught by exogenous shocks. Political pressure led the authorities to provide wider groups of unemployed with bare maintenance after careful screening. In interwar Britain, unemployment caused maintenance payments via the political process, as well as the payment shifting the labour supply function. Changes in benefit remain part of the explanation for unemployment in the late twentieth century, if not the main part.

The REH does not imply that expectations are free of error but that these errors are random. Predictions may not hit the targets of actual outcomes but rational predictions do not consistently cluster in the same area of misses. Such a bias would be spotted and corrected. In modern jargon, the extent of the misses is called 'noise'. When the misses are randomly distributed about the target but with the target in the centre, this is 'white noise'.

The next example is of a *rational expectations equilibrium with misperceptions* (REEM). This involves an extention to the REH which hypothesises that people behave as if they know the theory which best predicts the future value of a variable and monitor the data which are relevant to the theory. A REEM takes into account that continuous monitoring is costly. The rational person seeks information only at those intervals which make the expected gains exceed the costs. If a surprising event occurs during an interval between monitoring, misperceptions appear. Given knowledge of the event, such misperceptions are explainable; even people who suffered from them realise why they made them and correct them as soon as they receive information about the surprising event.

Consider the results of a sudden monetary contraction or, more likely, a surprising reduction in the growth of the money supply. There is a fall in the volume or prices of the orders placed with firms. Initially, each firm interprets this as a decline in the demand for its product relative to others. It knows its own prices but has not yet realised the price falls for others' outputs. If faced with a price reduction, it reduces its quantity offered for sale. If it is a price-maker, it finds the quantity demanded reduced and responds by lowering its price. Whatever the degree of monopoly, its labour demand function shifts to the left. It offers job-seekers a lower nominal wage than they expect. These prospective workers interpret the signal as a decline in the local demand for their skills. They extend the area of their search and the time they spend job-hunting; the labour supply function shifts to the left. The markets for labour and goods clear but employment and output are reduced. Once firms realise that all output prices have fallen, they realise that the decline in demand at the expected price level was not due to a relative fall in the demand for their own product. Once job-hunters realise that all nominal wages are less than expected, they realise that there is no point in extending the area and time of their search. Finally, firms realise that they need pay less for their inputs, and households realise that goods cost less; all *relative* prices are perceived and the economy returns to equilibrium at the natural level of output and the natural rate of unemployment. During the interim, the economy was in a REEM, with lower output and higher unemployment than the full information equilibrium. The *general* level of prices was less than expected and this caused misperceptions about relative prices, wage differentials and the real wage.

The argument assumes that wages are flexible downward as well as upwards and that firms as well as households suffer from short-run misperceptions. It was used by Sargent and Wallace (1975) as an illustration of the way the REH could be combined with a standard simple model to show that monetary surprises are possible reasons for output changes. Predicted monetary changes would *not* affect output because firms and households would change absolute prices to keep relative prices at their equilibrium ratios, which would also be their perceived ratios. For example, if the authorities always responded to a rise in unemployment by increasing monetary growth according to some formula, this formula would soon be deduced from their actions. The anticipated policy would then be an ineffective policy.

The combination of the REH with the market-clearing hypothesis appeared when the authorities were struggling with ways of using demand policies to reduce the impact of the supply shocks of the mid-1970s. The improvements in computational facilities had allowed some econometric models to become ungainly, with excessive detail on the demand side which prevented clear understanding, and crude equations for the price level to proxy the supply side. There was much bath water to be thrown away; the problem was to preserve the babies. In the following decade there was intense theoretical research into the reasons why some prices and wages change infrequently, why contracts are valuable, why they are not all renegotiated at the same time, why different markets adjust at different speeds, why some sectors find a blend of adaptive and rational expectations an economical method of picturing the future. Empirical work confirmed the theoretical findings. Because contracts overlap, moderate monetary expansions can increase activity even when anticipated. Contractions reduced activity, although here the difficulty was to discover whether the contraction was anticipated, because this depended upon the credibility of the government which announced the forthcoming contraction.

Many forecasting models now incorporate the REH, either for financial markets only or for all markets. This ensures that the inflationary expectations which drive some of the equations conform to the actual inflation predicted by the model as an outcome. Most models incorporate the main contributions of economists from many different 'schools'. The next two sections show how the REH can be combined with a Keynesian model for a demand-constrained economy and a Neoclassical model for a fully employed economy. The final sections show that temporary misalignments following shocks can have long-term effects.

8.3 EXCHANGE RATE OVERSHOOTING WHEN OUTPUT LAGS

During the regime of floating exchange rates the movements in the rates have been far greater than were expected or than can be explained by comparing the purchasing power of two currencies. An event triggers an immediate change in the expected direction but apparently the change is too great because it is then followed by a slow reversal of part of the change. The currency has rapidly over-appreciated (or over-depreciated) to be followed by a slow depreciation (or appreciation). The explanation involves two distinctions between financial markets and goods markets. First, financial markets deal in stocks of existing assets: foreign exchange, bonds, equities. Goods markets deal in flows which have to be produced and marketed over a period of years. Second, there is far more homogeneity in financial markets. Dealers in currency or bonds buy and sell items which are indistinguishable from each other except by ownership. The total value of such deals dwarfs the cost of monitoring and processing information. The REH applies and asset markets respond to 'news' within seconds. A manufacturer combines heterogeneous inputs to sell to heterogeneous customers. Detailed investigation of each individual would be prohibitively costly. As experience demonstrates reliability, he offers more favourable contracts to workers, suppliers and customers. When market conditions change, he reacts within a year or two, not the minutes within which asset markets react.

This section examines how these different reaction speeds can affect the exchange rate when output is below its natural level. Financial capital is assumed to be internationally mobile and the domestic interest

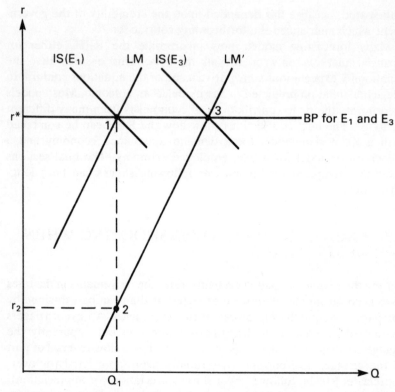

Figure 8.3 Adjustment is rapid in asset markets but slow in goods markets.
Point 1 is the initial equilibrium.
Point 2 shows asset markets adjusted to a monetary expansion before income
has had time to respond.
Point 3 is the final equilibrium. The horizontal BP locus implies perfectly mobile
financial capital.

rate is initially at the world rate r^*. The authorities then generate a
surprising increase in the money supply. Provided the goods market has
time to respond, the analysis is the same as Chapter 5. The changes are
illustrated in Figure 8.3. Over a year or two, the economy moves from
point 1 to point 3 where the rate of interest is r^* as before the change,
but the price of foreign exchange has risen and the trade surplus has
increased to generate more output. The dynamic story appears to be
that the shift in LM leads to a very small reduction in the domestic
interest rate which causes a capital outflow as bond purchasers move to
the higher world rate r^*. The currency depreciates until the price of
foreign exchange has risen from E_1 to E_3 which shifts IS until

equilibrium returns and even the small interest rate differential disappears. The markets for goods, money, bonds and foreign exchange are all in equilibrium. The move of LM seems to have pulled IS with it along BP as if the markets for goods and assets are adjusting at the same pace.

What happens to the exchange rate when asset markets adjust rapidly but goods markets do not? The sudden increase in the money supply occurs at the initial income and drives down the domestic interest rate (from point 1 to point 2 in Figure 8.3). Holders of domestic currency exchange it to purchase foreign bonds. Domestic bonds are willingly held only if the uncovered interest parity condition is met:

$$r = r^* + x \qquad (8.1)$$

where x is the expected depreciation of the domestic currency. With r below r^*, x must be negative, an appreciation. The domestic currency price of foreign exchange must be driven high enough to be expected to fall, but how high is this?

The participants in asset markets know the economy is below its natural level of output. They incorporate IS–LM–BP analysis into the REH and predict that the exchange rate will settle at E_3 once exports and imports have adjusted. Figure 8.4 shows the expected time path of E in the top diagram. Originally it was E_1 and is expected to become E_3. But asset market equilibrium involves an expected appreciation, hence E must overshoot to E_2.

The centre diagram of Figure 8.4 is labelled e, which is the rate of change of E predicted by the model. At point 1, the monetary expansion is noted and is followed by a positive blip in e (E rises at an accelerating then decelerating rate). For a moment e is zero then becomes negative (E stops rising and starts to fall; the model predicts the currency will appreciate). At point 2, the predicted negative e gives the expected appreciation to bring asset market equilibrium. With rational expectations, x *is* e. Between points 1 and 2, there is asset market disequilibrium which may be only a matter of minutes. After point 2, the rising demand for exports and falling imports are expected to appreciate the currency with time. At point 3, the impact of the monetary surprise has finished working its way through to goods markets and this has been anticipated by asset markets. Asset markets remain in equilibrium as the domestic rate of interest slowly returns to the world rate and x moves from negative to zero.

This section has combined the REH with standard Keynesian analysis to show how different adjustment speeds lead to exchange rate overshooting. The assumption was that domestic and foreign price

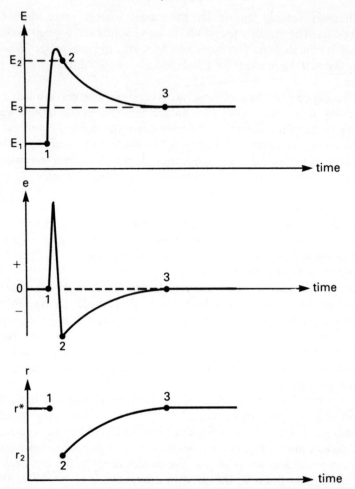

Figure 8.4   Exchange rate overshooting. A monetary expansion occurs at point 1. Asset markets move rapidly to equilibrium by point 2. This equilibrium changes as goods markets move slowly to equilibrium, which is not achieved until point 3.

Top. The price of foreign exchange moves rapidly up from E_1 to E_2 (depreciation) then slowly to E_3 (appreciation).

Middle. e is the rate of change of E. Immediately after point 1, e is strongly positive, then negative, but slowly becomes less negative until E ceases to change at point 3.

Bottom. The rate of interest is initially at the world rate r^*. Between 1 and 2 there is disequilibrium in asset markets. Between 2 and 3 there is dynamic equilibrium as described by uncovered interest parity.

levels remained unchanged so that a change in the nominal exchange rate was also a change in the real rate. The next section examines the case when output is not constrained by aggregate demand.

8.4 EXCHANGE RATE OVERSHOOTING WHEN THE PRICE LEVEL LAGS

This section considers the dynamics of the exchange rate when a surprising monetary expansion occurs in an economy which is at its natural level of output Q^n. For simplicity, any small rise in Q above Q^n is ignored to focus attention on the rise in P. The goods market does not respond immediately to news of the monetary expansion. Contracts have to be worked through. Price-lists are expensive to change. The process is faster and easier than quantity adjustment but it is not instantaneous. As P increases, there are two opposing effects on the exchange rate. The demand for money increases and raises the rate of interest, which appreciates the currency via interest rate parity (IRP). The rise in P also reduces competitiveness which tends to depreciate the currency via purchasing power parity (PPP). Hence IRP in asset markets and PPP in goods markets are pulling in opposite directions. The analysis for simplifying these complexities is due to Dornbusch (1976).

We first consider the range of possible equilibria in asset markets when the money supply is fixed at M. The demand for money depends upon three variables: P adjusts slowly; Q is held at the exogenously set value of Q^n; and r adjusts rapidly. With M and Q fixed, a rise in P causes a rise in r which keeps money demand constant.

$$M = Md\,(P, Q, r) \tag{8.2}$$

Financial capital is internationally mobile and the bond market adjusts immediately to ensure that uncovered interest parity holds:

$$r = r^* + x \tag{8.3}$$

Today's rate is E. Call the expected rate in, say, one year's time E_3. Then:

$$x = a\,(E_3 - E) \tag{8.4}$$

Here a determines the speed of adjustment. For example, if today's E is $1.50 per £1, E_3 is $2 per £1 and a is 2, then today's depreciation of the dollar is expected to be one per cent. If the expectation is realised, tomorrow's E will be $1.515 per £1 and tomorrow's x will be only 0.97 per cent.

Asset markets respond rapidly to a rise in P: the increase in r lowers E (an appreciation) to the level where the expected depreciation brings interest parity. In Figure 8.5 the locus marked AA shows the combinations of P and E which bring asset market equilibrium. An increase in the money supply would shift this locus upward: for each r and hence E, a higher P and hence Md can be accommodated at equilibrium.

The goods market maintains output at its natural level Q^n. For equilibrium, aggregate demand must also be maintained at this level. A rise in P would reduce competitiveness unless E rose in the same

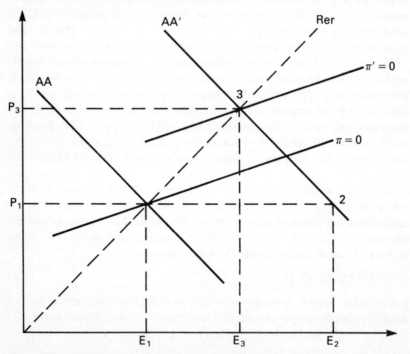

Figure 8.5 Exchange rate overshooting when output stays at its natural level but prices respond sluggishly to monetary expansion.
AA is the initial combinations of P and E for asset market equilibrium. The locus $\pi = 0$ shows the varying blends of aggregate demand resulting from varying combinations of P and E, with each blend giving aggregate demand to the natural level of output.
Point 1 is the initial equilibrium.
Point 2 shows asset market equilibrium immediately after the monetary expansion.
Point 3 is the final equilibrium. The exchange rate rises from E_1 to E_2 then falls back to E_3.

proportion. The dashed ray from the origin in Figure 8.5 gives an example of a constant real exchange rate, where

$$Rer = EP^*/P \tag{8.5}$$

The foreign price level P^* is assumed constant. The slope of this ray is P/E: the less steep the slope, the more competitive are exports. A movement along the ray would prevent the *switching* of demand caused by *relative* price changes when P increases. However, a rise in P also has an absorption-reducing effect: investment falls because of the rise in the rate of interest. To compensate for this, E must increase by more than P to ensure that the demand for domestic output stays constant. Goods market disequilibrium would cause changes in P. Equilibrium is the locus marked $\pi = 0$. Below the locus there is excess demand and π is positive. The slope of $\pi = 0$ is less steep than the ray marked Rer.

The assets and goods markets are at an initial equilibrium shown by point 1. Both the price level and the exchange rate are expected to remain at their actual levels. With no expected depreciation, the domestic rate of interest must be at the world rate r^*. There is then a surprising monetary expansion which leads to a rapid adjustment of assets markets shown by the shift to AA'. Initially, goods prices do not change and the new asset equilibrium is at point 2. Here the fall in the domestic rate of interest has led to a depreciation of the currency so that the price of foreign exchange rises as far as E_2. At E_2 an appreciation is expected.

At point 2, there is an excess demand for goods (the point is below the $\pi = 0$ locus). This is because there has been a rise in E but no rise in P: competitiveness has increased. (The ray from the origin to point 2 is less steep than that marked Rer.) The excess demand causes P to rise, although the adjustment is much slower than that of E and r in asset markets. The excess demand remains until point 3 is reached, where the economy returns to its original real exchange rate. At point 3 aggregate demand no longer exceeds the natural level of output and inflation ceases. If the price level had moved above P_3 there would be an excess supply of goods and prices would fall, unless the rise in P is accompanied by a greater rise in E as shown by the new locus $\pi' = 0$. At point 3, both the rate of interest and the real exchange rate have returned to their previous values, but the nominal exchange rate overshot on the way.

A fiscal expansion has a very different effect when financial capital is perfectly mobile and output stays at Q^n. A surprising tax cut with a constant money supply has a rapid impact on the goods market. The excess demand for all goods (not just domestic production) is illustrated in Figure 8.6. Goods market equilibrium was initially at point 1 on

$\pi = 0$. The fiscal expansion raises the locus of equilibria to $\pi' = 0$ which would make the combination of P_1 and E_1 unsustainable. The constant money supply holds the price level constant and the rate of interest stays at the world rate. The budget deficit is financed by foreign lenders and the currency appreciates. The price of foreign exchange falls immediately with asset markets adjusting from AA to AA''. Domestic producers switch from exports to providing goods for domestic consumers, responding to the loss of competitiveness as the real exchange rate falls from Rer_1 to Rer_2. The theory provided a ready explanation of the appreciation of the US dollar in the early 1980s. (The repeated and mounting budget deficits resulted in the United States becoming a net debtor in 1985. The subsequent depreciation of the dollar resulted from anticipation of monetary expansion when asset

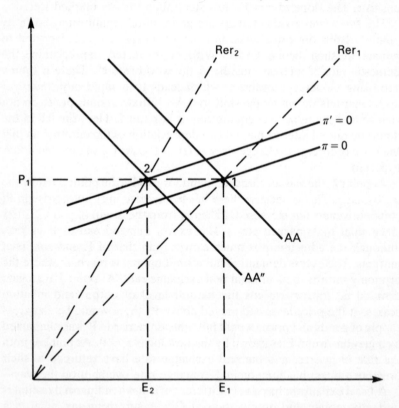

Figure 8.6 A fiscal expansion financed by borrowing moves the exchange rate directly from E_1 to E_2 with no over-shooting. The goods market moves from $\pi = 0$ to $\pi' = 0$ and the asset markets from AA to AA''. Equilibrium moves from point 1 to point 2.

markets took the view that the deficits were unsustainable by bond-financing alone.)

The models of this and the previous section can be combined to incorporate slow price adjustment and slower quantity adjustment in goods markets, with rapid adjustment in asset markets but capital mobility which is less than perfect. They form an important part of the explanation for the volatility of exchange rates.

8.5 HYSTERESIS AND TRADEABLES

Firms producing tradeables can usually cope with an over-appreciation of the currency for a few months. They maintain the competitiveness of their products by cutting the price in domestic currency. They maintain costly production teams and distribution networks, hoping that the flow of losses will be short-lived. If it is not, some firms cease trading. Their production, research and distribution teams are disbanded and equipment is scrapped. A subsequent depreciation which returns tradeables to their original competitiveness does not lead to a rapid return to the previous level of output. Forming a successful team takes much longer than disbanding it. For many years, the equilibrium output will be less than before the over-appreciation. The low actual output of the recent past has affected the natural level of output. When past values of a variable affect the current equilibrium, the process is known as *hysteresis*, which is the Greek word for 'arriving late'.

There are two main supply effects in this process. First, a distribution network is often a large fixed cost for a firm and requires some years of high expected sales to justify the expenditure. Second, much technical progress is the result of learning by doing and provides incumbent firms with the advantage. Some of the implications of these effects were considered in Chapter 7 for the case when manufactures are affected by the exploitation of a depleting natural resource.

There are also demand effects in the process of hysteresis. A new product has to find its niche. Even if the product is different in price, quality or type from apparently similar products, potential customers will be uncertain about the advantages and remain loyal to known brands. If the new product is itself an input, the firms which are potential customers are cautious in switching suppliers. The new equipment may be incompatible, maintenance service tardy, or delivery dates uncertain.

The causes of a transitory appreciation of the currency are various:

monetary squeeze, fiscal expansion, 'rational' overshooting via asset markets, speculative bubbles, mineral exploitation. Bean (1987) has suggested that the long-run costs are considerable, whatever the cause. The two main overvaluations of sterling in the twentieth century occurred in 1925 and 1980. Their main effects seem to have taken (or are taking) about a decade to work through. Temporary misalignments have long-run effects. The policy implication is that an overvaluation for more than a few months should be followed by a similar period of undervaluation to generate the signals and incentives which allow the tradeables sector to rebuild its lost advantages in supplying and attracting demand for its goods.

8.6   HYSTERESIS AND UNEMPLOYMENT

Changes in the unemployment rate in a particular year can sometimes be explained by comparing the recent growth of real wages with labour productivity. A rise in this *real wage gap* increases unemployment because a relative price has been set too high (a movement along the conventional labour demand function).

In countries where wage-setting is sensitive to excess labour supply, current unemployment can usually be explained by the recent growth of output. Unemployment rises above its natural rate if output growth falls below its natural rate:

$$u = u^n + b(q^n - q) \tag{8.6}$$

where u is the per cent of the labour force unemployed, q is the per cent per annum growth of output and b is a coefficient. The relation is known as *Okun's Law*. As originally stated it implied that the demand for labour was derived from the demand for output. Firms would respond to falling orders by first reducing output and overtime working. Then recruitment would fall and job-hunting by the unemployed would take longer, a slowing of the flow out of unemployment. Finally, some workers will be sacked, an increased flow into unemployment. The implication was that output creates jobs in a Keynesian sequence. Okun's Law can also be written to imply the neo-classical sequence that workers create output:

$$q = q^n + (1/b)(u^n - u) \tag{8.7}$$

An aggregate demand expansion should reduce unemployment by either raising prices to reduce the real wage or generating a derived demand for labour. However, during the last two decades many economies have reacted perversely to such policies. Their labour markets display strong resistance to reductions in the growth of real wages. Statistical 'explanations' of current unemployment are weak when unemployment is related only to the real wage gap or output growth. They become strong when past unemployment is used as an additional 'explainer' of current unemployment. There are two puzzles. First, why is current unemployment difficult to explain without incorporating past unemployment in the explanation? Second, why are many labour markets unresponsive to an excess supply of labour? In Australia and many European countries, particularly Britain, hysteresis has applied to unemployment for two decades; the natural rate of unemployment has been affected by past actual rates.

The long-term unemployed seem to have a negligible effect on real wage growth. Signals of excess supply from this group do not seem to be received by employers. One possible reason is that the signals are not sent. Either the unemployed are content with the income maintenance provided by the state, or they lose heart at the continuing lack of success in their hunt for jobs. In Britain, the ratio of unemployment benefit to wages fell over the period. If long-term unemployment is caused by supply behaviour, it seems to be because the intensity of job-search falls as people become discouraged. One policy suggestion is to subsidise employers who recruit people who have been unemployed for more than a year.

The alternative explanation is that the long-term unemployed send signals of excess labour supply by job-hunting, but the signals are not received by employers. The demanders of labour treat a record of long unemployment as an indicator that the job-seeker has lost the habit of work. He is not perceived as a supplier of labour. State schemes which create jobs for such people can produce both current output and a work record which enables future jobs to be obtained. Employers may also consider that a person becomes deskilled if he is unemployed for more than a few months. Publicly financed training schemes can counter this type of stigma, if it is a misperception, or correct the loss of human capital if it is a correct view by employers.

Whether the causes of long-term unemployment are due to labour supply or labour demand, schemes to reduce it need not have an impact on inflation. The new jobs create output without generating an excess demand for labour. Since the long-term unemployed are not perceived as part of labour supply, their employment shifts both the labour demand and supply functions and leaves the wage adjustment process unaffected.

8.7 SUMMARY

Keynes emphasised the importance of expectations and adjustment speeds. His view was that the flow of loanable funds would be reduced if interest rates are 'unusually' low, implying what is now called adaptive expectations. The loanable funds market would appear to be in equilibrium but costly disequilibria would develop in the markets for goods and labour. The cause was thought to be the speculative demand for money, which reduced spending just at the time when investment expenditures were also reduced because of business pessimism. Although the data do not support the hypothesis, it is an important theoretical example of how asset markets (here treated as flows rather than stocks) can exacerbate shocks.

In the late 1960s, the adaptive expectations hypothesis formed part of the analytical base for the criticism of crude expansionary policies. The criticism seemed to extend to any stabilisation policy when rational replaced adaptive expectations, and the assumption of market clearing replaced that of disequilibrium. Fluctuations in output and employment could be explained by misperceptions following policy surprises. Predictable demand policies seemed ineffective policies. The model of Rational Expectations Equilibrium with Misperceptions generated a decade of theoretical and empirical research in expectations, adjustment speeds and misperceptions.

Rational expectations can be incorporated into Keynesian or neoclassical models. Whether output is constrained by demand or supply, slow adjustment in goods markets and fast adjustment in asset markets provide part of the explanation for the volatile movements in exchange rates.

A temporary misalignment of the exchange rate can have permanent effects on the supply and demand conditions for tradeables. The fall in actual output causes a fall in the subsequent equilibrium level of output. The current equilibrium is not independent of past actual outcomes. Hysteresis can also appear in labour markets when high unemployment raises the natural rate. In Britain in particular there is strong evidence of its existence. It entails significant psychological costs as well as lost output.

PROBLEMS FOR CHAPTER 8

1. The demanders of bonds form their expectation about the interest rate by the following adaptive process.

$$r^e_{t+1} = 0.6\, r_t + 0.4\, r^e_t$$

where r^e_{t+1} is the expected rate for next month,

r_t is the current rate, and

r^e_t is the expectation that was formed of the rate which would now prevail.

The rate had been stable for many months at 3 per cent. It fell to 2 per cent in the current month. What is it expected to be next month? A perpetuity promising to pay £1 per annum costs $1/r$. What is the expected capital loss if such a bond is bought now and sold next month?

2. A surprising monetary expansion raises the price level above that currently perceived by firms. Employers raise wages above the level currently perceived by households. Explain how increases in output and employment might result. Why are the increases temporary?

3. An economy is producing below its natural level of output. There is perfect mobility of financial capital. The authorities hold the money supply constant and reduce taxes, financing the deficit by borrowing. What happens to output as a result of this policy?

4. An economy is producing at the natural level of output. The authorities expand the money supply to a surprising extent. Why do output prices respond less rapidly than the exchange rate and the rate of interest?

5. Give some of the possible causes of hysteresis as applied to the natural rate of unemployment. What information would you require to discover which policy to reduce long-term unemployment would have the greatest impact in your country? Would such a policy increase inflation, or raise the rate of interest, or increase output?

FURTHER READING

Leijonhufvud (1981) is certainly worth reading if one is interested in the history of economic thought and will also appeal to those intrigued by the economic effects of misperceptions and resulting disequilibria.

Shaw (1984) provides an introduction to rational expectations. Sheffrin (1983) gives a useful survey. Sargent (1986) relates the REH to specific historical periods. The feel of the debate involving the New Neoclassicists is well conveyed in Klamer (1984). Chrystal (1983) is a short and clear text on controversies in macroeconomics. Chapter 4 of Krueger (1983) summarises research on the influence of the capital account of the balance of payments on exchange rates. Chapter 10 of Williamson (1983) gives a fuller algebraic exposition of Dornbusch-type overshooting. Koromzay et al. (1987) discuss the peculiar behaviour of the dollar.

Hysteresis in the tradeables sector is suggested (convincingly) in a preliminary paper by Bean (1987). Bruno and Sachs (1985) give regressions for the main countries which are helpful summary descriptions of the varying extent of hysteresis in labour markets. Blanchard and Summers (1986) investigate its influence on European unemployment.

9 Towards Harmony

This chapter would be irrelevant if relative prices moved rapidly to their market-clearing values, if quantities adjusted rapidly to changed relative prices so that aggregate demand stayed near the natural level of output, if dramatic monetary changes were impossible, if bond-financed budget deficits were too low to affect real interest rates, if absorption stayed near income, if information were accurately transmitted and perceived and if temporary misalignments did not have long-lasting effects. Macroeconomists would be like astronomers who study laws of motion and observe from curiosity but do not seek to influence what they observe. However, macroeconomic problems are generated more by unpleasant events than by intellectual curiosity. The chapter discusses policies which could reduce the incidence of such events or minimise their harmful effects if they occur.

9.1 HARMONIOUS MONETARY POLICIES

Each of the three main currencies is more important than implied by the shares of world trade and output of the United States, Japan and West Germany. The US dollar is used as a medium of exchange by currency dealers. For example, a holder of Swedish crowns who wants South Korean won may first change the crowns for dollars in a routine market then the dollars for won in another routine market. A direct deal from crowns to won would be less routine and subject to more friction than using dollars as an intermediate stage. The US dollar is a *vehicle currency*. When used in this role it has a spectacular velocity of circulation, but as the value of such deals is also spectacular the stock of dollars required by dealers is high.

Although the output of the West German economy is smaller than that of Japan, the mark is the key currency of the European Monetary System. This gives it a greater weight than the yen in the world monetary system. The yen's importance is partly due to the high savings propensity of the Japanese, who save even more than Japanese firms invest and are the main suppliers of loanable funds to the international market.

During the 1970s the Central Banks of Germany and Japan responded to US monetary growth by echoing it. Monetary expansion in the United States triggered an over-depreciation of the dollar. The threatened loss of competitiveness for German and Japanese exports caused the authorities in these countries to buy dollars with new marks and yen, although aversion to inflation kept their monetary expansions more modest than in the United States. The result was a decade of world inflation. This experience led to a change in preferences in the main industrialised countries. Eliminating inflation became preferred to maintaining the previous rate of growth of tradeable output. During the 1980s, Central Banks echoed each other's caution in monetary growth to an extent which led to a mild but long-lasting demand recession.

As a suggestion for avoiding these follow-my-leader policies, McKinnon (1984) proposed that the three Central Banks should agree that a weighted average of their currencies would grow in the range of 5–7 per cent. This range would keep the world tradeable price index roughly constant without discouraging output growth. As an illustration of the possible weights, he suggested:

.45 (US monetary growth rate)

+ .35 (German monetary growth rate)

+ .20 (Japanese monetary growth rate)
= 5–7 per cent   (9.1)

Each country's monetary growth rate is initially set to encourage price stability within that country's tradeables sector. This implies higher monetary growth in Japan where the non-tradeables sector generates a high proportion of output but has a lower rate of growth of labour productivity than the tradeable sector. (See section 7.3 for the relation between productivity and inflation in the two sectors.) International price stability for tradeables entails modest inflation in the non-tradeables price index in each country.

With a monetary policy which brings price stability, the next objective is to encourage exchange rate stability. This involves an initial stage of mutually managed floats to discourage the extremes of speculative bubbles and over-shooting. The three countries agree on the exchange rates which seem approximately right taking into account the slow correction of trade surpluses and deficits. Since their agreed view may be wrong, they do not announce it. Since it is an approximation, they take action only if the market moves exchange rates by more than 10 per cent from their view of the correct rate. The action involves the monetary authorities: an excessive depreciation of the dollar, for example, is met by a reduction in US monetary growth. Condition (9.1) is preserved by increasing monetary growth in Germany and Japan, thereby widening interest rate differentials. If the depreciation of the dollar had been triggered by the expectation of US inflation, the changes in monetary growth remove it. From time to time, the three countries will make small changes in their agreed view of the 'true' equilibrium exchange rates. Such changes will be based on medium-term forecasts. The extreme effects of 'news' on the exchanges will be limited to plus or minus 10 per cent. The band can be narrowed as the market experiences stability and the authorities' view of the equilibrium rate is improved. In the longer run there will be changes in the weights of the monies in condition (9.1).

The result is to recapture most of the advantages of a one-money world such as the Gold Standard or the Dollar Standard, by using a three-monies standard with some flexibility. The main pressures on such a system would result from differing savings propensities between countries and unsustainable budget deficits. The next sections consider these aspects of the move towards harmony.

9.2 HARMONIOUS FISCAL POLICIES

When two countries trade mainly with each other and both consider that output is constrained by insufficient aggregate demand, there are several policy options. Country A may expand by increasing its budget deficit, assuming that country B will not. If the assumption is correct, A increases output by more than B but at the cost of a trade deficit, and B increases its exports with no budget deficit. If, however, B used fiscal policy to expand aggregate demand on the wrong assumption that A would not, then both A and B generate large budget deficits; both import more and trade deficits need not arise, but the combined effect of each expansion reinforcing the other may generate inflation if the monetary authorities respond to the increased demands for the two monies. If monetary conditions remain tight, the bond-financed deficits may drive up interest rates and slow the future growth of each economy's aggregate supply. Sharing information at the stage when the policies are being formulated allows a reiterative process of adjusting each country's planned expansion in response to the other.

Some illustrative outcomes are given in Table 9.1 where the bottom number in each box shows the pay-off to country A, the top right the pay-off to B. Each gain 5 if both pursue an active cooperation policy. The pay-offs are zero if each waits for the other to act. If B is active and

A passive, B's pay-off makes this just worthwhile. The effect of the fiscal expansion outweighs the problems of the budget deficit and the trade deficit. However A gains almost as much by being passive as active; its exports increase with no budget deficit to leave a legacy of problems to the next period. Nevertheless, an active policy for A is always better: 5 rather than 4 with B active; 1 rather than 0 with B passive. Likewise for B, and a concerted expansion is mutually profitable.. There is no incentive for each to wait for the other to act. The incentive is to cooperate.

Table 9.1   Cooperation pays

	B active	B passive
A active	5 5	4 1
A passive	1 4	0 0

The above example implies that moderate Keynesian policies applied in cooperation will encourage output growth. It is the view of the world in the late 1980s shared by most academic economists in Australia, Britain, Japan and the United States and most government economists in France and Japan. Provided the budget deficit was small before the expansion, an increase now will raise the tax base in future years and present no problems of debt servicing. A combined expansion will preserve equilibrium exchange rates. An isolated expansion would change exchange rates but not by enough to negate all the advantages. The increase in absorption outweighs the fall in the trade surplus and income expands.

An alternative view is that an isolated fiscal expansion could lead to exchange rate overshooting with an immediate and excessive appreciation of the currency. The loss of competitiveness has severe effects on the tradeables sector and a dislike of government activities inhibits the compensating growth of non-tradeables. The country which runs a budget deficit and trade deficit loses, and the passive country gains. Table 9.2 illustrates the resulting dilemma. The total pay-offs are 10 for a concerted action and 5 if A or B act in isolation. The individual pay-offs are such that neither country expands. If B is active, A gains 5 if active but 6 if passive. If B is passive, A loses 1 if active but 0 if passive.

Table 9.2 Dilemma

	B active	B passive
A active	5 5	6 −1
A passive	−1 6	0 0

Therefore A is passive. B reacts in the same way.

The dilemma disappears if there is trust. A and B promise each other to run active fiscal policies and believe each other. A published agreement then enhances credibility.

9.3 ABSORPTION, SWITCHING AND THE FEER

The preceding section referred to short-run fiscal stimuli and agreements to ensure that they did not cause current account imbalances. In the medium run fiscal policies are in harmony only if they avoid excessive interest rates which crowd out investment. This is an objective which applies to the total of all governments' borrowings. It ensures that current account imbalances are not eliminated by surplus countries increasing their budget deficits with no corresponding reduction by countries with current account deficits.

The problem is illustrated by comparing Japan with the United States in the late 1980s. Japan produces more than it absorbs because very high saving exceeds high investment and the budget deficit is modest. Without distinguishing between tradeables and non-tradeables:

$$\text{Absorption} \equiv C + I + G \tag{9.2}$$

Domestic production equals expenditure when

$$Q = C + I + G + X - Z \tag{9.3}$$

The production becomes domestic income which is completely allocated as:

$$Q \equiv C + S + T \tag{9.4}$$

Combining definition (9.4) with equilibrium condition (9.3):

$$(S - I) - (G - T) = (X - Z) \tag{9.5}$$

For Japan, both $(S - I)$ and $(X - Z)$ are large. Since the right-hand side is entirely tradeable it can be illustrated as in Figure 9.1 which shows the production point P vertically above the absorption point A by the amount of the trade surplus. For the United States, the signs of 9.5 are changed to give

$$(G - T) - (S - I) = (Z - X) \tag{9.6}$$

where both the budget deficit and the trade deficit are large. The right diagram of Figure 9.1 shows US absorption exceeding production.

During the early 1980s, the US ran a budget deficit which was seen as sustainable for a few years. Loanable funds are not perfectly mobile between countries, but only a small differential of the US rate of interest over the world rate was required to attract funds. The dollar appreciated but the loss of competitiveness did not outweigh the fiscal stimulus. At this stage, the interest rate differential drove the exchange rate (with many other influences on the timing of changes).

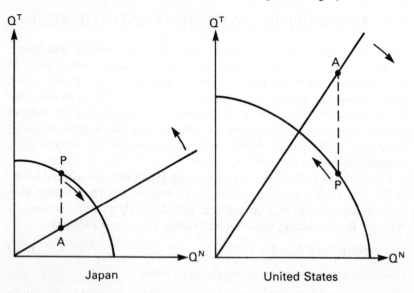

Figure 9.1   *Unbalanced current accounts with balance in the non-tradeable sectors. Japan produces at P and absorbs at A.* The vertical distance from A to P is the trade surplus. The *United States* absorbs more than it produces, the trade deficit being the distance from P to A. The fall in the yen/dollar rate by 40 per cent during 1985–87 moves the P points along the production frontiers in the direction of the arrows, maintaining full employment. The absorption lines swing in the opposite directions but the main effects on absorption are on the proportions of Q^N and Q^T demanded. Policies are required to attain the appropriate amounts of absorption.

By 1985, the accumulation of past US borrowing from overseas exceeded US ownership of foreign assets. The US became a net debtor. Increasing amounts of dividends, interest and profit flowed from the US. The deficit on the current account of the balance of payments exceeded the capital account surplus and the dollar depreciated. During the late 1980s, the exchange rate is driven by the current account. Rational expectations amongst currency dealers cause rapid responses to news about import and export volumes and values, the importance of volumes depending on the J-curve effects of a depreciating currency.

The arrows in Figure 9.1 show the effects of a fall in the yen/dollar rate. However, with no reduction in the US budget deficit the depreciating exchange rate will generate an excess demand for both tradeables and non-tradeables. (See section 7.2 for the analogous case of the 1967 sterling devaluation.) The floating exchange rate causes switching but a policy response to deal with absorption is also required. Without a reduction in absorption there will be inflation. The Latin American experience of high inflation illustrates the result of relying solely on depreciation to correct current account imbalances. Once the expectation of inflation develops, predictions of Purchasing Power Parity drive the exchange rate.

An objective of policy-makers is to reduce exchange rate volatility by reducing current account imbalances. This would encourage the world production of tradeables. The problem is how to reduce the US budget deficit without causing a recession. One view is that it should be reduced only after Japan has engaged in fiscal expansion, thereby generating a market for US tradeables. Yoshitomi (1987) has pointed to the disagreement about the way the world works in the short run. An increase in absorption in Japan by 2 per cent would raise imports but have little short-run effect on exports. The Japanese current account surplus might fall from $90 to $85 billion. One fifth of Japanese imports are from the US, and the US deficit would be reduced by a negligible amount from $140 to $139 billion.

The US economy is twice the size of the Japanese. A fiscal contraction which reduced US absorption by 1 per cent is the equivalent to the Japanese increase of 2 per cent. However, the US has a high import propensity and the current account deficit would be reduced by $15 billion. The Japanese share of US imports is two-fifths, and the Japanese surplus would fall by $6 billion. The different import propensities and trade patterns of the two countries cause different numerical effects. Comparing a US contraction of absorption with a Japanese expansion by the same amount, the former has 15 times the effect of the latter on the US current account deficit and also has a slightly greater effect on the Japanese surplus.

A medium-term objective of fiscal policies is to avoid crowding out investment. Dumas (1985) argues that such crowding out has occurred in most countries except Japan. He points to high real rates of interest as indicators of the large demand for loanable funds generated by governments at a time when investment in most countries is a low proportion of total expenditure.

If each country has its appropriate blend of private consumption, investment and government consumption expenditures, this need not entail current account balance. A country with a high savings propensity may send a flow of loanable funds to a country with low savings but high investment. If Japanese savers finance US investment the yen/dollar exchange rate is higher than it would be if both countries had balanced current accounts. The rate which takes into account the influences of exports, imports and long-term capital flows is known as the Fundamental Equilibrium Exchange Rate (FEER). It ignores the influence of short-term financial flows which finance unsustainable levels of consumption by households or governments in the receiving country. Estimates of FEERs differ slightly from estimates of exchange rates based on PPP because the country supplying long-term funds bids up the price of foreign exchange. FEERs take into account that a lending country is exporting in exchange for the realisable promise of future imports.

9.4 INSTITUTIONS

A crucial ratio within the domestic economy is that between the exchange rate and the nominal wage. There are two reasons for this. First, the Law of One Price (LOOP) is a long-run tendency which moves the domestic price of tradeables towards the foreign price, hence the real wage will slowly move to

$$W/P^T = W/EP^* \tag{9.7}$$

If exchange rates were determined by Purchasing Power Parity, the LOOP would always apply because E would adjust. However, E can be strongly influenced in the short run by interest rate differentials, speculative bubbles, 'rational' overshooting, changing demands for different monies by foreign Central Banks and corporate treasurers of multinational companies, and 'news' about fiscal and monetary policies. Firms producing tradeables have to adjust P^T to E instead of leaving the currency market to adjust E to P^T. With foreign prices constant, a fall in the price of foreign exchange entails either a fall in P^T or lost orders. A fall in P^T entails a fall in W or reduced employment in the tradeables sector.

The second reason why W/E is important is the labour intensive nature of non-tradeable production combined with the less competitive pricing practices in this sector. In the short run, there is a strong influence from W to P^N. Hence an increase in W/E also increases P^N/P^T. Firms respond by seeking to increase the proportion of non-tradeables produced but households reduce the proportion demanded. Job losses in the tradeables sector are not compensated by gains in non-tradeable employment.

For the individual firm or worker the informational requirements are often too great for wages and output prices to respond appropriately to exchange rate changes. Even under a regime of fixed exchange rates, the matching of real wage increases with productivity growth is imprecise. Institutional arrangements develop which emphasise notions of 'fairness' in the sense that familiar arrangements are acceptable. Negotiations between employers' and workers' organisations result in nominal contracts which can be as influenced by conventions as by swings in relative prices.

Balance requires the appropriate level of absorption as well as appropriate relative prices. The fiscal authorities are part of the institutional background along with employers and workers. In some countries, reliable guidelines result from discussions amongst the three groups. Data are shared, processed according to accepted theory; pronouncements are credible and agreements are kept. Social cohesion allows rapid responses to exogenous shocks and high output growth in the absence of shocks. Such cohesion does not seem to be limited by an economy's size: both Sweden and Japan are examples of rapidly adjusting economies with well-developed formal and informal communication amongst groups. Contracts may be implicit as when guidelines are accepted. Explicit contracts cannot be designed to mimic a world of perfectly flexible prices. Credible institutions and cohesion between groups allow the worst effects of shocks to be avoided as new guidelines are accepted. When information flows are constrained and negotiators process limited data with different primitive theories, the negotiating process is painful; only the agreement seems valuable and one party usually refuses to renegotiate during the period to which the agreement applies.

9.5 SUMMARY

Harmony requires some shared objectives by groups within a country and by the authorities of groups of nations. The realisation of these objectives usually entails different actions by different decision-makers. Moderate growth of the world's total of monies requires that increased growth in one country's money is matched by reductions in others. Combined fiscal expansions will snowball unless each country takes account of the expansion of others. Budget deficits which are unsustainable in the medium run cannot be countered by depreciation alone, nor by other countries also moving into unsustainable budget deficits.

Within some countries, relations between government and industry and between employers and employees involve conflict about the distribution of output, the availability and accuracy of data, the theories used to process the data, and the credibility of those involved in attempts to achieve agreements. In others, minor conflicts are dominated by common objectives, including a shared view of the trade-off between the short run and the medium run.

PROBLEMS FOR CHAPTER 9

1. Assume that Central Bankers consider 150 yen per US dollar is approximately the medium-run equilibrium exchange rate. The rate rises to 165. What actions should the Japanese and US Central Banks take to move the rate towards their notion of equilibrium?
2. Assume that 2 Deutschemarks buy the same bundle of tradeables as 1 US dollar. If German savers start to finance US investment, which way would the exchange rate move? Define Purchasing Power Parity and the Fundamental Equilibrium Exchange Rate.

   If German savers have financed US investment for a decade, and the outflow of dividends, interest and profit from the US becomes significant, which way would the exchange rate move?
3. Are trade deficits caused by overvalued currencies, or low savings propensities, or high budget deficits?
4. Why do high budget deficits financed by bond sales cause appreciation in the short run but depreciation in the medium run?
5. Why might short-run misalignments of exchange rates have medium-run effects on the growth of world output of tradeables and world unemployment?

FURTHER READING

Threats to international financial stability are discussed in the papers edited by Portes and Swoboda (1987). McKinnon (1984) presents proposals for monetary and exchange rate stability. Buiter and Marston (1985) contain more theoretically advanced papers outlining the difficulties of policy coordination. Williamson and Miller (1987) advocate target zones for exchange rates. Yoshitomi (1987) compares the relative effects of a possible fiscal contraction in the US with the actual expansion in Japan in 1987. The problems which arise when policy-makers share objectives but hold different models of how the world works are discussed in Frankel and Rockett (1987).

The importance of institutions in explaining the speed of recovery from shocks is emphasised in Black (1982) and McCallum (1983).

Bibliography

Alexander, S. S. (1952) 'Effects of a devaluation on a trade balance', *International Monetary Fund Staff Papers*, April.

Barro, R. J. (1974) 'Are government bonds net wealth?', *Journal of Political Economy* 82: 1095–117.

Beach, W. E. (1935) *British International Gold Movements and Banking Policy 1881–1913*, Boston: Harvard University Press.

Bean, C. (1987) *Sterling Misalignment and British Trade Performance*. Discussion Paper 177 London: Centre for Economic Policy Research.

Benjamin, D. K. and L. A. Kochin (1979) 'Searching for an explanation of unemployment in interwar Britain', *Journal of Political Economy* 87:441–78.

Benjamin, D. K. and L. A. Kochin (1982) 'Unemployment and unemployment benefits in twentieth century Britain: a reply to our critics', *Journal of Political Economy* 90: 410–36.

Berndt, D. and D. Wood (1979) 'Engineering and econometric interpretations of energy-capital and complementarity', *American Economic Review*, June.

Bickerdike, C. F. (1920) 'The instability of foreign exchange', *Economic Journal*, 30: 118–22.

Black, S. W. (1979) 'The political assignment problem and the design of stabilisation policies in open economies', in A. Lindbeck (ed.), *Inflation and Employment in Open Economies*, Amsterdam: North Holland, pp. 249–68.

Black, S. W. (1982) 'Effects of economic structure and policy choices on macroeconomic outcomes in ten industrialised countries', *Annales de l'INSEE* 44–48: 279–300.

Black, S. W. (1985) 'Learning from adversity: Policy responses to two oil shocks', *Essays in International Finance*, 160, Princeton University.

Blanchard, O. J. and L. H. Summers (1986) 'Hysteresis and the European unemployment problem', *Macroeconomics Annual*, National Bureau of Economic Research, 15–19.

Brunner, K. (1983) 'International debt, insolvency and illiquidity', *Journal of Economic Affairs*, 3: April, 160–6.

Bruno, M. and J. Sachs (1979) 'Macroeconomic adjustment with import price shocks: real and monetary aspects', *Working Paper 340*, National Bureau of Economic Research.

Bruno, M. and J. Sachs (1985) *Economics of Worldwide Stagflation*, Oxford: Basil Blackwell.

Buchanan, J. M. (1958) *Public Principles of Public Debt*, Richard C. Urwin, 1958.

Buiter, W. H. and R. C. Marston (eds) (1985) *International Economic Policy Coordination*, Cambridge: Cambridge University Press.

Butler, E. (1985) *Milton Friedman: A Guide to his Economic Thought*, Aldershot: Gower Publishing.

Cagan, P. (1956) 'The monetary dynamics of hyperinflation' in M. Friedman (ed.)

Studies in the Quantity Theory of Money, Chicago: University of Chicago Press.

Chick, V. (1983) *Macroeconomics after Keynes*, Oxford: Philip Allan.

Chrystal, K. A. (1983) *Controversies in Macroeconomics*. Oxford: Philip Allan.

Cobham, D. and J.-M. Serre (1985) 'Monetary targeting: a comparison of French and UK experience', mimeo, Department of Economics, University of St Andrews, June.

Cohen, B. J. (1978) *Organising the World's Money*, London: Macmillan.

Congden, T. (1978) *Monetarism*. London: Centre for Policy Studies.

Corden, W. M. (1977) *Inflation, Exchange Rates and the World Economy*. Oxford: Clarendon Press.

Corden, W. M. (1981) 'The exchange rate, Monetary policy and North Sea oil: the economic theory of the squeeze on tradeables', in W. A. Eltis and P. J. N. Sinclair (eds), *The Money Supply and the Exchange Rate, Oxford Economic Papers*, Vol. 33, Supplement, pp. 23–46.

Corden, W. M. and J. P. Neary (1982) 'Booming sector and de-industrialisation in a small open economy', *Economic Journal* 92: 825–48.

Crump, Thomas (1981) *The Phenomenon of Money*. London: Routledge and Kegan Paul.

Davidson, J. E. H., D. F. Hendry, F. Srba and S. Yeo (1978) 'Econometric modelling of the aggregate time-series relationship between consumer's expenditure and income in the United Kingdom', *Economic Journal*, 88: 661–92.

Dennis, G. E. J. (1981) *Monetary Economics*, London: Longman.

Desai, M. (1975) 'The Phillips curve: a revisionist interpretation'. *Economica* 42: 1–19.

Desai, M. (1981) *Testing Monetarism*. London: Frances Pinter.

Dornbusch, R. (1976) 'Expectations and exchange rate dynamics'. *Journal of Political Economy* 84: 1161–76.

Dornbusch, R. (1986) 'Inflation, exchange rates and stabilization', *Essays in International Finance 165*, Princeton University.

Dornbusch, R. and S. Fischer (1984) *Macroeconomics*. Third edition, New York: McGraw-Hill.

Dumas, C. E. (1985) 'The effects of government deficits: a comparative analysis of crowding out', *Essays in International Finance 158*, Princeton University.

Dunn, R. M. (1983) 'The many disappointments of flexible exchange rates', *Essays in International Finance 154*, Princeton University.

Eagly, R. V. (1971) *The Swedish Bullionist Controversy: P. N. Christiernin's Lectures on the High Price of Foreign Exchange in Sweden 1761*, Philadelphia: American Philosophical Society.

Evans, P. (1987) 'Interest rates and expected future budget deficits in the United States', *Journal of Political Economy* 95: 34–58.

Fetter, F. W. (1965) *Development of British Monetary Orthodoxy*. Boston: Harvard University Press.

Fleming, J. M. (1962) 'Domestic financial policies under fixed and floating exchange rates', *International Monetary Fund Staff Papers*.

Flemming, John (1976) *Inflation*, Oxford: Oxford University Press.

Frankel, J. (1985) 'Six possible meanings of over-valuation', *Essays in International Finance 159*, Princeton University.

Frankel, J. and K. Rockett (1987) 'International macroeconomic policy coordination when policy-makers disagree on the model', *Working Paper 2059*, National Bureau of Economic Research.

Friedman, M. and Laidler, D. E. W. (1975) *Unemployment versus Inflation?* Occasional Paper 144, London: Institute of Economic Affairs.

Frisch, H. (1977) 'Inflation theory 1963–1975: a second generation survey', *Journal of Economic Literature* 15: 1289–317.

Gordon, R. J. (1987) *Macroeconomics*, 4th edition, Boston, Mass.: Little, Brown.

Grubel, H. G. (1984) *The International Monetary System*. Harmondsworth: Penguin Books.

Guttentag, J. M. and R. J. Herring (1986) 'Disaster myopia in international banking', *Essays in International Finance 164*, Princeton University.

Hacche, G. and J. Townend (1981) 'Exchange rates and monetary policy: modelling sterling's effective exchange rate 1972–80', quoted in W. A. Eltis and P. J. N. Sinclair (eds), 'The Money Supply and the Exchange Rate', *Oxford Economic Papers*, vol. 33 Supplement, July, pp. 201–47.

Hallwood, P. and R. MacDonald (1986) *International Money*, Oxford: Basil Blackwell.

Hamilton, J. D. and M. A. Flavin (1986) 'On the limitations of government borrowing: a framework for empirical testing', *American Economic Review*, 76: 808–19.

Havrilesky, T. M. (1985) *Modern Concepts in Macroeconomics*. Arlington Heights, Illinois: Harlan Davidson Inc.

Hicks, J. (1974) *The Crisis in Keynesian Economics*, Oxford: Basil Blackwell.

Hillier, B. (1986) *Macroeconomics*. Oxford: Basil Blackwell.

Hogan, W. P. and I. F. Pearce (1982) *The Incredible Eurodollar*. London: George Allen and Unwin.

Isard, P. (1977) 'How far can we push the Law of One Price?', *American Economic Review* 67: 942–8.

Johnson, H. G. (1957) 'The transfer problem and exchange stability', *Journal of Political Economy*, 64.

Jones, J. H. (1933) 'The Gold Standard'. *Economic Journal* 43: 551–74.

Keynes, J. M. (1936) *The General Theory of Employment Interest and Money*. London: Macmillan.

Kilpatrick, A. and B. Naisbitt (1984) 'A disaggregated analysis of the slowdown in productivity growth in UK manufacturing industry in the 1970s', *Working Paper No. 12*, London: National Economic Development Office.

Klaymer, A. (1984) *The New Classical Macroeconomics: Conversations with New Classical Economists and their Opponents*. Brighton: Wheatsheaf Books.

Koromzay, V., J. Llewellyn and S. Potter (1987) 'The rise and fall of the dollar', *Economic Journal* 97: 23–43.

Kravis, I. B. and R. E. Lipsey (1978) 'Price behaviour in the light of balance of payments theories', *Journal of International Economics*, 8: 193–246.

Krueger, A. E. (1983) *Exchange-Rate Determination*. Cambridge: Cambridge University Press.

Laidler, D. (1982) *Monetarist Perspectives*. Oxford: Philip Allan.

Leijonhufvud, A. (1981) *Information and Coordination: Essays in Macroeconomic Theory*. Oxford: Oxford University Press.

Lever, H. and C. Huhne (1985) *Debt and Danger: the World Financial Crisis*, Harmondsworth: Penguin Books.

Llewellyn, D. T. (1980) *International Financial Integration*, London: Macmillan.

Marris, S. (1984) 'Managing the world economy: will we ever learn?', *Essays in International Finance 155*, Princeton University.

McCallum, J. (1983) 'Inflation and social consensus in the seventies', *Economic Journal*, 93: 784–805.

McCulloch, R. (1983) 'Unexpected real consequences of floating exchange rates', *Essays in International Finance 153*, Princeton University.

McKinnon, R. I. (1984) *An International Standard for Monetary Stabilisation*, Institute for International Economics. Cambridge, Mass.: MIT Press.

Miller, P. J. (1985) 'Higher deficit policies lead to higher inflation'. Chapter 13 of Havrilesky (editor).

Miller, P. J. and T. J. Sargent (1984) 'A reply to Darby', *Quarterly Review* Federal Reserve Bank of Minneapolis, Spring: 21–6.

Mundell, R. A. (1963) 'Capital mobility and stabilisation policy under fixed and flexible exchange rates', *Canadian Journal of Economic and Political Science*, 29: 475–85.

Muth, J. F. (1961) 'Rational expectations and the theory of price movements'. *Econometrica* 29: 315–35.

Norton, W. E. (1982) *The Deterioration in Economic Performance*: Occasional Paper 9. Sidney: Reserve Bank of Australia.

O'Brien, D. P. (1975) *The Classical Economists*. Oxford: Clarendon Press.

Officer, L. H. (1986) 'The Law of One Price cannot be rejected: two tests based on the tradeable nontradeable price ratio', *Journal of Macroeconomics*, 8: 159–82.

Okun, A. M. (1981) *Prices and Quantities: A Macroeconomic Analysis*, Oxford: Basil Blackwell.

Phillips, A. W. H. 'The relation between unemployment and the rate of change of money wages in the United Kingdom 1861–1957'. *Economica* 25: 283–99.

Polak, J. J. (1957) 'Monetary analysis of income formation', International Monetary Fund *Staff Papers*, November.

Portes, R. and A. K. Swoboda (eds) (1987) *Threats to International Financial Stability*. Cambridge: Cambridge University Press.

Ricardo, D. (1951–55) 'The funding system', in P. Sraffa with M. H. Dobb (eds) *Works and Correspondence of David Ricardo*, vol. IV, Cambridge.

Ricardo, D. (1951) *Principles of Political Economy and Taxation*, (ed. P. Sraffa with M. H. Dobb). Cambridge University Press.

Rivera-Batiz, F. L. and L. Rivera-Batiz (1985) *International Finance and Open Economy Macroeconomics*. New York: Macmillan.

Roberts, D. L. and E. M. Remolona (1987) *Finance for Developing Countries*. London: Group of Thirty.

Sargent, T. J. (1986) *Rational Expectations and Inflation*. New York: Harper and Row.

Sargent, T. J. and N. Wallace (1975) 'Rational expectations, the optimal monetary instrument, and the optimal money supply rule', *Journal of Political Economy* 83: 241–54.

Serre, J. M. and D. Cobham (1985) 'The new system of credit control in France', *Discussion Paper 8503*, Department of Economics, University of St Andrews.

Shaw, G. K. (1984) *Rational Expectations: An Elementary Exposition*. Brighton: Wheatsheaf Books.

Sheffrin, M. S. (1983) *Rational Expectations*. Cambridge: Cambridge University Press.

Stewart, M. (1986) *Keynes and After*, 3rd edition. Harmondsworth: Penguin Books.

Stewart, M. (1986) 'The world economy: some medium term perspectives', *Discussion Paper 8610*, Department of Economics, University College, London.

Taylor, C. T. (1979) 'Crowding out: its meaning and significance', in S. T. Cook and P. M. Jackson (eds), *Current Issues in Fiscal Policy*, Oxford: Martin Robertson.

Thomas, S. H. and M. R. Wickens (1987) 'Vehicle currencies, bank debt and the asset market approach to exchange rate determination: the US dollar 1980–1985', *Discussion Paper 180*. London: Centre for Economic Policy Research.

van Wijnbergen, S. (1984) 'The Dutch disease: a disease after all?', *Economic Journal*, 94: 41–56.

Williamson, J. G. (1964) *American Growth and the Balance of Payments*. Chapel Hill: University of North Carolina Press.

Williamson, J. (1983) *The Open Economy and the World Economy*. New York: Basic Books.

Williamson, J. and M. Miller (1987) 'Targets and indicators: a blue print for the international coordination of economic policy'. Washington: Institute for International Economics.

Wrightsman, D. (1970) 'IS, LM and external equilibrium: a graphical analysis', *American Economic Review*, 60: 203–8.

Yoshitomi, M. (1987) 'Heading off a monetary depression', *Economic Eye 8* (September): 4–7.

Yusuf, S. and R. Kyle Peters (1985) *Capital Accumulation and Economic Growth: the South Korean Paradigm*. Washington: World Bank.

Author Index

Alexander, S. S. 155, 202

Barro, R. J. 69, 202
Beach, W. E. 30, 202
Bean, C. 168, 186, 190, 202
Benjamin, D. K. 174–5, 202
Bickerdike, C. F. 126, 154, 202
Black, S. W. 161, 201, 202
Blanchard, O. J. 190, 202
Bruno, M. 190, 202
Buiter, W. H. 201, 202
Butler, E. 64, 202

Cagan, P. 54, 202
Chick, V. 82, 203
Chrystal, K. A. 189, 203
Cobham, D. 142, 203
Cohen, B. J. 30, 203
Congden, T. 64, 203
Corden, W. M. 151, 168, 203
Christiernin, P. N. 47, 65, 203
Crump, T. 64, 203

Davidson, J. E. H. 142, 203
Dennis, G. E. J. 126, 203
Desai, M. 64, 203
Dornbusch, R. 142, 181, 203
Dumas, M. 64, 203

Eagly, R. V. 65, 203
Evans, P. 82, 203

Fetter, F. W. 30, 203
Fischer, S. 142, 203
Flavin, M. A. 82, 203
Fleming, J. M. 126, 203
Flemming, J. 55, 203
Frankel, J. 65, 201, 203
Friedman, M. 36, 38, 53, 64, 133, 204
Frisch, H. 168, 204

Gordon, R. J. 126, 141, 204

Grubel, H. G. 30, 204
Guttentag, J. M. 82, 204

Hallwood, P. 82, 204
Hamilton, J. D. 82, 204
Havrilesky, T. M. 82, 204
Herring, R. J. 82, 204
Hicks, J. 141, 204
Hillier, B. 141, 204
Hogan, W. P. 82, 204
Huhne, C. 82, 204

Isard, P. 30, 204

Johnson, H. G. 155, 204
Jones, J. H. 30, 204

Keynes, J. M. 86, 169, 188, 204
Klamer, A. 189, 204
Kochin, L. A. 174–5, 202
Koromzay, V. 190, 204
Kravis, I. B. 30, 204
Krueger, A. E. 161, 189, 204

Laidler, D. 64, 204
Leijonhufvad, A. 189, 204
Lever, H. 82, 204
Lipsey, R. E. 30, 204
Llewellyn, D. T. 126, 204

McCallum, J. 161, 201, 205
MacDonald, R. 82, 204
McKinnon, R. I. 64, 192, 201, 205
Marston, R. C. 201, 202
Miller, M. 201, 206
Miller, P. J. 64, 82, 205
Mundell, R. A. 126, 205
Muth, J. F. 174, 205

Neary, J. P. 168, 203
Norton, W. E. 142, 205

O'Brien, D. P. 30, 205
Officer, L. H. 30, 205
Okun, A. M. 141, 205

Pearce, I. F. 82, 204
Peters, R. K. 30, 206
Phillips, A. W. 39, 43, 64, 205
Polak, J. J. 155, 205
Portes, R. 201, 205

Remolena, E. M. 79, 205
Ricardo, D. 68, 82, 205
Rivera-Batiz, F. L. 126, 205
Rivera-Batiz, L. 126, 205
Roberts, D. L. 79, 205
Rockett, K. 201, 203

Sachs, J. 190, 202
Sargent, T. J. 82, 176, 189, 205
Serre, J. M. 142, 205

Shaw, G. K. 189, 205
Sheffrin, M. S. 189, 206
Stewart, M. 82, 126, 206
Summers, L. H. 190, 202
Swoboda, A. K. 201, 205

Taylor, C. T. 82, 206
Thomas, S. H. 82, 206

Wallace, N. 176, 205
Wickens, M. R. 82, 206
van Wijnbergen, S. 164, 206
Williamson, J. G. 30, 206
Williamson, John 82, 126, 190, 201, 206
Wrightsman, D. 126, 206

Yoshitomi, M. 197, 201, 206
Yusuf, S. 30, 206

Subject Index

Absorption 8, 195
  and oil exploitation 164–7
  vs switching 150–5, 157, 183, 197
Adaptive Expectations Hypothesis 54, 76
Aggregate demand 8, 85
  and price level 127–9
Aggregate income 7
Aggregate supply 3
  and price level 43–6, 130–1

Balance of payments
  capital account 21, 87–8, 196
  current account 23, 87, 197
  equilibrium 19, 23, 88
  identity 19, 23, 89
  as policy constraint 87–9
Balanced budget multiplier 106
Bond market 70–2, 94–5
Budget deficit
  bond-financed 71–2, 196
  loan-financed 77–80
  money-financed 58–60
  sustainable 60, 72–4, 197

Competitiveness *see* Real exchange rate
Consumption 8, 136–8, 142
Cost-push 130–2, 133–4, 157
Crowding out 67–9, 82, 198

Deindustrialisation 160
Demand-pull 130, 133–4, 157
Devaluation 109–14
  of sterling 150–5
Disposable income 8, 89, 136–8
Domestic demand *see* Absorption
Dutch Disease 161–7

Elasticities
  in aggregate demand function 128–9

of imports and exports 15, 110–3, 129
Exchange market operations 35, 166–7
Exchange rate 15, 61–2, 74–7, 109–13, 116–9, 151–5, 160, 166–7, 191–3, 195–9, 201
Exchange rate overshooting 177–85, 194
Exchange risk premium 76–7
Expectations
  adaptive 54, 76, 136, 139
  backward-looking 28, 53, 63
  forward-looking 27, 53, 169
  gear-changes in 55
  rational 76, 169, 174–85, 189
Expectations-augmented Phillips curve 55
Expected depreciation 76, 179, 181

Fiduciary money 34
Fiscal expansion
  with fixed exchange rates 101–4
  with floating 116, 183–5, 201
Fixed exchange rates 15, 19, 97–107
Floating exchange rates
  dirty 124
  freely 122
  managed 123
Foreign trade multiplier 105
Fundamental Equilibrium Exchange Rate 198

Gold 12, 34, 62
Government's budget 9, 141
  see also Budget deficit
Government participation 28, 30, 62–4, 80–1, 108, 140, 200

High-powered money *see* Monetary base
Hysteresis 185–8, 190

Imports 8
and exchange rate 61, 109–13, 128–
    9
and income 87
and price level 16
as withdrawals 90–2
Income multipliers 104–6
Inflation 133–6, 168
and devaluation 152–4
and depreciation 197
and exchange rate overshooting
    183
expected 53–6
and Purchasing Power Parity 61–2,
    75–6
structuralist theory of 155–7
Interest rate
in bond market 71–2
in loanable funds market 10–11, 18–
    19, 67–9, 170–2
in money and bond markets 99–100
Interest rate parity 75–7, 82, 179, 181–
    5

J-curve 114, 197

Keynesian 9, 85, 103–4, 126, 139–40,
    172–3, 194

Labour, demand for 4, 172–3, 186–7
Labour hoarding 86
Labour productivity 51, 136, 155–8
Labour supply 5, 187–8
Law of One Price 16, 156, 198
Law of Supply and Demand 20, 40
Leads and lags 99–101
Learning by doing 164, 185
Liquidity ratio 13, 53, 59
Loanable funds market
domestic 10
international 20
and speculative demand 170–2

Marshall-Lerner condition 110–3,
    126
Medium of exchange 12, 18, 191
Misperceptions
by firms and household 174–7
by households 44–6
by loanable funds market 170–2

Monetarists ix, 64, 140
see also Expectations-augmented
    Phillips curve, New Quantity
    Theory, Monetary Rule,
    Purchasing Power Parity
Monetary approach to balance of
    payments 18
see also Fixed exchange rates, Price
    specie-flow mechanism
Monetary base
fiduciary 34
gold 12
multiplier 13
Monetary base control
and monetary rule 51–3
and uncertainty 119–22
Monetary rule
for one currency 51–3, 131–3
for three currencies 192–3
Money, demand for
New Quantity Theory 36
Old Quantity Theory 13–4
Precautionary 53
Speculative 170
Transactions 13–4
and wealth 116, 119
Money illusion 46–7
Money supply 13
and bank failures 33
demand-determined 63, 135
Multipliers
Foreign trade 105
Income 104–6
Monetary base 13

Neoclassical synthesis 140
Neoclassicists
New 28, 174–7
Old ix, 27
New Quantity Theory 36–9
Nominal wage resistance 134, 160
Non-bank financial intermediaries
    80
Non-tradeables 145, 149–68, 197, 199

Oil exploitation *see* Dutch Disease
Oil price rise
and deindustrialisation 158–61
and stagflation 134, 168
Okun's Law 186

Old Quantity Theory 14
Open market operations 35, 167
Organisation of Petroleum Exporting
Countries (OPEC) 78, 134, 159

Phillips curve 39–43, 55, 63
Price specie-flow mechanism 16, 26
Propensity
to consume 90
to import 87, 105–6, 197
to save 90, 105–6, 195–6
Purchasing Power Parity 61, 76, 183

Rational Expectations Hypothesis 76,
169, 174–85
Real exchange rate 14, 61, 75–6, 128–
9, 183–5
Real wage gap 186
Real wage resistance 134, 162
Reserves of foreign exchange 34–5,
114, 122–5, 150, 166

Saving
as disposal of income 8
as non-spending 90–3, 170–2
in Japan and US 195–6
Senorage (or seigneurage)
from new bonds 72–3
from new money 58–60

Stagflation 134
Sterilising deficits 101
surpluses 99
Supply shocks 130–1, 134, 158–61,
201
Supply side 18, 134
Switching 150–5, 183, 197

Taxation 8–9, 28, 90–2
Trade deficit/surplus 15, 111–3, 117,
196
Trade, gains from 148

Unemployment
and exchange rate 167
long-term 136, 186–7
natural rate of 40, 57, 139
and stagflation 134–6
and wages 40–3

Vehicle currency 191

Wages
and exchange rate 167, 198–9
nominal 4, 40–1, 56–7
real 5
Wealth
and demand for money 53, 116, 119
and government bonds 69